Imperfect Alternatives

Also by Dale Turner:

Different Seasons
Grateful Living
Another Way
Free to Be

Imperfect
Alternatives

Spiritual Insights for Confronting
the Controversial and the Personal

Dr. Dale Turner

High Tide Press
Homewood, IL

Published by High Tide Press Inc.
3650 West 183rd Street, Homewood, Illinois 60430

Turner, Rev. Dale E., Imperfect Alternatives: spiritual insights
for confronting the controversial and the personal /
by Rev. Dale E. Turner – 1st Ed.

ISBN 1-892696-35-5

Book design by Frank Alatorre

Proceeds from the sale of this book go to help people
with mental and developmental disabilities.

Printed in the United States of America

First Edition

With gratitude to my friend and colleague,
Tim Williams,
without whose help my books
would still be in manuscripts and drafts.

Table of Contents

Foreword

During my time in service as dean of Yale Divinity School, I have had the opportunity to meet with many of the alumni of the school, to hear of their lives of service and see the ways in which theological education at Yale has borne fruit in lives of loving service. I have also had the opportunity to read many of the written contributions that our alumni have made to the world of theological discourse, and I have learned from all of them. Hence, I was delighted to have the opportunity to read the collected sermons of Rev. Dale Turner, YDS '43, who has had a long and distinguished career in the pulpit ministry.

What I found here was the voice I would hope to hear in the pulpit, a voice of faith and of reason, united in the common effort to make the fullest sense possible of human life. The sermons in this collection encapsulate a life of learned reflection on the meaning of the Christian gospel for the contemporary world. Their tone is conversational and familiar, neither directed to an elite cultural coterie, nor reduced to crude emotional appeals. They are rhetorical pieces to be sure, but verbal pyrotechnics are restrained and held in harness in the service of calm, but theologically informed reason.

Yet theological discourse is not utterly unadorned. One common feature of these homilies is their appeal to poetry to provide the most appropriate expression to a particular insight. A recent incumbent of the prestigious Beecher lectureship at Yale, Rev. J. Barrie Shepherd, appealed to practitioners of the homiletic art to do just that. He could well have pointed to Rev. Turner's sermons as a prime example of poetry in service to the word.

Rev. Turner's artful prose addresses a wide variety of issues that were on the minds of the congregation that he served as pastor. Some of the issues that he addresses are of large political significance. What should we do about issues of war and peace? Although he initially addressed that issue prior to September 11, 2001, his concerns remain vital in the midst of our continual "war on terror." Other issues, particularly revolving around sexual ethics, continue to be highly sensitive in many mainstream denominations today. On such issues, Rev. Turner offers a voice of reason and moderation, decidedly liberal in sensitivity–he and his congregation are "open and affirming"–but aware of the challenges to his position.

Some sermons deal with complex ethical problems, such as genetic experimentation, with careful attention both to moral principles and scientific practice. Some issues are more narrowly focused on the political and social situation of Rev. Turner's congregation. Should the "drinking age" be lowered in the State of Washington? Rev. Turner responds to this and similar controversial issues, with the kind of analysis that one would expect of a serious pastoral theologian, a response that takes into account both the traditional sensibilities of various Christian denominations and current socio-logical data. Other sermons deal with perennial or common human problems: grief, the art of giving, the nature of prejudice, the need for independent thought, and even creative doubt.

These sermons draw on a wide variety of sources for inspiration. Scripture, of course, is behind many, although the sermons themselves are seldom expository. Allusions to history and literature abound, reflecting a widely read and inquisitive mind. Theological giants from Martin Luther to Paul Tillich make cameo appearances. The sermons are clearly rooted in a long theological tradition, which is presented without pedantry or pretension. It is gratifying to hear the names of some prominent Yale faculty–Roland Bainton, Liston Pope, H. Richard Niebuhr–who would all be pleased with what this alum of their beloved school has done in the pulpit.

These sermons, which begin with God and end with love, will provoke their readers to reflection on serious matters of faith and morals. It is significant that they usually end in prayer. Though perhaps a convention of the genre, these prayers reveal both the ground and the ultimate goal of the whole sermonic enterprise. They come from and finally aim to promote faith, an intelligent and reflective faith, but a faith firmly focused on the One who makes all sermons possible.

Harold W. Attridge
Lillian Claus Professor of New Testament and Dean, Yale Divinity School
Guilford, CT
July 31, 2004

Publisher's Note

The Trinity Foundation is a not-for-profit, public benefit corporation, 501(c)3, formed in 1989 with the mission of supporting and funding work related to improving the quality of life for individuals with mental illness and developmental disabilities. High Tide Press is owned and operated by the Trinity Foundation. The goal of High Tide Press is to provide the best print resources in development, mental and learning disabilities, as well as leadership, management and organizational development.

Since 1997, we have published the works of Dr. Dale Turner. At first glance, this may not seem a particularly good fit. A deeper look, however, suggests otherwise. All of Dr. Turner's writings focus on the keys to living a full and abundant life–what High Tide Press likes to think of as spiritual wellness. His immensely popular debut was *Different Seasons: Twelve Months of Wisdom and Inspiration.* While that book offers an inspirational tour of the year, *Grateful Living* (1998) is a collection of stories on faith, activism, love, grief, forgiveness and humor. *Another Way:*

Open-Minded Faithfulness (2001) is a collection of quotations that express the breadth and depth of Dr. Turner's ministry. *Free to Be* (2003) is Dr. Turner's thoughtful book of children's stories. First offered as sermonettes during a church service, these teaching stories are enjoyed by children from age five to ninety-five.

Imperfect Alternatives now takes its place alongside the first four books. High Tide Press is particularly pleased to publish this work. Dealing with such difficult topics as suicide, genetic experimentation, war, racism and grief, Dr. Turner demonstrates an extraordinary ability to take a strong position while reaching out with love and compassion to anyone who feels otherwise. The book provides spiritual insight into difficult life situations and, by example, demonstrates a loving tone that is so needed in our sharply splintered society.

As a not-for-profit organization, the Trinity Foundation relies on the generous support of groups and individuals. We are grateful that substantial support for publishing *Imperfect Alternatives* has come from friends and supporters of Dr. Turner and the Bill and Melinda Gates Foundation.

Art Dykstra
Editor-in-Chief
High Tide Press

Preface

At the hour of my graduation from Yale Divinity School in the spring of 1943, I had no close ties with any denomination. I had graduated from West Virginia Wesleyan, a Methodist College in Buckhannon, West Virginia, and while in college I was the custodian in a United Brethren Church. But my ties to Methodism or the United Brethren Church were not strong.

I was determined to find a denomination where I would feel at home and one that would be able to accept me. While still in the search for a denominational tie, I was visited at Yale by Robert Bartlett, minister of Plymouth Congregational Church in Lansing, Michigan. He wanted me to join his staff as minister to youth and Christian Education. He explained to me that in the Congregational Church the goal is to find unity of spirit without uniformity of conviction.

This approach appealed to me and so I was ordained in the Congregational Church. I have remained in the denomination for my sixty-one years of ministry. During this time, I have never been told what I could preach and what I could not. While I was open to input from parishioners, my selections were ultimately based on what I believed was important and reflected the vital role that Christianity ought to play in our lives.

In this collection of sermons given in Lawrence, Kansas and in University Congregational Church in Seattle, I chose to tackle many controversial issues and tried to deal with them as fairly as I knew how. It always seemed to me that to avoid important, controversial topics in pursuit of harmony was an act of ministerial cowardice. Moreover, topics that seem controversial are often the ones that most need to be discussed. And, in almost every case, that discussion is most helpful if it occurs in the context of the Christian message of love and forgiveness.

Parishioners were usually not hesitant to voice their disagreement. When anyone disagreed with my conclusions, my practice was to invite them to lunch or dinner where I would encourage them to tell me why they disagreed and what it was they believed. I have learned much from these sessions.

The sermons in this book were preached as now published with no alterations from what was given at that time. I hope that as you read these sermons that you will value the opportunity to explore openly and lovingly the topic under discussion. Please feel free to either agree or disagree. I have never believed that a difference of conclusion is reason for the repudiation of a friendship. It is important for all of us to learn to disagree agreeably. I am proud of the hundreds of members of our church who, in spite of our different conclusions on some issues, maintained membership and steadfastly continued to provide support for the ministry of our church.

My hope is that we will remain friends even if you disagree and, should we have the chance to meet, that we can discuss our differences in a manner that allows us both to find joy in our friendship.

Dale Turner

A Personal Journey

Life's Imperfect Alternatives

❦

God, in his love and trust, has granted to each one of us the high and wonderful privilege of choice. He does not govern our lives from without, but we determine our destinies from within by the choices of attitude or action that we make. We are co-creators with God in an unfinished world. Creation is not ancient history because each day is a new time of creation. What our nation and world become and what we become as individuals is determined in large measure by the choices that individuals make. If we choose a particular road, we determine our destination. If we pick up one end of a stick, we pick up the other also.

It is a beautiful compliment to be so trusted, but it is not without its agonizing aspects. There is a well known story of a youngster seeking employment who was hired by a farmer and given a job sorting potatoes–the small ones in one basket, the large ones in another and the medium potatoes in still another container. After several hours, the farmer returned to see how the boy was doing.

He found him stretched out on the ground, exhausted beside the potato pile. "I'm sorry, son," said the farmer. "I didn't think the job would be so strenuous."

"True," responded the tired youngster, "it wasn't all that hard, but making the decisions done me in." Making decisions can "do us in." Even so, choose we must.

Another aspect of decision making is illustrated by a cartoon I once saw. A man is pictured at the door of a home, taking a public opinion poll. The woman of the house is saying, "I think I'm undecided, but I'm not sure." But, no one can remain undecided. Not to decide is to decide. William James once observed that when a person has to make a choice and doesn't make it, that in itself is a choice.[1]

One of the disconcerting aspects of nearly all decision making is that the situations wherein choices must be made are seldom completely simple or clear cut. Rarely do we face a choice where one situation is completely ideal and the other situation completely un-ideal. Most situations are neither wholly right nor wholly wrong–neither all desirable nor undesirable. Often, it is not a choice between good and bad, but between two goods. But this does not release us from the necessity of choice. It only makes the decisions more complicated. It is precisely because we are in the nature of our creation confronted with imperfect alternatives that I want to share with you some of its haunting implications–its problems and its possibilities.

We are confronted with imperfect alternatives because we do not live in a world that is static and fixed. Heraclites, a Greek philosopher who lived in the sixth century B.C., reminded us that life is in a continual state of flux–the same man never steps in the same river twice.

In the biological world when an organism faces a novel situation, old responses will not suffice; a new response is called for or failure results. This is just as true in the social world. The greatest tragedies of history have occurred when theories persisted which no longer fit the facts, and decisions were made on the basis of a former condition, which is now altered.

Dr. Harry Overstreet has made the judgment that one hero, long accorded an accolade for his heroism as the boy who stood on the burning deck, was not really a hero at all. He was just a person who didn't have enough gumption to adapt to a changing situation. If the church ever dies, it might well be that the dagger in its back could be the sermon. But the seven last words of the church could also be the words of the laymen who say, "We have always done it that way."

James Russell Lowell gives better advice:

> *New occasions teach new duties*
> *Time makes ancient good uncouth.*[2]

Choosing in the presence of imperfect alternatives is further complicated by the fact that we are finite beings with limited knowledge. We do not have the wisdom of Solomon, nor do we have a crystal ball in hand. We know the present imperfectly and know only probabilities for the future. God has not so ordered our lives as to permit us to see over the hills or around the corners. We do see through a glass darkly.

We are forced into a choice between imperfect alternatives by the passing of time. Some of us might suppose that the perfect opportunity and fulfillment of our lives would be in retaining and living in the full vigor, health and activity of the late teens or early twenties. But in these early years, experience has not had enough time to bring us the wisdom we need if we are to live wisely. But the passing of time, which gives us much of this wisdom, inevitably takes its toll on physical vigor as it gives us the asset of experience. It's a tradeoff—energy for the wisdom of experience. One man describing his experience said, "All my get up and go got up and went." The question is: Will we attempt to act as if we still had the capacity for the physical activity that we knew and possessed in our early twenties, or will we accept the physical limitations that come and try to live directed by the deeper wisdom that time can bring?

One can accept, adapt to, and even find joy within the imperfect alternatives of lessened vigor and agility of movement, or he can play the fool and try to defy time and possibly destroy himself. Lady Astor, on her eightieth birthday said, "I used to dread getting older because I thought I would not be able to do all of the things I wanted to do, but now that I am older, I find that I don't want to do them."[3]

An individual is inducted into the world of imperfect alternatives early in life. Follow the life of one person and see illustrations of this reality. Here is a young lad who moves into the age of discretion, a time when life is not parent-directed, and he has to make conscious decisions on his own. He may not be aware of it or think of its implications, but his character is formed at the forks of the road where decisions are made in the presence of imperfect alternatives. And those decisions are the hinges of his destiny.

We are proud of that young man when, eager to be with his pals, he refuses to go to the movie with them, as appealing as that prospect might be to him, until his responsibilities at home are discharged–his bed made, the dishes done, his homework completed or whatever else was his to do. Tackling those tasks seemed like a far less pleasing alternative. But in following through with what seemed right, though less attractive, he grew by renunciation toward a more mature manhood, developing both self-respect and social responsibility.

When I was a young man, a friend conveyed the philosophy to me that I have captured on a card. It reads: "Do the thing you have to do, when you have to do it, whether you feel like it or not." I hate this card, but I keep it beneath the glass that covers my desk!

At school this young man is faced with an examination. Again the imperfect alternatives are present. On the one hand, he might gain an A or a B by copying the work of another or cheating in some other manner. Without these dishonest methods, he might receive a C or D or even failure. So he is confronted with an imperfect alternative. The A would look good, but may cost him his self-respect and integrity. If he chooses not to cheat, the C, D or failure could be a great source of embarrassment. But in the long run, one wonders if the embarrassment of mediocrity or failure might not contribute more beneficially to that young man's life. It could become a prod to better preparation or a warning against procrastination.

In the dating process, this young man will experience the normal desires for intimate expressions of love. To restrain brings frustration of desire, but to express his affections physically carries some negative repercussions.

Neither decision offers the fulfillment for which he longs. He is confronted with imperfect alternatives. He is caught in the middle. But in choosing patterns of restraint, self-denial, and sublimation, he develops patterns of control that are translated into other areas of life. There can be no virtue without temptation to immorality. Maturity is the ability to surrender the pleasures of the moment in the interests of a larger good.

When the prospect of marriage comes, he finds he has not escaped the dilemma of imperfect alternatives. If he decides to marry, he runs the risks of additional responsibilities and the possibility of being hurt, for in reaching out to encompass another in his love, he increases his points of vulnerability. But if he chooses to remain alone, he runs the risks of loneliness–no one with whom to share intimately. Socrates saw the imperfect alternatives clearly. When asked if it were better to marry or not to marry, he responded, "Whichever you do, you will regret it."

Once in marriage, imperfect alternatives are ever present. Decisions made, when alone, are often very complicated, but decisions are compounded when commitment is made to another. It is no longer I, my, mine, me; it is we, ours, us. Couples must make decisions that are neither totally ideal nor un-ideal:

> *Shall we live here or there?*
> *Shall we buy property now or wait?*
> *Where shall we spend our vacation?*
> *How shall we spend the money that we do have?*
> *Shall I change jobs or stay with the one I have?*
> *Shall we send our child to a private school or have*
> *   her remain in the public schools?*

Sometimes marital discord comes. What was at one time a duet becomes a duel. Shall we stay together and work through our problems, or shall we go our separate ways? Either choice is something less than perfect because there are so many complications. How in the world can we cope, we ask, and how can we make wise decisions in the presence of so many imperfect alternatives? We might well wish, as did Oliver Wendell Holmes, that we could be a clock wound and set ticking through calm and storm.

Let me share with you the wisdom of one who chose wisely in the presence of imperfect alternatives. His name was Henry Drummond. He lived in Scotland from 1851 until 1897–a relatively brief life, but a life of high quality and deep faith. Dr. Drummond was a geologist, and he made many visits to America to lecture in the field of science, but more importantly to witness for his Christian faith in countless student assemblies.

Mark Twain called him the most effective speaker in college chapels and assembly meetings that he had ever met. He counseled hundreds of students individually, young men and women who stood in the presence of imperfect alternatives in vocational choice, sexual dilemmas, marital decisions and religious commitments. He was wise, loving and discerning, and thousands of students said of him, "He lighted my candle. He showed me the way."

Dr. Drummond, like the rest of us, had to make decisions in the presence of imperfect alternatives, but he was singularly successful in making wise choices. His procedures in decision-making are worthy of emulation. First of all, he said, "Pray. Seek for wisdom and counsel from the one who created us all."[4] He firmly believed in the truth conveyed in Proverbs 3:5-6: "Trust in the Lord with all thine heart and lean not unto thine own understanding. In all thy ways acknowledge him and he shall direct thy paths." Jesus promised that they who follow him shall not walk in darkness but shall have the light of life. The testimony of the saints is that it is truly astonishing how bending the knees will clear a mental fog. Lincoln was aware of the need for God's guidance. On leaving Springfield for the White House with the burden of office heavy on him, he told his friends and associates, "I hope you will all pray that I may receive that Divine assistance without which I cannot succeed, but with which success is certain."[5]

Secondly, Dr. Drummond suggested, "Think! God gave us a mind to figure out a few things for ourselves."[6] Get all the facts from all the sides. Analyze, compare and decide; then act. There are two ways of getting through the world; one is to stop thinking, and the other is to stop and think.

Next, he said, "Talk to wise people, but do not consider their decisions or counsel as final. Let it be grist for the mill, an alternative for consideration."[7] I suggested in a sermon entitled "Choose Your Counselors with Care" that it is often not wise to seek counsel from your best friends, for in their love for you, it may be difficult for them to be totally objective. "Beware of the bias of your own will," he continued, "but do not be afraid of it. Do not let analysis paralysis stymie you into immobility."[8] But, he also encouraged balanced action. "True," he said, "look before you leap but remember, too, that he who hesitates is lost."[9] Launch out bravely with confidence. One never gets to second base by keeping a foot on first.

The football team at the University of Alabama has consistently been a winner. The success of the Crimson Tide is traceable in no small measure to Bear Bryant, the coach. Behind his desk in the athletic office, there is a framed copy of the motto: "Always begin somewhere. You can't be a champion on what you intend to do."

Sometimes, even an imperfect alternative can become a perfect alternative based on its results. The imperfect alternative offers us an opportunity to make something positive of the choice we do make. That is why we should go ahead and do something that needs to be done even when we don't feel like it or when the prospects for success are much less than one hundred percent.

Old time baseball fans remember Walter Johnson as the "Big Train." One day late in the 1920 season, Johnson arrived at the ball field in Washington, DC, complaining of a sore arm. The game scheduled that day with the Boston Red Sox had an important bearing on the standings, and the stadium was filling rapidly. Clark Griffith, manager of the Washington Senators, knew that many who were in the stands were visitors to the nation's capitol and had come especially to see Walter Johnson pitch. He did not want to disappoint these fans. So he told the Big Train to go in and pitch the first inning. "If your arm gives you trouble, I will take you out," he promised.

Johnson pitched the first inning and retired the side without a hit. Although his arm pained him, he agreed to go in for the second inning, and then the third. And so on for the full nine innings. But the remarkable thing is this: while working with a sore arm, he pitched the only no hitter of his twenty-year, major league career, a career that included more than four hundred victories.

There is something inspiring about a person who takes an imperfect alternative–a situation something less than ideal–and makes of it something fine. That is why the poem written by Edwin Rowland Sill captures our imagination.

> *This I beheld, or dreamed it in a dream;*
> *There spread a cloud of dust along a plain;*
> *And underneath the cloud, or in it, raged*
> *A furious battle, and men yelled and swords*
> *Shocked upon swords and shields. A prince's banner*
> *Wavered, then staggered backwards, hemmed by foes.*
> *A craven hung along the battle's edge,*
> *And thought, "Had I a sword of keener steel–*
> *That blue blade the king's son bears, but this*
> *Blunt thing!" He snapped and flung it from his hand*
> *And lowering crept away and left the field.*
> *Then came the king's son, wounded, sore bestead,*
> *And weaponless, and saw the broken sword,*
> *Hilt buried in the dry and trodden sand,*
> *And ran and snatched it, and with battle-shout*
> *Lifted afresh he hewed his enemy down*
> *And saved a great cause that heroic day.*[10]

Dr. Drummond concludes his counsel to us all by saying, "When you have made your decision, never reconsider, but press on. You will probably not find out until afterwards, perhaps a long time afterwards, that you have been led at all."[11]

The most significant consideration of all is not so much whether we succeed or fail in the venture we have undertaken, but what is it doing or what has it done to us as persons? It is not what happens to us as a result of our considered choices, but what happens in us that supremely counts. Whenever we conquer our own fears or timidity in choice and do with love and courage what is ours to do once the choice has been made, then we are victorious and are counted as those who have been successful in the eyes of God no matter what the results may seem to be at the moment.

❧

Where Life's Victories Are Won

❧

E very sermon ought to have an object as well as a subject. The object of this sermon today is to speak of one universal truth, a truth about which we do not so much need to be informed as to be reminded. That truth is this: great events or occasions in our lives–events that are either joyful or tragic–do not make or break us. They merely reveal what we have become in hours of solitude and seclusion. The important issues of life are decided in secret, in privacy, behind closed doors, without the blowing of trumpets or the waving of banners. It is in hours of isolation and withdrawal that we prepare ourselves for whatever life may bring.

It is easy to see this truth in some areas more than in others. We are all aware that preparation is a necessary prelude where any physical skill is developed and maintained. Before a team runs onto the field, there are hours spent in conditioning through calisthenics or running and sharpening of skills. What happens in the game reflects the mental and physical preparation that has gone on before. The untutored eye sees only the performance. The wise spectator knows the staggering number of hours and the rigorous disciplines behind the scene that are required if there is to be any excellence.

The battle of Waterloo, it is said, was won on the fields of Oxford where young men had developed their bodies and had learned through spirited, aggressive play what makes a great soldier. Military victories are won behind the scenes. Before guns are fired, military strategists are at work behind closed doors with maps, diagrams, sketches and toy soldiers. They are studying the terrain and every conceivable condition that might be present. What goes on behind the scene conditions and, to a great extent, determines the outcome of the battle.

Last year, several hundred of us sat here in this sanctuary enraptured during a piano concert by a twenty-six-year old pianist and professional musician, a son of parishioners. We all were thrilled by and marveled at his skill and precision. The standing ovation at the concert's close simply reflected the hard work of the hours, days, months and years before. The young man began to acquire his skill when, as a boy of nine, he began his quest for excellence and has been unrelenting in that pursuit, practicing countless hours each day behind closed doors, the place where excellence is achieved. He mastered his skill and won the acclaim before the standing ovation ever occurred. His career is only in its ascendancy, for he is willing to pay the price to make it so. He is well aware that anyone who attracts success and competence must carry with him the magnet of preparation.

I was inoculated with piano lessons at an early age, but the lessons never took. I was so intent on play and games that I neglected practice on the piano behind closed doors. and to my regret, a marvelous instrument stands in the chancel, seductive in its silence. And now, try as I will at this late hour, I cannot induce from it any recognizable melodies. However, one enterprising mother, capturing her son's interest in sport and linking it to a musical skill, told the youngster that the practice of violin would strengthen his pitching arm, and he seldom put the bow down.

Long before a student walks into a classroom for an examination, he earns the A, B, or C that he gets. In some secluded nook or cubicle of a library, or in whatever privacy he can find, he battles for mastery of the subject and the grade he receives. The exam offers no terror if he has paid the price of study. He has the poise of preparedness. He can be almost jaunty: "I just dare that professor to ask me something that I don't know." Yet, for those whose preparation is not thorough, usually the professor discovers just how to ask that question! He seems to lift up an obscure chapter of the book that the student found unworthy of closer scrutiny.

Each of us, regardless of age, is intrigued by magic. It has been a hobby with me for many years. As you know, magicians do not reveal their secrets lest the performance lose its charm and fascination. But since you are here this morning and since we are a family grouping, I am going to transgress that tradition of confidentiality and let you in on one of the secrets of the trade, provided, of course, that you do not carry it beyond these walls.

Magicians cannot pull a rabbit out of a hat unless they have concealed a rabbit in the hat in the first place! They can't draw one out if they haven't put one in. I'm sorry to spoil your illusion, but I tell you this to point out as well that we cannot draw information out of a mind beneath a hat if it has never been put there in the first place. To hope and even pray for success academically and neglect the laws of learning–to refuse to study behind closed doors or plant information in the mind through reading or attentive listening–is to make a mockery of the laws by which we learn. It is not enough to desire a mastering of the subject. We must be willing to pay the price it requires. That which costs us nothing is worth just that–nothing. Dirt is relatively cheap, but we must dig for gold. The island of excellence is surrounded by a sea of sweat.

The teacher who has occasion to lecture knows that she must brood over the material privately before she presents it publicly if she is to be an exciting and helpful teacher. Sometimes, even with the most careful preparation, she fails to register. But, with consistent preparation behind closed doors, she increases her effectiveness. If she is going to penetrate a student's defenses against learning, she has to plan in solitude every conceivable method of delivering the lecture and not simply getting it off of her hands. A hit or a miss is usually a miss. Consider all of the methods Jesus used to convey truth to the minds of his listeners–metaphor, simile, epigram and stories. What a fantastic teacher he was! His truth was portable. It went home with the people. He chose his words with care in hours of meditation and seclusion.

Those of us in the ministry must try to understand this truth. What goes on in the pastor's study conditions what goes on in the pulpit and in the pew. Make of the study a lounge, and the pulpit becomes an impertinence. Our private evasions become public liabilities, and our laziness is shouted from the housetops. There are preachers who take the Bible too literally and believe that it will be given to them at preaching time what they should say. One honest minister did say that the Holy Spirit spoke to him once in the pulpit. It was when he started down the steps after a very disjointed and rambling sermon. The Spirit uttered only three words, "Heinrich, you're lazy!"

We who have the awesome responsibility of preaching should at least try to be prepared. "A haze in the pulpit does make a fog in the pew." Regardless of his talent, popularity, experience, reputation and past successes, a wise preacher builds each of his sermons on the rock of preparation and not on the sands of overconfidence and carelessness. By failing to prepare, he is preparing to fail. There is nothing sadder than an empty preacher pouring himself out to a full house. One woman said of her minister, "He had nothing to say and he said it."

The lawyer knows that the bigger part of his work is done in the privacy of his study. "Cases," goes an old proverb, "are won in chambers." That is behind the courtroom scene, where in silence and isolation, the lawyer organizes his brief and formulates a logical argument. He chooses his words with care, words that do not sprawl, but march into the mind of the jury with persuasive and compelling power. His eloquence in the courtroom is simply logic on fire. He has won his case behind closed doors. The argument of the moment reflects the concentration of the previous hours.

Without a den of refuge we cannot achieve either tranquility or greatness. Thomas Jefferson wrote the Declaration of Independence in a quiet rooming house in Philadelphia. The soaring ideas that went into it evolved during hours of reading and contemplation in a secluded library. Had there been a TV in the guest room, the United States might still be a colony. Nothing worthwhile or creative is accomplished in a crowd. We grow when we are alone. Victories are won behind closed doors.

We have seen that seclusion is necessary in the realization of physical prowess and intellectual accomplishment. This is likewise true in the realm of the spirit and morals. The secret thoughts we cherish, the inner companionship of ideas that we harbor, and the pictures that we hold in our minds lie behind what ultimately becomes action in our lives. A man steals in his mind before he steals with his hand.

The battle for high ideals and clean, wholesome morals is not won alone or mainly in the hour of temptation, in a parked car or a darkened room. Rather, the battle is won in a decision made, a noble resolve, a dedication of a life to God at a summer camp—or on vision hill, at a vesper point, or in a church service. Or, victory becomes reality in the quiet of a room where high commitments are made and in hours of silence and meditation where they are nurtured and where they mature.

If there are no high resolves, no strengthened purposes, then the emotions and desire of the moment sweep over a life like a mighty tide engulfing and destroying, for there is no invisible well of resistance built in quieter hours of dedication. Quietly, and often unknown to others, we make those decisions and nurture the attitude of mind that prepares us for whatever tragedy or joy life may bring. Noah built the ark before the floodwater came.

There are times when spontaneity spoils the reputation of an individual, for at an inopportune moment thoughts that he has been harboring spring from his life to reveal what he might have wished to conceal. The development of the wholesome, genuine, good life is done quietly behind the scene. In hours of thought, prayer and meditation, we can lay up treasures of integrity and high character where "neither moth nor rust doth corrupt, nor thieves break through and steal."[1] The subconscious mind makes a note of every thought and every kind act, and plays it back like a record through the years. It was in the silence of the Tekoan Hills that Amos became a prophet of the invisible realities. In the loneliness of the long night watches, David became a poet and Moses a seer.

Many who worship with us today have seen the incredibly beautiful stained glass windows in the University Chapel at Stanford University. If you have been in that magnificent building, you may remember the window that depicts Jesus as a boy in the carpenter shop. Beneath the window are engraved the words:

> *The highest service may be prepared for and done in the humblest surroundings. In silence, in waiting, in unnoticed offices, in years of uneventful, unrecorded duties the son of man grew and waxed strong.*

In the adult life of Jesus, we see this principle of isolation and solitude so very clearly. It was what he practiced and taught. Many times we read, "Jesus departed into a quiet place and was alone."[2] In calm he prepared the compass of his life for the storms that were sure to come. Before Christ faced Pilate, he faced God and found the tranquility and assurance that enabled him to stand before the Roman leader—not with the air of a martyr, but with the courage of a conqueror. Jesus encouraged his followers to enter into their closets to pray in secret. The results of private prayer, he said, would be revealed in the public lives they lived.[3] I have long known that a pastor's prayers in public reveal the nature of his inner prayer life. He cannot pray skim milk all week and expect to pray cream on Sunday.

You see, it is true. Great occasions and events in our lives that are either joyful or tragic do not make or break us; they merely reveal what we have become. We are able to meet with triumph or disaster and treat those two impostors just the same if time apart, reflection, prayer and meditation have a part in our daily lives. Every life has its great days–its Palm Sundays of Triumph and Good Fridays of Cross-bearing–and these seem to be where the battle is fought. But, when one searches for the secret of tranquility in the midst of storm or modesty in the hour of success, the secret lies in the unrecorded hours, as the sources of an abundant river lie hidden in some nook among the hills. For in quietness and confidence is our strength, and it is behind closed doors that life's victories are won.

May God grant us the wisdom and the discipline to fully prepare ourselves for a life of triumph.

◌ℛ◌

The Purpose of Life

The last time I stood in this pulpit, if you were here you may remember that I preached on the subject "The Greatest Text in the Bible." How could anyone be so audacious as to presume to know which of the 31,173 texts in the Bible is the greatest? I chose Micah 6:8.

> *He has showed you what is good*
> *and what does the Lord require of you,*
> *but to do justice, and to love kindness*
> *and to walk humbly with your God.*

Today the subject is "What Is the Purpose of Life?" a title even more presumptuous than the last. This is a question that has puzzled the world's keenest minds since the beginning of time. Some may be thinking if we ever invite Dale Turner again his title will no doubt be "A Sermon About the Universe and Other Things!"

Even so, is it not wise to launch out into waters that can never be fully fathomed? We do not learn to swim in the shallows. The purpose of life has puzzled us all. Many would say with Piet Hein, the writer of *Grooks*:

> *I'd like to know*
> *what this whole show*
> *is all about*
> *before it's out.*[1]

Life is a game, the object of which is to find the object of the game.

Unfortunately, the majority of people never succeed in finding the object of the game. It is sad, as Isaac Watts wrote, that:

> *Most people creep into the world*
> *and know no reason why they were born*
> *except to consume the corn and the fish*
> *and leave behind an empty dish.*[2]

Matthew Arnold's lines, in his famed poem "Rugby Chapel," are similarly pessimistic.

> *What is the course of the life*
> *Of mortal men on earth?–*
> *Most men eddy about*
> *Here and there–eat and drink,*
> *Chatter and love and hate,*
> *Gather and squander, are raised*
> *Aloft, are hurl'd in the dust,*
> *Striving blindly, achieving*
> *Nothing: and then they die–*
> *Perish;–and no one asks*

Who or what they have been,
More than he asks what waves,
In the moonlit solitudes mild
Of the midmost Ocean, have swell'd,
Foam'd for a moment and gone."[3]

These deep themes deserve our consideration, but they must not engage the whole of our time. We must get on with living. Concentrating too much on imponderables can be immobilizing.

The centipede was happy quite
Until the toad, for spite, said
Pray tell me which leg comes after which?
This wrought his mind in such a pitch
He lay distracted in the ditch.
Considering how to run.[4]

And, I think of the old man with a long, white beard. A youngster asked him if he slept with the beard on the inside of the covers or out? He hadn't thought about that and that night he couldn't sleep–first tossing his beard outside the covers, then tucking it in.

Puzzling as the purpose of life may be, there are three simple guidelines that, if not an answer to all the questions, still can direct us to a more purposeful life, rescuing us from meaningless existence. We need a goal fit to live for, a self fit to live with, and a faith fit to live by.

When John Wanamaker, the great Christian merchant of Philadelphia was asked, "What is the greatest lack in the young people of the day?" he responded immediately, "Purpose, a sense of purpose; they have no goal for which they aspire."[5]

If his assessment is true it is sad, for goals are essential. No wind is favorable to a sailor who does not know into which port he is trying to sail. Yet, a goal per se is not enough. Not all goals are worthy of the time and energy that is expended. It was recorded of one of the princes of France that his chief occupation and goal in life was to capture weasels in barns. There are still plenty of weasel chasers in the world–people setting out to accomplish inconsequentials, striving for goals that are really not fit to live for.

There are those who have climbed the ladder of success only to discover it has been leaning against the wrong wall and there is no real fulfillment in their lives. Fortunately, many people have had or do have worthwhile goals–goals fit to live for. Thomas Macaulay, the great British historian, desired above all to live amiably with those with whom he lived most intimately. That was the central goal of his life.

A freshman student at a small Midwestern college was visiting in the hall between classes with the president of the school. He asked her why she had enrolled at that college. She said, "I come to school to be went with but I ain't yet." Her grammar left something to be desired, but her goal was a good one. A meaningful relationship with another is a worthy goal.

Early this month, I was in Minneapolis speaking at an automotive convention. The leader of the convention was Bill Smith, a longtime friend, who owns the Gopher Engine Rebuilding Company in Minneapolis. He took me on a tour of his plant where we went from bench to bench as he greeted his eighty-five employees by name. There was genuine affability between Bill and those employees.

It was obvious they loved him and were not threatened by his presence. They bantered and joked with him and delighted in the relationship with Bill which was theirs.

While driving back to the conference I said to him, "Bill, you have certainly learned how to be the top banana without losing touch with the bunch."

I'm not sure he thought the figure of speech or analogy was all that great, but he said, "That's it exactly. Those people you met today are my dear friends as well as employees. I want them to know I care about each one of them, and if they can love me for my fairness and concern, that will be a large part of any compensation that might come." When those who know us best can love us most, we've attained one of life's highest goals. What a worthy goal for one in an executive or leadership position!

On the other hand, I've known executives who know little or nothing about those who work for them. The bottom line is all that matters. A young man once said to me, "Mr. Turner, the only time my boss ever notices what I do is when I don't do it."

It is no mystery why Steve Largent is so highly regarded and loved by so many on the football field and off. He has a sense of purpose that infuses the whole of his life. He has taken 1 Corinthians 9:24-27 as the goal for his play. It reads:

> *Do you know that in a race all the runners compete, but only one receives the prize? So run, that you may obtain it. Every athlete exercises self-control in all things. Now, they do it to receive a perishable wreath, but we are imperishable. Well, I do not run aimlessly, I do not box as one beating*

> *the air; but I keep my body, and bring it into subjection, lest*
> *that by any means when I have preached to others, I myself*
> *should be disqualified.*

I received correspondence from Steve from his home in Tulsa in which he tells of his concern to teach his children honesty, humility, responsibility and perseverance. These are wonderful goals, fit for all to live for.

When our immediate goals are seen in the context of a larger goal all goals, glow with deeper meaning. The Apostle Paul was a tentmaker, a preacher, a writer of letters and organizer of churches. There was much that engaged his hand and mind. Writing to the Christians in Philippi, he said:

> *Brethren, I do not consider that I have made it, but*
> *this one thing I do, forgetting what is behind and*
> *looking forth to what is before, I press on toward*
> *the goal for the prize of the high calling of God in*
> *Christ Jesus.*[6]

In other words, the goal of my life is to be so committed to Christ that His spirit shall infuse the whole of my life. That is a goal fit to live for. The purpose of life is to have a goal fit to live for and a self fit to live with. We are aware that no one of us is only one self. We are many selves. Sometimes I feel like a mob with many contending selves. I know what Edward Sanford Martin meant when he wrote:

> *Within my earthly temple there's a crowd;*
> *There's one of us that's humble, one that's proud,*
> *There's one that's broken-hearted for his sins,*

There's one that's unrepentant sits and grins;
There's one that loves his neighbor as himself,
And one that cares for naught but fame and pelf.
From much corroding care I should be free.
If I could once determine which is me.[7]

The purpose of life is to live in such a way that our best self dominates the maximum amount of time. It is important that our best self dominate for we give to others not only what we have, but what we are. Nothing can prevent us from visiting our virtues or our vices upon those around us.

I think of Saul, the reprobate, in John Masefield's poem "The Everlasting Mercy." His words have come to mind on several occasions: "the harm I've done by being me."[8] Sometimes, when I've done a stupid or foolish thing I think of that phrase. Oscar Wilde said, "Some cause happiness wherever they go; others whenever they go."[9]

I was with several people a couple of days ago where one of the group was talking about Rabbi Rafael Levine, who meant so much in the life of our city. He often spoke in their church and many of you knew him well. When Rabbi Levine went into a room, it was as though a fire were kindled or a lamp were lit. He carried with him the contagion of glad goodwill. In a way, he was a third testament bridging the Old Testament and the New. He made the world brighter and better because he lived in it. He is gone now. The light is out, but the glow remains. Great personalities such as Rabbi Levine and others encourage us to be better than we are.

Personality is not so much like a structure as like a

river; it flows. To be a person is to be in a perpetual process of becoming. It takes a long time to become what we aspire to be. William James was seventy-seven when he said, "I'm just now becoming fit to live with."[10]

I like the bumper stickers that say, "Be patient; God is not through with me yet."

Sometimes simple lines from the pen of a writer of verse can encourage us in the direction of improvement, as Edgar Guest wrote:

> *I have to live with myself, and so*
> *I want to be fit for myself to know;*
> *I want to be able as days go by*
> *Always to look myself straight in the eye;*
> *I don't want to stand with the setting sun*
> *And hate myself for the things I've done.*
>
> *I don't want to keep on a closet shelf*
> *A lot of secrets about myself,*
> *And fool myself as I come and go,*
> *Into thinking that nobody else will know*
> *The kind of man that I really am;*
> *I don't want to dress myself up in sham.*
>
> *I want to go out with my head erect,*
> *I want to deserve all men's respect;*
> *But here in the struggle for fame and pelf,*
> *I want to be able to like myself,*
> *I don't want to think as I come and go*
> *That I'm bluster and bluff and empty show.*
>
> *I never can hide myself from me,*
> *I see what others may never see,*

I know what others may never know,
I never can fool myself—and so,
Whatever happens, I want to be
Self-respecting and conscience free.[11]

To give our lives purpose we need a goal fit to live for, a self fit to live with and a faith fit to live by. No vital religion is possible unless three aspects of it are developed:

The inner life of devotion,
The outer life of service, and
The intellectual life of rationality.

The purpose of the church and its ministry is to make God real to each succeeding generation and help us know God by other than hearsay. It would be helpful and perhaps more conclusive if each of us could have a burning bush experience like Moses or a Damascus Road conversion in the manner of the Apostle Paul. But, for most people the religious pilgrimage is not so dramatic.

For most of us, growth in the Christian faith is a gradual process mustered by prayer, meditation and the daily practice of the presence of God. When I was in the early years of my Christian commitment, I was puzzled by the Apostle Paul's admonition "pray without ceasing."[12] I wondered how I could be praying all the time when I had so many other things to do. Gradually, I came to see that he was encouraging Christians to live in an attitude of prayer, an attitude of commitment to God at every point where life was lived.

A worship service such as we are sharing sensitizes us to God's presence. The hymns, scriptures, prayers, anthems and sermon all are planned to make us aware of God so that when we go from this place we carry with us a desire to experience a sense of God's presence wherever we are. This is one of the reasons why church attendance is so important.

Jesus never substituted a prayer in a garden for worship in a synagogue or the temple. But he brought the habitual experience of reverent reflection to the garden and it, too, became a place of prayer.

Vital religion requires the inner life of devotion and the outer life of service. What is learned on Sunday must be lived on Monday. There must be a correlation between what is professed and what is practiced. What is explained must be applied. Not all believe we are serious in living our faith each day. A cynical writer describing Christians wrote:

> *They're praising God on Sunday,*
> *But they'll be all right on Monday.*
> *It's just a little habit they've acquired.*[13]

Adlai Stevenson used to tell about a preacher who had so moved one of his hearers that the latter jumped to his feet and said, "Use me, Lord. Use me, Lord–in an advisory capacity!"[14] There is a ready supply of that kind of declaration: God does not need more advisors as much as He needs those who will give practical and effective support by their prayers, service and gifts.

The quality of our contributions to life can be assessed by asking not how much we have got, but how much we have given; not how much we have won, but how much we have done; not how much we have saved, but how much we have sacrificed; how much have we loved and served, not how much have we been honored. How well and how often do we do the little amenities that are the best portion of a good person's life?

Dr. Charles Mayo was not only a fine doctor but a great teacher of doctors. He tried to help his students see the value of little kindnesses that went beyond the required. He taught a "flavors for the living" philosophy.

> *An ounce of taffy is better than a pound of epitaphy.*
> *One genuine tear of compassion for the living*
> *is better than a face full of tears for the dead.*[15]

No vital religion is possible without the inner life of devotion, the outer life of service and the intellectual life of rationality. Religion is more than its intellectual formulations, but its intellectual formulations are important. Since we become like that which we worship, it is important to think of God right. It is better to have no idea of God than an idea that is unworthy of Him.

Well-ordered beliefs provide the stability we need. They serve as an inner gyroscope that makes steadiness possible in a world of rapid transition. Many are vulnerable to gurus and charlatans because they have never hammered out their own faith.

Margaret Mead complained that the young had been forced to make a mish-mash of all the religions of the world because their own tradition had not been successfully transmitted to them. Gandhi observed that true religion is essential, though it has been exploited and distorted.[16]

I never cease to be amazed at the unbelievable things some people believe. I sometimes think density of the population has a double meaning. In the book of Job, we read of those who darken counsel with words without wisdom. The Apostle Paul spoke of those who have zeal without knowledge. Nothing is more dangerous than energetic ignorance.

I have become leery of those who have everything neatly packaged and ribboned. Things seldom are. I often find myself praying, "O, Lord, lead me to the one who is in search of truth and deliver me from the one who has found it!"

The greatest need in our day is a combination of open-mindedness that works for progress with the loyalty to convictions that conserves the best contribution of the past. "The object of opening the mind," said G. K. Chesterton, "as of opening the mouth, is to shut it again on something solid."[17]

One of the many reasons I prefer the Congregational tradition is that we have no claim to all the truth, nor do we believe we have all of the answers. But, we hope we are asking the right questions. We do not believe we have arrived, but we want to be on the way. We do not believe we are the saved, but we do want to be among the saving. We want to be open and accepting to everything that is just and good, and provide a listening ear and helping hand to all who are in a similar search for truth.

J. Studdert Kennedy was one of the outstanding English chaplains in World War I and the private chaplain to King George V. His understanding of the last judgment involved only one question. When he stood before the eternal judgment seat, he expected God to ask, "Well, what did you make of it?"

The question will not be: Did you actually achieve everything you set out to do and be? It will be: Did you give yourself to worthwhile goals, and did you let your light shine to make it a better world? What did you make of yourself? What did you do with the raw materials that were yours? Did yours become a life fit to live with? And was your faith intelligent and loving? Those are questions that could be asked of us all: Well, what did you make of it?

Isn't it strange
That princes and kings,
And clowns that caper
In sawdust rings,
And common people
Like you and me
Are builders for eternity?

Each is given a bag of tools,
A shapeless mass,
And a book of rules;
And each must make,
Ere life is flown,
A stumbling-block
Or a stepping-stone.[18]

If we conscientiously set out to have a goal fit to live for, a self fit to live with and a faith fit to live by, our lives will never become stumbling blocks for ourselves or others. They will become stepping stones to higher, finer personal satisfaction and greater public usefulness. To this end we dedicate ourselves this day.

The Difference One Life
Can Make

❧

O ur technological age, with its accent on size and
numbers, has the tendency to make the individual feel insignificant. Many never find a sense of
fulfillment in their work. They spend days, weeks or
months sitting at benches or tables endlessly packing
things in boxes, pounding typewriters, writing letters,
washing dishes, ironing or a hundred and one other
things that seem little more than mundane and routine.
Some feel they are just one more little cog in a huge,
impersonal wheel or simply an extension of an inani-
mate machine. A sign in a department office in
Washington, DC, warns, "Look alive! You can be
replaced by a button."

It is true that some have more confidence in their own
worth and indispensability than the facts would warrant.
A manager said to a dismissed office boy, "What are you
doing here? I fired you two weeks ago."

"I came back," said the office boy, "to see if you were
still in business." Not all are so confident of their worth.

Students in many of our larger schools often feel lost in the crowd. They seem like little frogs in a big puddle or a number from an IBM machine. We all see the magnitude of the problems that confront our own city, state and country. And, the contribution that one person can make seems so trivial that half of the eligible voters do not go to the polls at all. One woman caught this sense of uselessness and futility when she penned lines that reflect the mood and conclusion of many.

Sometime when you're feeling important,
Sometime when your ego's in bloom,
Sometime when you take it for granted
You're the best qualified in the room;
Sometime when you feel that your going
Would leave an unfillable hole,
Just follow this simple instruction,
And see how it humbles your soul.

Take a bucket and fill it with water,
Put your hand in it up to the wrist;
Pull it out, and the hole that's remaining
Is a measure of how you'll be missed.
You may splash all you please when you enter,
You can stir up the water galore,
But stop and you'll find in a minute
That it looks quite the same as before.

The moral of this quaint example
Is do just the best that you can
Be proud of yourself, but remember
There's no indispensable man.[1]

True, there is no indispensable man, but like so many proverbs and poems, this bit of verse expresses only a half-truth. One life can make a difference–and a great difference!

Most of us can date significant turning points in our own lives by our meeting with one person, a person under whose influence our lives were radically changed for good or ill. Perhaps it was a mother, father, brother, sister, uncle, aunt, grandparent, friend, teacher, coach, scout or campfire leader, girlfriend, boyfriend, husband or wife. A young woman may say all men are alike, yet she is careful which one she chooses–or she ought to be–for that one person can make all of the difference in the world.

Most of us here have lost loved ones by death and have experienced the aching void of loneliness and despair. It happened to Alfred Tennyson. His close friend Arthur Hallam was claimed by death, and Tennyson mourned his loss for the remainder of his days. He wrote his immortal poem "In Memoriam" to honor Hallam. He also penned these lines as he pondered the gravity of his loss.

> *Break, break, break,*
> *On thy cold gray stones, O sea!*
> *And I would that my tongue could utter*
> *The thoughts that arise in me.*
>
> *O well for the fisherman's boy,*
> *That shouts with his sister at play!*
> *O well for the sailor lad,*
> *That he sings in his boat on the bay!*

And the stately ships go on
To their haven under the hill;
But O for the touch of a vanished hand,
And the sound of a voice that is still.

Break, break, break
At the foot of thy crags, O sea!
But the tender grace of a day that is dead
Will never come back to me.[2]

Generations rise and pass away and each one of us, like Tennyson, experiences how agonizing the death of a loved one can be. We discover in their absence how very important a single life really was to us. But life does go on, and we all have a mission to fulfill.

Each person born into the world has a part in God's plan that no one else can fill. Each of us is unique in God's creation. There is no one quite like us in all the world. In a book entitled *Why We Act That Way,* John Homer Miller suggests that if you ever get discouraged about yourself, just hold up your thumb, look at it and say, "There is no other thumb just like that thumb in all the world."[3]

Something came into the world when you were born that had never been here before and will never be here again. God is trying to do in and through you what He never tried before and what He can never try again. If you do not become your truest, strongest, deepest self, there is one place in the world that will never be filled and some work that will never be done. You were meant to be yourself at your best. That is the only original thing that you will ever do.

Each of us has wished to be someone else at one time

or another. "If only," we have thought, "I were more talented, could speak, sing or write like someone else." But God does not want you or me to be someone else. If He had, He would not have made you and me. He wants us to be ourselves, to make whatever contribution we can make, even though our talents are average or mediocre. The smallest hair casts its shadow.[4] He wants us to use our talents now, where we are, all the time, as best we know how.

Dwight L. Moody said, "There is no man living that can do the work that God has got for me to do. No one can do it but myself."[5] However, many feel that what they could do would be so insignificant that they do nothing at all.

In Jesus' story of the talents, the man who had but two talents and used them heard the same words as the one who had five: "Well done, good and faithful servant."[6] It was the man who buried his talent who received the scorn, not because he had only one talent, but because he did not use it. He buried it! God holds us accountable only for what we can do.

The risk of the five-talent man is conceit; the risk of the two-talent man, envy; and the risk of the one-talent man is hopelessness. How often we bury the talent we have, and no good is accomplished. Some have power but no purpose. They are all dressed up with an education or a position, but they have nowhere to go. Like wax fruit, they may be good to look at, but are not nourishing or helpful to anyone.

Certainly, your attitude and mine pervade the homes in which we live. One person can set the tone of a household. One man told me, with tongue in cheek, that he had an evergreen marriage. "When I am away from home," he said, "she pines. When I am at home, she needles." Needling and nagging is what we don't need; encouragement and love is the order of the day. Each person needs love and acceptance, and it's in the home that he should find it.

> *No matter what,*
> *No matter where,*
> *'Tis always home*
> *If love is there.*[7]

Nathaniel Hawthorne discovered that love in his home at a critical hour in his life. He was dismissed from his government job in the Custom-House in 1849 and went home in despair. His wife listened to his tale of woe, set pen and ink on the table, lit the fire, put her arms around his shoulders and said, "Now you can write your book."[8] Hawthorne did, and literature was enriched with *The Scarlet Letter*, one of the best from an American writer.

A study of history reveals that often men and women of ordinary talents have been those who have altered history's course in significant ways. The little book written by John F. Kennedy called *Profiles in Courage* makes us aware that great social movements have had behind them the impetus of one man or woman who was on fire with enthusiasm and convinced of the worth of a particular cause.

If I were to ask you who more than any other one man stopped the British slave trade, whose name would come to the fore? The majority of you would say, "William Wilberforce." Wilberforce was a sickly man who, for more than twenty years on doctor's orders, took opium to keep body and soul together and had courage never to increase the dose. He is buried in Westminster Abbey and above his grave one reads, "The Attorney General of the Unprotected and of the Friendless."

Wilberforce was a man unusually short of stature, but a giant of a man in commitment. Boswell went to hear him speak and said afterward, "I saw what seemed a mere shrimp mounted upon the table; but as I listened, he grew, and grew until the shrimp became a whale."[9] The stand we take or refuse to take in ordinary conversation encourages either the true or false, the good or the bad; we make it either easier or harder for others to have the courage to stand.

One student, professor or teacher can influence the whole of a student body. Students sometimes project the hour of their service to humankind to a date in the future. But, just because a person is young is no guarantee that he will have a future. There are some things a student can do today no matter how seemingly insignificant his talent may be. For instance, on Friday of this past week I received a letter from Martin Bailey, editor of our denominational magazine, *A.D.* He told me that he had received a letter from a college girl in our church who had received the last issue of *A.D.* Without request or encouragement from anyone, she wrote a letter of commendation that lifted Martin Bailey's spirit.

Teachers and professional administrators, too, can make a difference. When the great Timothy Dwight took over the presidency of Yale College in 1795, not one student would admit publicly to faith in Christ. When Dwight ended his presidency twenty-two years later in

1817, the entire intellectual and spiritual climate had changed. It changed because Timothy Dwight did something about it. Emerson was right; "Every great institution is the lengthened shadow of one man."[10]

What you and I are called to do may be nothing dramatic or spectacular. It may be very mundane and seemingly inconsequential, but it may make more difference than we would ever suspect. Perhaps some little, nameless, unremembered act of kindness and of love will make a significant difference in the life of someone else.

I once read the story of a gentleman who passed by a department store window that was decorated beautifully. Interrupting his own schedule, he followed his impulse and went into the store to commend the manager. "I would like to compliment the one who decorates your windows. I am not interested in buying anything, at least now, but I would be remiss if I did not say to you that it is a beautiful display." The manager, not used to such comments, looked at him in amazement and thanked him.

The gentleman went on his way, but sometime later, he received a letter from a young man who wrote, "Because of your kindness in stopping to tell our manager that you liked my window display, I have been advanced in position and given a substantial raise. I want you to know how grateful I am for your thoughtfulness." It is true that others may not be greatly swayed by our thoughts, but they could be deeply moved by our thoughtfulness. The greatest sin against ourselves is to have a good impulse and then fail to act on it.

In the organizational structure of a church, committees serve a useful purpose, but they are often given bad press. A committee, we are told, is a group of people who individually can do nothing, but collectively decide nothing can be done.[11] Or, a committee is a group of people who spend hours producing minutes. When Lindberg flew the Atlantic in 1927, an office employee ran into the office of Charles Kettering and shouted, "Lindberg flew the Atlantic! Lindberg flew the Atlantic! ALONE!"

The grand old man of General Motors, Mr. Kettering responded, "Oh, that's nothing. Let him try it with a committee!"[12]

Committees do aid the democratic process and offer opportunities for the participation of many people. However, we all know there are times when committees obstruct decision making, and an individual, acting on his own, can affect positive changes that committees don't bring to pass without violating democratic procedures. There are times when I think if Moses had been a committee, the Israelites would still be in Egypt!

In this church, we have one who, in her work with refugees, illustrates what one person can do. She would say, "There are others, too–my husband, children and many others–who teach and provide help in many ways." This is true, but still this one has planned and coordinated our efforts in magnificent ways, and we are all grateful for the inspiration she is to us all.

In the long run, Christianity will not be defended nor propagated by philosophers, theologians and pastors alone–important as they may be in verbalizing and formulating what it is we believe. Instead, Christianity will be kept alive and its truth spread abroad by common people. It is undoubtedly true that in every generation there are a few exceptionally gifted people–the four-leaf clover, as it were, in the field of life. But the clover that keeps the fields green, feeds the cows and bees, giving us milk and honey, is the plain folk.

"I must do something" will always solve more problems than "something must be done." You and I can do something if we will. Edward Everett Hale said it for us all.

> *I am only one,*
> *But still I am one.*
> *I can't do everything;*
> *But still I can do something;*
> *And because I cannot do everything*
> *I will not refuse to do the something that I can do.*[13]

May God grant us the strength to do the best we can, with what we have, where we are, all the time.

✧

Developing an Intelligent Faith

⚜

I have in my hand this morning one of the books I was privileged to read this past summer. It was written by Alastair Cooke and is titled *Six Men*. Here we have brief biographical sketches of six men who have made significant contributions in various ways. I was particularly interested in the biography of H. L. Mencken. He has long been one of my favorite writers–not because it is comfortable to read his writings, but precisely because it is not. He was a biting, sarcastic and caustic commentator on the human scene. Many of his conclusions were in opposition to what I have long believed. When he drove a nail, he often split the wood of my preconceived ideas, but he hit the nail on the head so often that I have found myself reading his writings over and over again. In one of his books, he said:

> *We take pride in the fact that we are thinking animals, and like to believe that our thoughts are free, but the truth is that nine-tenths of them are rigidly conditioned by the babbling*

that goes on around us from birth, and that the business of considering this babbling objectively, separating the truth in it from the false, is an intellectual feat of such stupendous difficulty few men are able to achieve it.[1]

When Harold Macmillan, the former prime minister of England, was asked about the education policies of his cabinet, he used to quote one of his Oxford professors. The distinguished old scholar would greet each new class with the same speech on educational philosophy.

Gentlemen, you are now about to embark upon a course of studies which will occupy you for two years. Together they form a noble adventure. But nothing that you will learn in your studies will be of the slightest possible use to you in years to come save only this: That if you work hard and intelligently you should be able to detect when a man is talking rot, and that in my view, is the main, if not the sole purpose of education.[2]

He was right. We must not be sponges absorbing all as true simply because it is said or written. It is important that our critical faculties be developed. I have long felt that every college curriculum should include a course called "The Non-Appreciation of Literature." The student would be encouraged to figure out which books bore him and for what reasons. The writing of a well-argued term paper on "Why I Cannot Stand Paradise Lost" might well lead to a finer appreciation, enjoyment and assessment of other kinds of poetry. For we learn by what we reject as well as by what we accept. We need the analytical mind to move wisely through the events of our time.

The tasks of social change are for the tough-minded and competent. Those who come to the task with the currently fashionable mixture of passion and incompetence only add to the confusion. There is nothing more terrible than energetic ignorance.[3]

When we come to ideas in the realm of religion, it is equally important that we learn what to reject as well as what it is to which we should subscribe. God did not baptize ignorance. His own son was crucified by stupidity. Ignorance is not bliss. The Creator is concerned with accuracy, not error. In the book of Job, we read of a discussion Job had with three of his friends. There is in their discussion much meaningless meandering of mind, and in the midst of their cocksure conclusions, they hear the voice of God: "Who is this that darkens counsel with words without wisdom?"[4]

Furthermore, Jesus was selective in his conclusions. He didn't accept everything as true or worthwhile simply because it was said or was a part of tradition. "You have heard it said, but I say unto you this–"[5] He saw the fallacies in the reasoning of his adversaries. They tried to back him into a corner and flail him with their logic, but his brilliant perceptions enabled him to explode their arguments so deftly that they didn't know what was happening until the pieces began to fall at their feet.

The Apostle Paul, in his letter to the Romans, speaks of those who do damage because they have zeal without knowledge–heat, but no light. In his second letter to his spiritual son Timothy, he admonishes him to study to show himself "approved unto God, a workman that needeth not to be ashamed, rightly dividing the word of truth."[6] That word *rightly* looms large. And, we need to hear and heed that counsel today.

There are some atrocious ideas circulating today in the realm of religious interpretation. I never cease to be dumbfounded by the unbelievable things that people believe. Every other pulpit in America is occupied by a person who never graduated from an accredited seminary. It is not that education, per se, guarantees freedom from error, but it is at least a safeguard.

I read of the evangelist Bob Harrington, who said, "I not only believe every word of the Bible, I even believe that the leather is genuine."[7] Such gullibility. A bare assertion is not necessarily the naked truth.

I had opportunity this past summer to listen to radio and television preachers more often than time ordinarily permits. Some were very inspiring and helpful, but others were not. I remember one in particular. He certainly had an oily tongue and a slick mind. He had it all together. He knew exactly when the end of the world would come and who would be saved, and predictably, he was one of them. He knew the last word about everything and the first word about nothing. He not only had a closed mind, but he was sitting on the lid. James Thurber, writing of one of similar ilk, said, "While he was not dumber than an ox, he was not any smarter."[8]

Sir William Osier observed that the "greater the ignorance, the greater the dogmatism."[9] Often, "egotism is the anesthetic that dulls the pain of stupidity."[10]

I am well aware that we define ourselves most clearly when we comment about another; and, I define myself when I comment upon a colleague as I have. President Harry Truman said, "I rather think there is an immense shortage of Christian charity among so-called Christians."[11]

I do not want to be uncharitable, but I don't want to be identified, either, with what I conceive to be outlandish interpretations of the gospel to which I am committed. Frankly, I think that radio preacher was talking "rot." And, I not only disagree, I protest!

One major newspaper published the comments of the Reverend Bailey Smith, recently elected president of the thirteen-million member Southern Baptist Convention and pastor of the fourteen-thousand-member First Southern Baptist Church of Del City, Oklahoma. Speaking to a group of preachers at a meeting in Dallas in July, the Reverend Bailey Smith said, "God Almighty does not hear the prayers of a Jew."[12] I do not question Mr. Smith's sincerity, his devotion or the depth of his commitment. He must have many fine qualities to have gained the leadership positions that are his, but such an absurd observation as he made makes clear how preposterous it is to be a literalist. As he explained in subsequent interviews, he takes literally what the Bible says in Acts 4:12: "There is no other name under heaven whereby we must be saved than the name of Jesus."

How presumptuous and arrogant it is for any human to assume the role of God and presume to know whose prayers God will hear and which ones he will not. God asks us to play the game and not keep the score. I have too many marvelous friends who are Jews or are of other religions to believe that somehow the God in whom I believe turns a deaf ear to their prayers. In my understanding of God, Bailey Smith was also talking "rot."

And what do we make of the so-called Moral Majority, the new radical right, people who are involving themselves aggressively in political activities? What right, some ask, do religionists have in politics? I believe that most of us would affirm the separation of church and state and would interpret such a reality to mean that Congress will not force citizens to pay for established religion. But the separation of church and state does not separate a Christian from his politics. We hope that morality can inform our politics as well as our personal lives.

Certainly, we liberals welcome conservatives willing to join the political process. Through legislation, we all may seek to implement Christ's injunction to feed the hungry, clothe the naked at home and abroad, aid the rich, rehabilitate the prisoner, welcome the refugee and stranger to our shores, and beat our swords into plowshares by working for arms limitation and nuclear disarmament.

This so-called moral majority or radical right, however, seems less interested in attacking these public evils than in legislating private morality and, in so doing, imposing its standards and values on all citizens. This tendency we view with grave concern. It deserves to be challenged. Our pluralistic nation is comprised of many people who emigrated from Europe to escape the regimented life and gain our basic freedoms. Yet, the radical rights crusaders, Jerry Falwell and a host of others, seek to restrict our channels of communication by censoring anything they view as pornographic. They would deprive women of equal rights by opposing the ERA; prohibit freedom of choice for the termination of pregnancies; run roughshod over the feelings of all groups other than Christians by inserting Christian prayers in the public schools; and encourage us to harass adults for their unconventional sexual preferences. They are against abortion, but quite indifferent to aborting the whole human race, which is exactly what the arms race is threatening to do. They seem to fear the Russians more than they fear God. In their view, the meaning of patriotism is to secure our privileged position in the world and those who doubt the rightness of our privileged position are called unpatriotic. Listening to them, you'd sometimes think Jesus Christ was our Secretary of Defense.

I do not deny the right of Jerry Falwell and the others in Moral Majority to their political opinions, but we have to be careful about identifying our voices with God's, and this they do.

Where does all of this leave those of us who are of a more liberal persuasion? I believe that somewhere between intransigent dogma on the one hand and skepticism on the other, there is another way: open-minded uncertainty. This does not mean that our minds are so open that everything has fallen out. There is much to which we cling and believe deeply. We believe in God's reality, His creative power, His continuing concern for His world and all life, His will of love for us, the revelation of Himself in the person of Jesus Christ and in all souls who do His will. We believe in His availability through the power of prayer and His continuing presence with us always.

Why do we think we must understand the whole of God in order to believe? A God small enough to be fully understood would not be big enough to meet our needs. If we understood all, where then would faith be? Is it not better to understand a little rather than to misunderstand a lot? It could well be that if we feel we have our feet firmly planted on the ground, our education has failed us. Sure things seldom are.

Will Durant said:

> *Sixty years ago I knew everything. Now I know nothing.*
> *Education is the progressive discovery of our own ignorance.*[13]

And many of us have lived long enough to take a second look at what we believed so readily at first glance.

I believe that somewhere between the dogmatism that cannot stand the insecurity of uncertainty and the indecision that cannot stand the insecurity of commitment, there is the possibility of faith and courage adequate for our times. We will not easily capture it, but if we cease to flee from it, such a faith may capture us.

May God grant to us the earnest quest of mind and soul that will enable us to discover the truth that shall surely set us free.

∽❦∽

Handling Our Handicaps

❧

Most of us do not travel very far in life before we are well aware that we have handicaps or limitations that prevent or hinder us from being all we would like to be. The race of life is run in fetters and chains, and we never see the day that we are not without some impediments.

Handicaps come in a variety of forms. They may be physical, mental, emotional or temperamental. We are either too tall or too short, too heavy or too thin, too young or too old. We may even be too poor. It may be wild temper leaping out at inopportune moments, a temper we can't seem to harness or control. Or, it may be a lethargy that prevents us from expressing as much concern as we know we ought to feel. It could be shyness, bashfulness or a feeling of inferiority that makes us miserable in the presence of others. It may be an insatiable appetite for food or drink. It could be a love affair or a marriage that has us baffled and is less than we had hoped it would be. It can be a chronic illness, or loneliness resulting from the death of someone we loved deeply. These are some of the handicaps everyone encounters at some time or another. The good life does not guarantee an easy road, free from handicaps.

The Apostle Paul writes of a thorn in the flesh that plagued him. There have been many guesses as to what it was, but nobody knows. We only know that he had to handle a limitation from which he prayed to escape. However, though handicapped, he was radiant in personality and successful in work. "I have learned," he said, "in whatever state therewith to be content."[1]

The story of history is the story of those who refused to accept a handicap or use it as an excuse for not contributing something worthwhile to life. They did not merely tie a knot in the end of the rope and hang on, but became masters instead of victims of circumstances. They went ahead with what needed to be done whether they felt like it or not. A library of books could be assembled that tell of men and women who have surmounted handicaps. Milton, Beethoven, Handel, Sir Walter Scott, Helen Keller and Robert Louis Stevenson are but a few of those who are better known. They did not accept the limitations of their lives as an excuse for mediocrity or failure.

Many years ago a freshman came to Dean Briggs of Harvard to explain his tardiness in handling an assignment. "I'm sorry," he said, "but I was not feeling very well."

"Young man," replied Dean Briggs, "please bear in mind that the greater part of the world's work is carried on by people who aren't feeling very well."[2]

See that eight-year-old boy seated at his desk in school? Could anyone be more unattractive or unpromising than this lad? He is pale and emaciated. He has poor eyes, buck teeth and a frail, weak body. But who can measure that boy's heart? Who could guess what Teddy Roosevelt would become? Nevertheless, he became a symbol of ruggedness and manliness. But Teddy Roosevelt, with every excuse for an undistinguished career, refused to use them.

What is the secret of such a response in the presence of handicaps? How do we handle our handicaps? First of all, we need to be aware of what our handicaps are. We must be honest with ourselves. We must know what we can reasonably accomplish and what is likely to be beyond us. A person ought not try to move in areas where his or her abilities do not have some relationship to the demands of the task. God has endowed us with certain native abilities that are likely to respond to cultivation more readily than some others.

Sometimes, we can either develop a skill commensurate with the demands, or we can eliminate some of the impediment that handicaps us. The best of medical and counseling help is available to us these days. These men and women are God's missionaries, too; they are our allies. They are devoting their lives to the work of setting conditions right for health and healing. Handicaps that some people have could be minimized, if not eliminated, by competent medical care or wise counsel.

We recall the story of the farmer in Maine who was seated on a wagon drawn by two horses. "Tell me," he called out to a bystander. "How long does this hill last?"

"Hill nothing," was the reply. "Your hind wheels are off!"[3] Even the casual observer was able to help that man know of his handicap. Sometimes, a friend's or an enemy's comment can make us aware of ours.

Professional doctors, lawyers, counselors and social workers, who are trained and have the skills to help us, can be even a greater aid.

We must learn to see each handicap in the perspective of the whole of life and not magnify its inhibiting power out of proportion to what ought to be. A little child breaks a toy, and his whole world is shattered. He is unable to see this one incident in perspective to the whole of life.

Sometimes, we become frustrated, anxious and defeated by inconsequential handicaps that become the center of our lives. We need to see the positive aspects of each situation. The fact that we do not have one thing can be the very stimulus for gaining another good that is of equal or greater value.

Charles Eliot, one of the great presidents of Harvard, was born with a face disfigurement. It could have been a source of great embarrassment to him, but he was fortunate to have a wise mother who said to him, "Son, it is not possible for you to get rid of this facial disfigurement. Surgeons say that nothing can be done. But, it is possible for you, with God's help, to grow a mind and soul so big that people will forget to look at your face." Dr. Charles Eliot did just that. He became a great administrator at Harvard and one of the leaders in American higher education.[4]

There are many who have overcome great handicaps by acting as though the handicaps didn't exist. Teddy Roosevelt captured health by acting as though he was healthy. He overcame fear by acting as though he was not afraid. He overcame lack of physical beauty by acting as though he was as attractive as anyone else. This is not to say that he believed that he was radiantly well, entirely courageous or handsome. He did not dupe himself. He recognized his defects and limitations, but he didn't dwell on them, nurse them or let them become an occasion for laziness, cowardice or feelings of inferiority.

Rest assured that God has a purpose for every life no matter how handicapped that person may think himself to be. It is no disgrace to have only one talent. The disgrace comes in not using it to the full. God holds us accountable only for what we can reasonably do, and our work is not judged on the merits of another's skills. If God has circumscribed us with limitations, there are, nevertheless, many things we can do for Him even with something less than the best of tools. If God has led us to this place and given us only limited talent, there must be something we can do with it.

A little grain of salt can help to bring flavor to life. A thin wire can carry a great message. A small window can transmit a great deal of light, and a small candle can overcome some of the darkness. We ought not to think that we have to be a "star" to shine. In one of Jesus' parables, we learned that it was by the ministry of a candle that the woman recovered her lost piece of silver.[5] We need never despair of our usefulness. Even those with handicaps or less skill can contribute to the whole in a helpful way. On the campus of one of our great universities, there is a monument near the athletic department dedicated to the scrub, who never quite made the varsity. It reads: "He never made the team, but he made the team."

Seek as we will for happiness in life, we may rest assured that there is no finer joy possible for any of us than to take a plot of life which is unattractive, barren, bleak and unpromising, and because of our concern and effort, make of it something productive and beautiful–something that except for our concern and hard work would never be a reality. This is one of life's highest fulfillments and joys.

God does not judge us in masses. Each one will have a private examination. True, others may surpass us in distance traveled, skills gained and good works done, but it's conceivable that many will hear him say, "Well done, good and faithful servant. Yours was a hard row to hoe; yours was a difficult situation; and you have handled it superbly." No matter how limited our outward situation may be, we can always make a spiritual contribution to the life of our times.

There is something that the integrated, fortunate, un-handicapped person can't do for us that the handicapped can. I visit a young man, only nineteen, at the university hospital. He was paralyzed from the waist down by a firearms accident last fall. I go to his room as a minister, but leave having been ministered unto. His radiant spirit and optimism pervade the room. He hopes he can, with the doctors' help, restore life to his limbs. But, he says, "If my legs can't carry me any longer, I'll carry them, and together we'll yet do something worthwhile."

Dr. Fosdick has said it well. "If you say it takes great faith to live like this, you are right. You will not get this quality of life out of the atheistic cults that some try to substitute for a profound religion."[6] If you say there are hours when you hate your handicaps, quite so! Even Christ prayed against the cross. That was a handicap. "If it be possible, let this cup pass from me."[7] Like Paul, he too prayed three times. But, as a matter of fact, as it turned out in the end, no cross would have meant no Christ. That handicap was his most shining instrument. It was not the Greek Apollo, charioteer of the victorious sun, that won the world. It was the handicapped and crucified Christ.

May God grant to each of us the ability and insight to move, through sustained effort, from acceptance of our handicap to a triumphant life.

⚬✄⚬

Dare to Stand Alone

❦

I have always been fascinated by stories. I recall a story I heard as a little boy that intrigued me some and even frightened me a little. The story came from Greek mythology. It concerned Procrustes, the grisly bandit who was not content merely to rob and plunder. His eccentricity was to make each of his victims lie down on an iron bed and be fitted to it. If they were too short, he had them stretched on the rack. If they were too long, he lopped off their extremities at the right point, for he insisted that no one should be any taller or shorter than he. Procrustes was his own standard of perfection.[1]

Now that my childhood days have long since ceased to be and I have become a man, I find it still frightening to know that the truth of the matter is that Procrustes is not a myth. He stalks the earth today under the guise of social custom, conformity and regimentation. He is still insisting on uniformity. Replicas of the iron bed are in mass production. We put a premium on conformity, like-mindedness. We often put a penalty on personal initiative, originality, distinctiveness and ingenuity. We are pressured from all sides to conform, to be like others in what we think, what we do, what we eat, what we drink and where we go.

Our minds are conditioned by press, radio, films and television. We do our thinking by ear and our acting by imitation. We tend to develop a society of people who simply parrot the ideas of those about them. We are people with opinions, but not convictions.

Individual man seems to be giving way to mass man. The motion picture dictates our styles and sometimes our morals. The columnist provides us with pre-masticated ideas. Book clubs select our reading. We live under a dictatorship of psychological pressure and social atmosphere. Wherever you look, the mass man is encroaching on the individual man.

Business and industry, for reasons good or bad, have been moving in the same direction. We have "teamwork" in science and business as well as politics, and you don't fit unless you are a part of the team. Industry has gone in for "brainstorming" and again the individual is depreciated in favor of group decision. The result may well be to cause extremely competent persons to lose faith in their own individual ability. Ralph Waldo Emerson put his finger on the weakness when he said that the price of group agreement is descent to the lowest common denominator.[2]

Of course, some group consensus and conformity is absolutely necessary; two heads are often better than one. Some group habits are essential to any well-organized business or society. All pressures toward conformity are not bad. Our prisons are filled with non-conformists. There are some group habits where no moral elements are involved. But, group conformity can become a very dangerous thing for character. It is well to remember that conformity is not the goal of life. If it were, God would have made us all alike to begin with–the same height, weight, color of eyes, talents and abilities. The way to please God is to develop whatever talents are ours and blend them with the talents and skills of others. The Apostle Paul gave us all wise counsel.

Don't be tossed about by every wind of doctrine.[3]

Don't let the world squeeze you into its mold, but let God remold your minds from within, so that you may prove in practice that the plan of God for you is good, meets all his demands and moves toward the goal of true maturity.[4]

The purpose of education is not merely to garner knowledge as though we were intended to be walking encyclopedias. The purpose of education is to teach us how to think, not what to think. Education should encourage us to turn things over in our minds, to listen, observe, remember and reflect. But, even in education, there is a pull toward conformity against which a student must continually be on guard. Sarah H. Wallada says,

Education was once a teacher on one end of log–a student on the other. Today we see a logjam with students astride their whirling floats heading toward the sawmill where they will be ground into pulp and reappear mass-produced into millions of identical wooden headed molds.[5]

That this does happen is borne out in the study conducted by two Purdue professors who looked at one hundred fifty thousand teenagers, over a seventeen-year period. Their conclusions are revealing and disconcerting. Seventy-five percent of those students felt that the main purpose of education was not primarily to learn to think as individuals, but to teach them how to get along with others. Would the adult generation have any different point of view? It is doubtful, for it seems that the philosophy of so many Americans is that the important thing in life is to have people like us.

The psychologist, David Riesman, author of *The Lonely Crowd,* asserts that today's parents make children feel guilty, not so much about violations of inner standards, as about failure to be popular.[6] Life itself encourages this desire. We are gregarious creatures. We crave friendship; we don't want to be friendless. More than half of those one hundred fifty thousand teenagers said they tried very hard to please their friends, and forty percent declared that the worst calamity that could befall a teenager is to be considered an "oddball." Not many of us want to be regarded as eccentric. The last thing we want to be is a killjoy, prude, poor sport or holier-than-thou. Sometimes, this normal, natural desire to be loved and accepted by our fellows leads us to lose our individuality by conforming to their desires.

In another study conducted by Yale Alcoholic Studies, over seventeen thousand college students were interviewed representing twenty-seven colleges from Maine to California. Among other interesting and enlightening information, the study reveals that the overwhelming reason why students drink is not for taste, but because of social pressure, the desire to be accepted by the group, their peers.

There are many students who have no inclination for or love of hard liquor, nor do they want to develop a free and easy attitude in the matter of sex. But, they feel that abstinence on their part will be construed as criticism and condemnation of those who do have the inclination. To maintain the friendship and respect of others and be able to say no when everyone else is saying yes takes tact and real moral courage, but it can be done.

It does take courage to be a non-conformist, to dare to stand alone. Unfortunately, some are like chameleons that take on the color of their environment. They have no more backbone than spaghetti. Standing for nothing, they fall for anything. They are not really persons, only echoes of their environment. They put their minds in neutral and go where they are pushed. Lord Chesterfield, in his book entitled *Letters to My Son*, wrote, "Always shrink yourself to the size of the company you are in."[7] That ought to take a Pulitzer Prize for poor advice.

Even a cursory study of history will reveal that those who have found deepest personal fulfillment and have counted for the most have never been merely echoes. They were men and women who refused to shrink themselves to conform to the pattern of those about them, nor did they drift with the crowd and let others do their thinking for them. They were "tall men, sun-crowned, who live above the fog in public duty and in private thinking."[8] They bearded Procrustes in his own den, did battle with him, and refused to be cut down or stretched to size. They remained distinctive, thinking persons–not puppets or pawns of society. They were not creatures of circumstance; they were creators. They were willing to face criticism, ridicule, ostracism or even death for a principle.

American history has its gallery of heroes–men and women who have not run with the crowd but have shown the crowd a new way. Washington, Jefferson, Franklin, Paine and, of course, Emerson, the great individualist. Hear him.

Envy is ignorance; imitation is suicide.[9]

Whoso would be a man must be a non-conformist.[10]

It is easy in the world to live after the world's opinion. It is easy in solitude to live after our own. But the great man is he who in the midst of the crowd keeps with perfect sweetness the independence of solitude.[11]

The Bible heroes were non-conformists. The prospects of a fiery furnace could not alter the conviction of Shadrach, Meshach, and Abednego; they refused to bow down to the golden image as commanded by Nebuchadnezzar.[12] Their loyalty was to God.

Daniel was thrown in the lions' den because he bowed the knee to his God.[13] Perhaps one reason the lions did not touch him was because most of him was backbone and the rest of him was grit.

The central personality of the Bible dared to stand alone. Jesus was alone in his challenge of the graft and corruption in the temple. Fearlessly, he turned over the tables of the moneychangers and openly opposed the temple authorities. He took the offensive and courageously waded in, against overpowering opposition, even with the virtually sure prospect of death.[14]

How desperately his cause needs disciples, followers who will stand up now and be counted for all the causes that are fine and constructive. The local church needs support in its programs at home and abroad. The cause of peace, minority rights, integrity, high moral standards, and many other worthy ideas and causes need courageous supporters. It is far better to stand alone if need be, to dare mighty things and win glorious triumphs–even though checkered with failure–than to take rank with those poor spirits who neither enjoy much nor suffer much because they live in the gray twilight that knows neither victory nor defeat.

Times like these demand men and women of integrity who have loyalty to God above all. It is better to die for something than to die of something. Maltbie Babcock wrote the words that are our marching orders.

> *Be strong!*
> *We are not here to play, to dream, to drift,*
> *We have hard work to do, and loads to lift;*
> *Shun not the struggle, face it, 'tis God's gift.*
>
> *Be strong!*
> *Say not, "The days are evil–who's to blame!"*
> *And fold the hands and acquiesce–O shame!*
> *Stand up, speak out, and bravely in God's name.*[15]

God gave us two legs to stand on. May we not use them simply as something with which to run from reality or danger, but may we:

Dare to be a Daniel
Dare to stand alone
Dare to have a purpose firm
Dare to make it known.[16]

May God teach us to serve, to give and not to count the cost,
to fight and not to heed the wounds, to toil and not to seek
for rest, to labor and not to ask for any reward save that of
knowing that we do His will.[17]

∞

The Power of Doubt

❧

W e have often heard preachers extol the virtues of faith. How often have we heard of the positive values of doubt? Perhaps not often enough. One of the tragedies of life is that far too many people are often wrong, but never in doubt. Doubt encourages us to question some widely accepted dogmas that are an affront to God and harmful in the practice of Christian ethics.

We will continue in our services to sing the praise of men and women of great faith because we need faith in and commitment to what is good and right. But today, we lift our prayers of thanksgiving for doubters, those who have the courage to stand in the presence of widely accepted falsehoods and cry, "I doubt that!"

Think of the good things that have come to us because someone doubted, because someone not only answered questions, but questioned answers. Look at it in the scientific realm. At one time, men believed that the earth was flat, but Galileo doubted. Men believed that the sun traveled around the earth, but Copernicus doubted. Because these and others doubted, a new day of understanding was ushered in. Every scientific advance begins with skepticism and doubt. Galileo was right when he called doubt the father of discovery.

Edgar Guest wrote lines to express the thought we are now considering.

If youth had been willing to listen
To the tales that its grandfathers told,
If the gray-bearded sage by the weight of his age
Had been able attention to hold,
We'd be reading by candles and heating with wood,
And where we were then we'd have certainly stood.

If youth had been willing to listen
To the warnings and hints of the wise,
Had it taken as true all the best which they knew,
And believed that no higher we'd rise,
The windows of sick rooms would still be kept shut
And we'd still use a cobweb to bandage a cut.

If youth had been willing to listen,
Had it clung to the best of the past,
With oxen right now we'd be struggling to plough
And thinking a horse travels fast.
We'd have stood where we were beyond question or
doubt
If some pestilent germ hadn't wiped us all out.

So, although I am gray at the temples,
And settled and fixed in my ways,

I wouldn't hold youth to the limits of truth
That I learned in my brief yesterdays
And I say to myself as they come and they go;
"Those kids may find something this age doesn't know."[1]

See, too, how doubt led to justice and social improvement in regard to slavery. Aristotle defended slavery on the grounds that slaves were "naturally inferior" to their masters. The great empires of Greece, Rome and Egypt had been built on slave labor. Some individuals owned as many as ten thousand slaves. The English-speaking world had long recognized slavery as a basic institution blessed by religion.

The Peace of Utrecht was signed in 1713, giving England a monopoly on the West African slave trade. The treaty was celebrated at St. Paul's by the singing of Te Deum, written by the Christian composer Handel especially for the occasion. Here in our country, slavery was likewise firmly established. In 1835, the governor of South Carolina declared, "Slavery is the cornerstone of the Republic Edifice. Destroy slavery and you put a stop to all progress."[2]

The same principle held in the North. A professor at Yale said, "If Jesus Christ were here on earth now, he would under certain circumstances be a slave holder."[3] In 1855, the moderator of the Presbyterian Church declared, "God has permitted slavery for wise reasons."[4]

At the time of the Dred Scott Decision most of the members of the Supreme Court were slaveholders, so:

The law honored it.
The church blessed it.

> *Business profited by it.*
> *The nation recognized and practiced it.*

Who, then, would have the audacity to doubt it? In England, William Wilberforce did. Here in America, William Lloyd Garrison did. John Greenleaf Whittier did. Harriet Beecher Stowe's *Uncle Tom's Cabin* solidified sentiment in the North against slavery. And, hundreds of others–known and unknown–stood up to be counted, and slavery came to an end because they doubted.

Consider doubt as it relates to our religious faith. If we inherit our religion, borrow it or swallow it without reflection, it is not really ours. Great faith, if it is to be firmly believed and possessed, must be fought for. Arguments against it must be openly and honestly confronted. We gratefully accept some conclusions that are ours, for they appear to us, after close scrutiny, to be both intellectually defensible as well as being emotionally satisfying. We must be ready to doubt what cannot be reasonably substantiated.

Tennyson reminded us:

> *There lives more faith in honest doubt,*
> *Believe me, than in half the creeds.*[5]

Who never doubted, never half-believed. Paul Tillich, the eminent theologian wrote, "Doubt is not the opposite of faith; it is an element of faith."[6] It is true–faith and doubt go hand in hand. There is a paradox here, but not a contradiction. The man of faith is the man of doubt. He must doubt something in order to believe with conviction something else. He must doubt the wisdom and practicality of polygamy in order to believe firmly in monogamy. He must doubt the wisdom of hatred in order to believe firmly in love. He believes in God because he doubts the credibility of atheism. Often, the religious man believes, not because he finds his faith easy, but because he finds its opposite incredible.

We sing the praises of men and women of great faith but most of them traveled through the land of doubt before they arrived at their destination of faith. Robert Louis Stevenson, for instance, called himself a "youthful atheist," but he did not remain that. His became a deep and compelling faith in God and His goodness. Luther had periods of doubt and disbelief. On one occasion, he wrote, "For more than a week, Christ was wholly lost. I was shaken by desperation and blasphemy against God."[7]

But he didn't remain in doubt forever. His hymn attests to his triumph over doubt: "A Mighty Fortress Is Our God–A Bulwark Never Failing." It was doubt that forced these two great leaders to think at greater depth.

Doubt was a dimension of Christ's life that is sometimes overlooked or minimized. Jesus was a great believer, but a magnificent doubter, too. In his day, there were many Jews who espoused and believed in a wild idea of war making. Jesus doubted the wisdom of military retaliation for Roman wrongs. He encouraged his followers to return good for evil.

There were Jews who called Samaritans half-breeds, an inferior people. Jesus doubted this evaluation. They, too, were God's children. He made a Samaritan the hero of his best known parable. Some of the contemporaries of Jesus saw lengthy prayers, rigid rules and dietary laws as the essence of religious expression. Jesus doubted that such a response was what God really wanted. There were more important concerns. He said:

> *You tithe mint, anise and cumin, but you neglect the weightier matters of the law—justice, mercy and faith. These you aught to have done and not left the others undone.*[8]

There are some frightening distortions or outright falsehoods walking around in our world today under the guise of religious truth. They deserve to be unmasked. It is no mystery why this is so. Every other pulpit in America is occupied by one who never graduated from an accredited seminary. They assume that all that is needed or required for the propagation of religion is a mouth. As a result, millions have been inoculated with erroneous or indefensible theologies. Some of the ideas relating to God are truly an affront to Him.

I never cease to be amazed at the unbelievable things that some people believe. There are those who never open their mouths without subtracting from the sum of human knowledge. They darken counsel with words without wisdom. All of the fossils are not underground; some of them walk and talk among us.

Sometimes, an isolated text becomes a theological stumbling block. For instance, in Acts 4:12, Luke quotes Peter's comment concerning Jews:

> *Neither is there salvation in any other; for there is no other name under heaven given among men whereby we must be saved.*

Well, for me, Jesus is my savior; if I follow him he leads me toward God and a fuller realization of the being God created me to be. But can I be so dogmatic as to say that all who don't go this route are lost? I question that conclusion. Not only that, I disagree with it. Can we say that Anwar Sadat, who prayed to his God four times daily, who risked his life for peace–indeed, lost it in the pursuit of peace–can we say he has no eternal salvation? Do we deny salvation to that great Egyptian leader who gave refuge to the Shah of Iran when he was being tossed about among the nations like a human hot potato? Does God reward that kind of human response with a denial of salvation? It is a great act of faith for each of us when we decide that we are not God, when we resign as General Manager of the Universe, when we play the game and not keep the score.

There are so many ideas about God–bandied about glibly among humans–that are at great odds with the God of whom the Hebrew prophets and Jesus spoke. It is better to have no idea of God than one that is unworthy of Him.

One time a young man came to Dr. Harry Emerson Fosdick, confessing that he was an atheist. "Tell me," responded Dr. Fosdick, "about the God in whom you do not believe."

The young man described God as he believed God to be, a concept long since discarded or never really held by enlightened Christians. When he had finished his description of God, Dr. Fosdick said, "Young man, I am an atheist too. I never could believe in that God! Now, let me tell you of the God in whom I do believe. Let me share with you my conception of the God revealed through Jesus. I believe you will find it possible to believe in that God. I do not believe," continued Dr. Fosdick, "that it is the true

God you are rejecting, but a stereotype that does not deserve your allegiance."[9]

A young man of Catholic faith had a similar experience with his religious leader. He confessed, "Father, I have lost my faith."

"Good," was the priest's response. "The faith you had should have been lost." And, like Dr. Fosdick, he shared with the young man a more solid and believable interpretation of God.

Paul Tillich once remarked, "Sometimes I think my mission is to bring faith to the faithless and doubt to the faithful."[10] I am aware that I should accept his counsel, for undoubtedly I do hold in my mind ideas that deserve to be challenged. I confess to you that I may not believe tomorrow what I believe today, but I hope it is not because I am fickle or wavering in faith, but because I, with you, know how complicated life can really be and must be ready to recognize the meagerness of my understanding.

A new phenomenon in recent years has been the entrance of ultraconservatives into the realm of politics. We do not fault them for the desire to apply Christian principles to political actions. Liberal activists have been doing this for years. The Moral Majority, for instance, under the leadership of Jerry Falwell, is the group with the most visibility. It is not their participation, but the answers and priorities that are theirs, that some of us question. In political controversy, those who disagree with us are not always less moral than we. They may have information we lack or experiences that are not ours. They may even have moral insights that we have missed. However, to claim the title "Moral Majority" as though others were not moral is, in itself, an immoral arrogance.

I question why, in all of the ethical issues that deserve to be addressed, should their priority be as it is. The Moral Majority, for instance, is opposed to abortion, the Equal Rights Amendment (ERA), sex education, gay rights, cuts in our defense budget, and Salt II. They are, however, for prayers in the schools. But why is so little said about hunger and starvation? Why nothing about human rights, the burden of poverty and unemployment, the extravagant and disproportionate use of the world's resources by our country, the crimes of the American penal system and torture of prisoners in many parts of the world?

I question and object to the list of issues that the religious right has identified as the moral agenda facing our nation. They are theologically and ethically inadequate. A Christian's agenda ought to reflect God's concern for the whole world. This kind of concern represents what Jesus called the "weightier matters of the law."[11] I regard the theology of the religious right, expressed in their choice of issues for concern, as unfaithful to the fullness of biblical witness, and I question many of the answers they give.

On March 22 of this year, I was scheduled to debate Cal Thomas, spokesperson for Moral Majority. He is Jerry Falwell's "right arm." Mr. Thomas had appeared on KOMO Television on Sunday night several months prior to March 22. Randall Mullins, Jim Thiebaut and I drove him to Sea-Tac Airport on Monday morning, where he was to board a plane for his home in the Washington, DC, area. It was our plan to share breakfast together and to set "ground rules" for the ensuing debate.

In the course of our meal, I said, "Mr. Thomas, I am sure that you are aware that your ideas and mine will be revealed in debate to be miles apart. I do not share Moral Majority's lack of confidence in the merits of ERA. I disagree with your belief that prayers should be introduced into the public schools. I believe in cuts in the defense budget, which, as I understand it, you do not. I believe in sex education in the schools. I do not 'write off' gays as sinners as you do. To me they are people whose sexual expressions are not mine, but they are still God's children as we are, and it is not our responsibility to point the finger of judgment.

"We shall have to discuss in the debate our varying interpretations of the Bible, for it will, in the main, be theological interpretation with which we will deal."

There was an awesome silence, and then Mr. Thomas became livid with rage. "Dr. Turner," he said, "I do not have the habit of engaging in arguments at the breakfast table, and I don't want to begin here. I have no intention of debating you in the area of theology. That is your field. I am concerned with issues. I have been an employee in national television since I was a young man, and it will be with issues, as I say, that we will deal!"

"But," I countered, trying not to be argumentative, "how can we talk about any of these issues without referring to the Bible from which you draw your scriptures to buttress the positions you hold?" Again a silence. Conversation ended. Pleasantries were exchanged, and the call for the boarding of his plane came over the public address system.

Well, I was not surprised when a call came canceling the debate. I do confess to you that I am often irked and irritated by what seems to me to be an intransigent and inflexible spirit among many fundamentalists. I'm sure they say the same of me. But I, with you, do not want it to be so. I want to heed the counsel of Mark Twain: "You ought to get [your brain] out and dance on it. That would take some of the rigidity out of it."[12] I am not impressed, per se, when I hear another described as one who has the courage of his convictions. So what? A bigot can have the courage of his convictions. What really takes courage is to be willing to continuously re-examine our convictions and alter them if new information would encourage us to do so.

I am confident that we are all trying to learn to live not only on tenets, but tentatives as well. It is intellectual suicide to subscribe to a creed, for a creed is an intellectual landmark. We may discover new truth in intervening years, and we do not want to be harnessed to a statement of the past which now in the repeating violates our integrity.

As I see it, living is a process of continuous rebirth. The tragedy of life is that many die before they are fully born. "We must," as Thomas Huxley said, "sit down before fact as a little child, follow humbly wherever and to whatever abysses nature leads."[13] For then, and only then, will we know the truth that sets us free.

May we all be delivered from the cowardice that shrinks from new truth, from the laziness that is content with half-truths, and from the arrogance that thinks it knows all truth.

∽⚬∾

A SHARED JOURNEY

The Grace of Receiving

❦

The practice of gift giving at Christmas time traces back to the wise men who came to the manger bearing gifts of gold, frankincense and myrrh to the Christ child. Now, nearly two thousand years later, we give gifts to those whom we love or know to be in need. In this yearly renewal of giving at the Christmas season, we discover anew the joys that giving can bring both to ourselves and others. We all wish we had more money so that we could buy bigger and better gifts for those whom we love. But, alas, for most people, money is in short supply. One man remarked that there were yet many days till Christmas, and already his disposable income had been disposed of. Perhaps some jingle bells because it is all they have to jingle. In answer to our query requesting his want list for Christmas, one of our sons responded, "Why not send money? It is so easily exchanged."

But there is good news for all who have limited resources with which to buy for others. We can be gracious receivers and that in itself is a gift to one who has been kind to us. Those who receive what is given with genuine joy, enthusiasm and deep appreciation contribute to the joy of the donor. We all know people who receive even the smallest of favors in such a gracious manner that we always wish we could give something more.

Jesus did say that it is more blessed to give than to receive, but he didn't say that it isn't blessed to receive. It is as important to know how to receive a gift as it is to bestow one. The manner in which we receive a gift makes a difference to us and to one who gives it. One of the genuine joys of giving is that it makes someone else happy. Sometimes, the manner of receiving can destroy some of the joy of the giver. A little girl received a gift of a pincushion from her grandmother. She wrote a thank you note, saying, "Thank you, Grandma for the pincushion. I've always wanted a pincushion, but not very much!"

Most of us have a few close friends who can be very frank with us, for we know that friendship is not threatened by constructive criticism. When in seminary, one of my best friends gave me the gift of a new book. It was an expensive book, a gift beyond my deserving, and I knew it cost more than my friend could afford to spend. I responded by saying, "Ed, you should not have done this. You don't even have such a fine book for your own." I could see he was crestfallen at my comments.

Then, after a moment of reflection, he said, "Dale, sit down. I want to say something to you that I hope you will never forget." He used a few strong words to cement it to my mind, but no purpose is served in calling them to your attention. I leave it to your imagination. The gist of his speech was this. "Dale, when someone loves you, cares for you, plans for you and even sacrifices something of his own to give you a gift, don't make him feel he should not have done it, that he has exercised poor judgment or made a mistake in giving you a gift. Let him know you appreciate it very much. Don't kill his joy by being a poor receiver."

And, warming to his lecture, I recall that he said one thing more. "When someone gives you a compliment in words, don't disagree or minimize what he says, for words are gifts, too. Accept them gratefully, even though you don't think you deserve them. Take it for granted that the one who commends is sincere in his commendation. Accept his words and cherish them, for you will hear plenty of another kind before you are through with this life. A compliment is a gift not to be thrown away carelessly unless you want to hurt the giver. I'm sorry," he concluded, "for this sermon, but I felt that it needed to be said."

That was forty years ago that I received that lecture, and although I have not always applied its truth as well as I should, I have, nevertheless, not forgotten it. It was for me a teachable moment. I saw then that it is thoughtful to pay as much attention to how a gift is received as it is to give one, for both receiving and giving are manifestations of Christian love.

My friend was right; words are gifts, too. George Bernard Shaw said, "My idea of a good conversation is to find someone who will listen to me."[1] That means someone who will graciously receive the gift of my words.

I was seated in a restaurant across from the booth where a high school girl and boy were sitting. He was talking and she was listening–really listening. She was giving him a look that you could have poured on a waffle. I assume he was telling her how wonderful she was. I hope so. The point is that regardless of what was being said, she was certainly a most gracious receiver.

At Madison Avenue Methodist Church in New York City, there was a woman who listened to Dr. Ralph Sockman each Sunday with rapt attention. One Sunday she went to him and said, "Oh, Dr. Sockman, I so enjoy hearing you preach. Every sermon is better than the next!" Dr. Sockman, great man that he was, knew what she meant and thanked her, but chuckled to himself and mused, "What she says, alas, may be all too true!"

When I was in college, I was the janitor of the administration building. Often, while sweeping in the library section of the building, long after I thought everyone had gone home, I would hear someone talking. At first I was startled; then I came to know it was Dr. Lewis Chrisman, the literature professor who had a habit of talking to himself as he browsed through the stacks. When I became better acquainted with him, I ventured to comment about his habit. "Dr. Chrisman," I said, "when I first heard you talking to yourself, I was surprised and startled. How did you come to develop such a habit?" I have never forgotten his answer.

"Dale," he said, "why should you have been surprised? It should not be embarrassing for anyone to be caught talking to himself any more than it is for people to sing to themselves, which many people love to do. Certainly, if you are not on speaking terms with yourself, you need to do something about it. And besides," he continued, "I have always loved to have an attentive audience, and I enjoy hearing an intelligent man talk!" That was answer enough for me! Now, if you see or hear me mumbling to myself as I walk across these spacious and beautiful grounds, it will not be because I love to hear an intelligent man talk, but it will be because I am still practicing a habit acquired from Dr. Chrisman years ago.

Jesus was a wonderful giver. He "came not to be ministered unto, but to minister and to give his life as a ransom for many."[2] But, Jesus was a great receiver, too! Matthew, Mark and John all record that a woman used precious ointment worth about six thousand dollars to anoint Jesus. The disciples criticized her for what they considered an unwise extravagance. "The ointment," they said, "could have been sold and the money given to the poor." But, Jesus praised her, for he knew of the love that was behind the gift. Jesus, the great giver, was the most grateful of receivers.[3]

How rich are those who know how to receive graciously, for we all receive in a lifetime more than we are able to return to others. For instance, we live in houses we did not build and sleep in beds we did not construct. We sleep beneath sheets or blankets we did not weave and wear clothes we did not fashion. We eat food we did not grow and read books and papers we did not write. We ride in cars we did not manufacture on roads we did not create, and we come to worship in buildings we did not erect.

God showers upon us more wonderful gifts than we can ever fully receive, gifts of beauty–the sky, sun, moon, stars, flowers, grass, lakes, streams and the mighty oceans. God's gifts are everywhere present and remain only to be received. Consider, too, the gift of music–how much less life would be without this precious gift! God gives us that gift tonight through voices and instrumentalists in their interpretation of Handel's incomparable "Messiah." How sad if we run all of the way to the grave without having been gracious receivers of all that God offers to us. It remains for us to be gracious receivers.

At this season of the year, we are sensitized anew to God's greatest gift of all, the gift of His Son. Centuries ago, God walked down the steps of heaven with a little baby in His arms–a marvel, His gift to our world. For the little baby grew to become a man who leads us to God, rescues us from meaningless meanderings and reveals to us the way in which our lives should be lived. "I am the way, the truth and the life; he that followeth after me shall not walk in darkness, but shall have the light of life."[4]

But, all in Jesus' day were not wise enough to follow. The fourth gospel reminds us that "Jesus came to his own and his own received him not, but as many as received him he gave power to become children of God."[5] To receive Jesus is to let his spirit rule our lives so that with the Apostle Paul, we can say, "I live; nevertheless, not I, but Christ liveth in me."[6]

Jesus does not force or thrust himself upon us today. He does not overpower us. He comes to us, but the initiative of response is ours. "Behold, I stand at the door and knock. If anyone hear my voice and open the door, I will come in and eat with him and he with me."[7] The latch is on the inside of the door. We must let Christ in.

This is what Phillips Brooks tried to make clear when he wrote the carol we will sing as our recessional hymn.

How silently, how silently, the wondrous gift is given;
So God imparts to human hearts the blessings of his Heaven.
No ear may hear His coming but in this world of sin
Where meek souls will receive him still, the dear Christ enters in.[8]

You Are as Good as Your Words

Among the many fascinating and distinguishing aspects of being a human being is the ability we have to use words to convey ideas. I imagine that a systematic, thorough study of the evolution of words would be one of the most thrilling and interesting of studies. From the grunts, groans and signals of primitive humans to the complicated, intricate language pattern that we now have is an intriguing pilgrimage. Of this journey, there is no end. New words are being coined continually. The English language has five times as many words today as it had in the day of Queen Elizabeth. New words are being born, and old words are undergoing change of meaning. It is difficult to keep pace with the modern lingo.

When I was a boy, certain kinds of music were described as being hot; today, the same music is described as cool, a complete reversal. It used to be that character was something a person had. Now, it is something he is. Square once meant dependable and honest. Now call a person square and you may lose a friend.

Many good words have passed out of popular usage. "Fellow traveler" was once a fine phrase to describe a companion on a journey, but now call one a fellow traveler, and there is the lifting of eyebrows. "Comrade," too, was once a fine word, rich in affection and closeness of spirit. Now, call another comrade and some see red.

Many euphemisms have also come into the language. I can recall when I was a child that I was afraid to encounter the truant officer. Now, he is the "Manager of Student Attendance Problems." Some words grow old and become threadbare. Such words as "dialogue," "relevant," "at this point in time" or "you know" soon become pretty old. One man remarked, "I wish that people who insist on using nonsense words like 'input' would 'upshut.'"

No doubt, each given word in its beginning had only one meaning. But words are so full of life that they are continually sprouting the green shoots of new meanings. For instance, the three-letter word "run" already has ninety dictionary definitions. There is a run in a stocking, a run on the bank and a run in baseball. The clock may run down, but you run up a hill. Colors run. You may run a race or run a business. You may have the run of the house or the run of things, and on and on it goes.

When we drive west on 45th or 50th streets and turn south onto I-5, we usually see hitchhikers thumbing for a ride. I marvel at the lack of imagination in the young people who are there. Most have no sign at all indicating where they want to go. Some have signs hastily and poorly prepared. With a little foresight and creativity, they could have prepared signs that would have made a ride more likely. For instance, I once gave a ride to a hitchhiker who had a huge, beautifully prepared sign, which read, "She lives in Denver!" Well, we all want to help the cause of love, so it was easy for me to stop. I have seen other signs, too, that revealed imagination and were effective in securing a ride. For example, "I had a bath this morning," and "Anywhere but here." Once I saw a couple whose sign read, "Drive with Caution and Care. I'm Caution, she's Care."

Since words are so commonplace, there is always the risk that we take them for granted or fail to realize how very important they are. George Buttrick, one of America's great preachers, knew the power of words. He tells of speaking at a high school commencement. At the bottom of the program, he noted the class motto, "Deeds, Not Words." Dr. Buttrick rebelled at this because he reasoned that words are deeds. We commonly think erroneously that the greatest way in which we can help others is through tangible gifts of money, clothing or food. But in reality, through the gift of memory, words of comfort and cheer reside in the mind to lift our spirits long after they were spoken. Mark Twain said, "I can live on a good compliment two weeks with nothing else to eat."[1] The poet was right.

> *Words are things, and a small drop of ink,*
> *Falling like dew, upon a thought, produces*
> *That which makes thousands, perhaps millions think.*[2]

Do you remember how Luther Burbank was converted to his life work? At the age of nineteen, still unschooled, he read Darwin's book, *Variations of Animals and Plants Under Domestication.* That does not sound emotional, but it converted Luther Burbank. That is to say that printed words gave him his vision, his idea of what he was going to do with his life, around which he marshaled his ambitions and desires, to which he gave his devotion and from which he never turned aside. The whole world seemed placed on a new foundation after he had read that book.

The tide of battle has turned on the oratorical skills of noted leaders. Early in World War II, waves of Nazis were beating on the shores of England, threatening to inundate that island of millions of people. On June 4, 1940, in the House of Commons, a bulky, tank-like man, whose trademark had become a cigar jutting from his lips like a turret gun on a tank, arose and spoke words of hope and courage to the many who were dispirited and afraid.

> *We shall fight on the beaches; we shall fight on the landing ground; we shall fight in the fields and on the streets; we shall fight in the hills. We shall never surrender.*[3]

Mere words, some may say, but ah, they set a tottering nation on its feet and gave hope to millions. Truly, Churchill mobilized the English language, enabling it to fight on behalf of peace.

Words, like all of God's great gifts, can be distorted and used to ends that alienate and divide rather than build community. Friendships have been strained or broken by the spoken word. When we were youngsters, we might have returned the taunt of another with, "Sticks and stones may break my bones, but words can never hurt me." But that's not true. Another's critical, biting words can hurt us deeply. We remember and experience the continuing pain.

The John C. Winston Publishing Company of Philadelphia some years ago decided to eliminate from its dictionaries all words that are used as uncomplimentary epithets in referring to different races and nationalities. Among the words omitted were nigger, dago, wop and coon. The decision was a good one, and we commend the spirit of it. But the dictionary does not create words or build a vocabulary. Words get into the dictionary because they come into the language. To get rid of them, we must begin at the beginning, not with the words themselves, but with the ideas that the words are intended to express. If a man has an ugly idea, he will eventually find a word to express it.

The heart of the matter is that speech is an index to the mind. The tongue reflects what the mind thinks. It shows where our minds have been feeding. When we use words, we are vocalizing our thoughts. A medical doctor sometimes says, "Let me see your tongue" to gain insight into physical health. A spiritual doctor might well say the same, for what the tongue speaks reveals spiritual health. Words reflect what is being thought. There are those who cannot be spontaneous, for they fear a wild dog will leap out at an inopportune moment and spoil their reputation.

It is not easy to bridle the tongue, but it is important that we learn to do so. Some have even cut their own throats with a sharp tongue as well as wounding others deeply. There is no merit in saying everything that comes to mind. Tact is the unsaid part of what we think. The Chinese have three gates through which words must pass in the mind before they can be uttered by the lips: Is it true? Is it kind? Is it necessary? Discretion, in speech, is more important than eloquence.

Sybil Partridge's prayer would be a helpful one to offer at the beginning of each day.

> *Let me no wrong or idle word unthinking say;*
> *Set thou a seal upon my lips just for today.*[4]

A card on the literature tables of the church also carries an important prayer.

> *O Lord, help my words*
> *To be gracious and tender today*
> *For tomorrow I may have to eat them.*

One needs to read only a little in the New Testament to see what high importance Jesus attached to words. Occasionally, we get a glimpse into how his mind worked. He seemed to weigh his words before he used them. "To what shall I liken this generation? To what shall I compare it?"[5] It is as though he were not willing to utter the first word that came to his mind. Like an astute general marshalling soldiers to accomplish a particular task, Jesus knew there were certain words that were better than others to carry God's message of love and goodwill.

He was not content to dress his speech shabbily. He dressed his thoughts in active, vascular words, teeming with life–words that walked up and down in the hearts of his listeners. He used parables, metaphors, similes and epigrams that stuck in the mind. He clothed his truth in illustration. He knew that naked truth has a way of running to hide.

In Matthew's account of the Beatitudes, there are one hundred nineteen words. Ninety of them are just one syllable. All of this had a marked effect on the reception accorded his message. "The common people heard him gladly."[6] The people of Nazareth marveled at the words of charm that came from his lips. The officer sent to arrest Jesus said, "No one ever spoke like this man,"[7] and he was right. Sometimes, I think that those of us who study to be spokespersons for His cause miss the lessons in simplicity that He would teach.

There is a story of an old missionary who had struggled by himself for many years in a remote area of the world. Finally, the mission board wrote to tell him that they had raised enough funds to send him an assistant. They sent a young fellow who had just completed seminary and had all the self-confidence and certainty that comes with being young and being right out of seminary. When he arrived at the mission station, they called together the chief and all the people of the tribe to welcome him. Then, they asked the young missionary to say a few words. He could speak only in English, so the old missionary stood up to translate.

The young fellow said something like this, "We must always remember that there is an infinite and qualitative distinction between the eternal gospel and all the historical manifestations of it under the contingencies of human existence."

The old missionary stood for a moment dumbfounded as the young man waited for him to translate that. Finally, the wise old missionary turned to the people and said, "Friends, he says he loves you, and he's glad to be here."

Theologians and ministers are often guilty of confounding the simple verities of the faith by clothing them in obscure and complicated garb. For instance, listen as St. Augustine explains the Trinity.

> *In that highest Trinity one is as much as the three together, nor are two anything more than one. And They are infinite in themselves. So each are in each, and all in each, and each in all, and all in all, and all are one.*[8]

My soul! If that wouldn't make an atheist or a Unitarian out of us, I don't know what would! If St. Augustine had wanted to confuse us, he certainly made his point.

I sometimes think that every profession declares a conspiracy in language usage to confound the laity. Lawyers wrap their words in legalese, a mix of ancient English and encrusted Latin. Doctors keep us wondering what really ails us as they describe our affliction in long and technical terms. Scientists keep us at bay by resorting to symbols and language that only the initiate can comprehend.

To shoot over the heads of those we address does not so much reveal that we are brilliant as it reveals us to be poor shots. "Though I speak with the tongues of men and of angels and have not clarity it availeth nothing."[9] Jesus did not put the spiritual food in high-sounding phrases so as to nourish only intellectual giraffes. He put it on the bottom shelf where all sheep could feed.

Professionals in religion are not alone in confusing issues with language. A woman left a note for her milk-man before she went to bed, "Please leave two quarts of milk today, and when I say today, I mean tomorrow for I am writing this yesterday."

What is important is not just smoothness of words and beauty of phrases, but the quality of life that underlies what we say. True, Jesus was a master in choosing the right word, but the words had credibility because He preached what He practiced. When Jesus finished speaking the words of the Sermon on the Mount, the recorder was not so much impressed by the matter as by the manner. "He spoke as one having authority and not as one of the scribes."[10] Socrates had said in the fifth century, "The quality of a man's character is more important than the content of his speech." Emerson said of Seneca, the moralist, "His thoughts are excellent, if only he had the right to say them."[11]

Most of us were introduced to Nathaniel Hawthorne's story of the Great Stone Face when we were early into our schooling. We remember that at the end of a valley there was a great rock formation that resembled a kind and benevolent face. Tradition had it that one day someone would come to the valley who would be the very image of the Great Stone Face. The attributes of love and kindness would be in his bearing, and his countenance would glow with goodness. Several celebrities came to the valley and were initially heralded as the ones to fulfill the prophecy, but they were soon seen as impostors, because they lacked the inner qualities of character and kindness that were so obvious in the great rock formation.

One evening, Ernest, one who had lived all his days in that valley–a life of kindness and caring–stood, as his custom was, to speak to the people as they gathered to share his words of wisdom. He stood at an elevation, silhouetted against the background of the rock formation. As he spoke, his face glowed, and his radiant, benevolent smile warmed the hearts of all who listened. As the people looked at him and then beyond to the mountain, they all acclaimed, "Ernest! Ernest! He is the very image of the Great Stone Face."[12] Then Hawthorne wrote these lines.

His words had power, because they accorded with his thoughts; and his thoughts had reality and depth, because they harmonized with the life which he had always lived. It was not mere breath this preacher uttered; they were the words of life, because a life of good deeds and holy love was melted into them. Pearls, pure and rich, had been dissolved into this precious draught.[13]

"Keep thy heart with all diligence," said Solomon, "for out of it are the issues of life."[14] The Apostle Paul builds on that counsel when he writes to the Philippians (counsel wise, then and now):

Whatsoever things are true, whatsoever things are honest, whatsoever things are just, whatsoever things are pure, whatsoever things are lovely, whatsoever things are of good report; if there be any virtue, and if there be any praise, think on these things.[15]

May God, who has given us a mind and a mouth, also give us the wisdom to keep the two connected. Let the words of our lips and the meditations of our hearts be acceptable in His sight, now and always.

When We Don't Get
What We Want

❧

O n Wednesday of this week, Lent begins. This is a period in the church year for penitence and preparation for the Easter season that is to come. It is a call to search our own hearts and lives to discover unfortunate habit patterns that should be discarded and learn how to give new priority to things of supreme worth.

One time, a little boy fell out of bed. His father hurried into the room to see what had happened. The little fellow, still half asleep, explained that he had fallen asleep too close to the edge he had gotten in on. Some do that in the church. They never get over into the middle of things, and before long, they are spiritual dropouts. By "getting over into the middle of things," I don't necessarily mean joining more groups, although for some people this could be a good thing. What I mean is to get into the scriptures with serious intent, pray with some degree of regularity and practice the Christian faith in the daily routine with more diligence.

My text for today's sermon is Philippians 4:11: "For I have learned in whatsoever state I am therewith to be content." In writing these words, Paul could not have meant that he was satisfied with all things as they were, or that he no longer aspired to be better himself. There is too much elsewhere in the record of his life to permit us to believe that. For example, "I count not myself to have attained," he wrote, "but I press on..."[1]

Nor did Paul mean that his contentment was based on always getting what he wanted or achieving every goal he desired. He wanted strong, robust health as we all do, but that didn't come to him. There was an affliction that plagued him throughout his life. He spoke of this affliction only as a thorn in the flesh. We don't even know what it was. How incredible that a person could write as many letters as he did and still not divulge the nature of his infirmity. That was magnificent restraint.

He did not get to be every place that he wanted to be. In the Acts 16, we read that he wanted to go to Bithynia. All of his plans were made in this direction, but he ended up in the city of Troas. The scripture simply says, "The spirit suffered them not to go to Bithynia."[2]

When we read the account of his life–shipwrecks, stonings, imprisonment, floggings, and all other manner of abuse–we marvel all the more that he could say, "I have learned in whatsoever state I am therewith to be content."[3] It is a secret we would do well to learn, for today millions of people are discontented with their lot in life and trying by every manner and means to escape from the situation in which they find themselves. Some take drugs, some overeat, and others drink to excess because alcohol seems the shortest road out of town. The sensual appetites run rampant, speaking not so much of their virility as of boredom, unhappiness and discontent.

Sometimes, the escape is gradual. Sometimes, it is a sudden, impulsive, overt course of action. Some of you may recall reading of an incident like this, recorded in our daily papers. A bus driver in the Bronx took the wheel of his bus, and instead of driving his route, which he had done conscientiously for sixteen years, week in and week out, he drove his bus right down to Florida. When he was questioned concerning this unscheduled tour, he simply said he was fed up with the daily routine and just wanted to get away from it all.

There are many who would feel that here is a kindred spirit. Indeed, there are occasions in each one of our lives when we think we would like to chuck it all, and break the bonds of habit and routine that become so overpowering day after day.

A witty bishop was once asked why he kept up a summer home that he seldom visited. "Do you not know," he replied, "that I must have some place where, though I never go, I can always imagine that I might be happier than where I am?" It is a strange quirk of human nature that so often we wish to be somewhere besides where we actually are or have something other than what we have.

> *As a rule a man's a fool*
> *When it's hot he wants it cool*
> *When it's cool he wants it hot*
> *Always wanting what is not.*[4]

In the fine book *Grand Hotel*, Vicki Baum describes this discontent. She writes:

> *The real thing is always going on somewhere else. When you are young you think it will come later. Later on you think it was earlier. When you are here, you think it is there. When you get there you find that life has doubled back and is quietly waiting here, here in the place you ran away from. It is the same with life as it is with the butterfly collector and the swallowtail. As you see it flying away it is wonderful. But as soon as it is caught the colors are gone and the wings bashed.*[5]

It is intelligent to recognize that there is some drudgery and routine associated with all of life. We must learn how to adjust to this fact and see that even in monotonous situations there are opportunities for creativity and service. One time, President Charles Eliot of Harvard was motoring in Canada in the spring of the year when the dirt roads were thawing. He saw a sign which read, "Choose well your rut; you will be in it for the next five miles."[6] We all get into ruts or habit patterns, and we are often in them not only for five miles or five years, but sometimes for an entire lifetime.

We tend to think of ruts as bad per se. But that is not necessarily so. Think of the great train, The Empire Builder. What a rut that train is in! Day after day, it is stuck in its four-foot, eight-inch groove. Over and over, it travels the same path–Seattle to Spokane to Whitefish to Fargo to Minneapolis to Chicago and back again. Some years ago, when this family of cars added a dome car as a part of its equipment, the old routine might have seemed dull. With the new asset, it could have felt qualified to wander a bit where the scenery was even more spectacular, say a trip down the Oregon Coast or into California or up north through Glacier Park. Fortunately for everyone aboard, The Empire Builder did not wander a single foot. Till the end of its days, the train will be in the same old rut–Seattle to Spokane to Whitefish to Fargo to Minneapolis to Chicago–and precisely because of that, it will continue to be a great and useful train.

One secret of contentment is to develop the habit of looking on the brighter side of things. There are those who have a difficulty for every solution. They continually see the hole and not the donut. We can learn to be pleased with everything: for wealth so far as it makes us beneficial to others; for poverty since we don't have too much to care for or keep track of; and for obscurity so we may live unenvied.

We might all wish for the outlook of the little boy who had an optimistic way of looking at defeat. He was playing alone with his baseball and bat one evening. "Hey, Dad! Watch!" he called, throwing the ball into the air and swinging fiercely only to miss it. "Wait, Dad," he said, "watch this one!" And a second time, he swung and missed. "Here's the one, Dad," he called out, yet the result was the same. But, the boy's ingenuity prevailed and triumphed. "Three strikes and out," he called. "Gee, Dad, aren't I a good pitcher?"

Samuel Johnson was right: "It is worth a thousand pounds a year to have the habit of looking on the bright side of things."[7] Yet, it will also help us if we will make an honest, sane analysis of our own situation and talents, and avoid continuously longing for something that is not within the realm of our possibility. True, our aim should exceed our grasp, but it is pure foolishness to set our aim so high that there cannot be even partial fulfillment. This leads only to continual frustration, disappointment and despair. We must learn to recognize our own limitations and learn how to live with them.

Dr. Harry Emerson Fosdick told of one boy who excelled in the community where he was born. He was the pride of his large family and also the handsomest, ablest boy in town. In everything he undertook, he was always first, captain of this and president of that. He grew into young manhood and became a serious, high-minded youth, headed for one of the major professions. But, he had a dangerous factor in his situation of which he was unaware–a dominant picture of himself as always a shining "first."

Then he went to a large university, where he found himself good, but not eminent. The expectations of peerless priority, built into him by his family and friends, proved fallacious. He suffered a serious nervous breakdown without knowing why. Only when he saw clearly the absurd tension between his actual and imagined self, and went through a thorough process of self-acceptance, did he get himself in hand and go on to make a credible and serviceable use of the self he really had.[8]

God doesn't expect us to be more than we are equipped to be. He wants us to see ourselves in the right perspective. Bishop Quayle and Merton S. Rice of Detroit were two close friends and often visited together. One time, Merton S. Rice said to him, "Quayle, how is it that even though your assignment is difficult and somewhat routine, you always manage to be so fresh and renewed?"

"Merton," said Quayle, "I am a farm boy. I've always found inspiration, revelation and renewal on a farm. When I am discouraged or low, or life is becoming too daily, I go to the farm, take off my shoes and walk through the soft grasses of the field. If it rains, I look up into it and am renewed and inspired."

"Well," said Rice, "I am a farm boy, too. I'll have to try that." And he did. He walked through the fields, sat and felt the cold rain down his neck, but no new revelation came at all, so he gave it up. Seeing Quayle later he said, "I did what you recommended, but to no avail. I just sat in the rain and thought, 'Rice, what a fool you are.'"

"Man," interrupted Quayle, "what more of a revelation do you want than that?"[9]

We do need to see ourselves in proper perspective. And perhaps each one of us needs to take his work seriously, but take himself with a grain of salt. We may never be what we once dreamed we might be, yet success in God's eyes is not what we achieve, but what the process of struggle does to us. What is important is not when we arrive or where we are, but what we are. What has life–with its frustrations, thwarted hopes and unfulfilled longings–done for us and to us? The quality of life that evolves from the struggle is the most important thing of all. It is not what a man actually accomplishes, but what he would accomplish and the manner in which he works at it, that distinguishes him.

There are two things that can happen to us in life. One is that we get everything we want, and the other is that we don't. It is better that the latter be true because if we got everything we wanted, there would be many fine qualities that might never come to the fore. Adversity and deprivation teach many lessons that we can learn in no other way. What an unmitigated tyrant or bore a person would be if he had never failed himself. If he were able to achieve everything he had set out to do, what unreasonable demands he would be led to make on all of us. It is undoubtedly good that we all bear in our bodies the scars of many defeats. Our own inability to reach all that we set out to attain or aspire to be ought to make us more patient and understanding with the shortcomings of others.

We have to learn to accept what comes to us and make of it what we can. If we don't get what we like, then we must learn to like what we get and make of it something positive and good.

Wordsworth, the poet, asks:

> *Who is the happy warrior? Who is he*
> *That every man in arms should wish to be?*
> *It is the one who, doomed to go in company with pain*
> *And fear, and bloodshed, miserable train.'*
> *Turns his necessity to glorious gain.*
> *In face of these doth exercise a power*
> *Which is human nature's highest dower;*
> *Controls them and subdues, transmutes, bereaves*
> *Of their bad influence, and their good receives.*[10]

Paul was such a happy warrior. Paul did not want Troas; he wanted Bithynia. But, as things turned out, Paul transformed that disappointment into positive gain, for Troas became the door through which Christianity moved into the Western world.

Paul did not want that thorn in the flesh. Thrice he prayed that it might be removed. It was not removed, but his infirmity was accepted in the confidence that in all things–even pain and suffering–God works for the good of those who love him.

Christ did not seek the cross. He did not want it. He prayed, "If it be possible, let this cup pass from me."[11] But he did not run from the prospect of the cross. He continued, "Nevertheless, not my will, but thine be done."[12] George Bernard Shaw, writing about what followed, said:

We have always had a curious feeling that though we cruci-fied Christ on a stick, he somehow managed to get hold of the right end of it, and that if we were better men, we might try his plan.[13]

One of life's chief joys is to take a little plot of land—barren, rocky and unpromising—and till it so conscientiously and with such imagination and creativity that something beautiful will grow where nothing beautiful had ever been. This is what Peter Milne did. His mission assignment placed him on the little island of Nguna in the New Hebrides.

What an unpromising situation that must have once seemed to be, but Peter Milne dedicated himself to it with such zeal and did his work in such an inspiring way that under his picture in the church he founded the natives placed the words, "When he came, there was no light. When he died, there was no darkness."[14]

Whoever we are and whatever the situation, there is something God can do through you and me that apart from us will never get done. Ours is a sacred trust. With characteristic insight, the poet John Oxenham penned words that set our lives in proper perspective:

Is your place a small place?
Tend it with care;

He set you there.
Is your place a large place?
Guard it with care;
He set you there.

Whate'er your place, it is
Not yours alone, but
His who set you there.[15]

∞

Giving Away the Sleeves
of Your Vest

❦

Next year, Protestant Christians throughout the world will celebrate the five hundredth birthday of Martin Luther. He was born in 1483. I am in correspondence with Dr. Roland Bainton, one of the world's foremost authorities on Luther and the Reformation. I have asked him to send me a list of books that might be placed in our library. I am eager to read more about Luther and have you share in the venture. Luther was one of life's "choice spirits." He was so totally alive and sensitive to his own frailties–sometimes almost too much so. In his pre-Reformation days, goes one story, Luther was such a compulsive confessor of moral peccadilloes that his priest, in exasperation, told him to go out and commit some interesting sins in order to relieve the tedium of confession!

The more I read about Luther, the easier I find it to compare him to King David in the Old Testament. Certainly, David, too, was a "choice spirit." He captures the imagination and in today's world would be described as a charismatic personality. Whatever David did, he went all out. When he sinned, he sinned boldly–no little peccadilloes. When he played, he played skillfully. When he fought, he fought vigorously. When he loved, he loved ardently. And when he worshipped, he did so with integrity, devotion and conviction. Small wonder that we think of David as a man after God's own heart.

The Scripture read today (2 Samuel 24:18-24) catches up with Israel's second king at the point where the nation was under divine judgment for attempting to take a census in opposition to the will of God. Just why this census was forbidden is not made clear. But, the pestilence that followed in its wake is all too clear and real. God, in his mercy, cut short the punishment. Out of a sense of profound thanksgiving, David determined to offer up a sacrifice. He approached a farmer by the name of Araunah, in the vicinity of Mt. Moriah. This humble citizen, awed by his master's intention, offered his threshing floor and oxen to the king free of charge. But, David insisted on paying. His words commend themselves to our consciences even to this day.

> *I will not offer to the Lord, my God,*
> *that which costs me nothing.*[1]

Incidentally, Araunah's floor went on to become the site of Solomon's magnificent temple.

We don't believe in sacrificing animals today. We do not look upon God as one who needs to be either placated or thanked in this manner. But, let us not assume in our sophistication that we have outgrown the need for honesty and generosity in our response to the Almighty. How easy it is to give what costs us nothing! This is like giving away the sleeves of our vests. Such an exercise allows us the sensation of doing something without diminishing us one whit. What a powerful sentence of scripture. Let it firmly take hold in our minds and spirits.

> *I will not offer to the Lord, my God,*
> *that which costs me nothing.*

There is much of this in our society, especially among folk who call themselves "liberals." I have in mind people who are willing, at the drop of a hat or a ballot into a box, to give away someone else's feelings and someone else's money. I once heard a rabbi say that the only thing upon which two Jews can agree is how much another Jew should give to charity. We sometimes find it easy to tell others what to do when we have nothing personally at stake.

I can recall several years back when many who lived nowhere near the area were saying that there should be a third floating bridge, glibly determining the destinies of those affected directly by such construction. In a similar attitude, some opt for the demolition of old buildings for which they have no feeling and in which they have not lived. In the interest of urban renewal, they decide to give away what belongs to those tenants–their memories, their associations, their livelihood and, yes, their identity. It is an easy thing for us to give away what costs us nothing. It's just like giving away the sleeves of our vests.

> *I will not offer to the Lord, my God,*
> *that which costs me nothing.*

Charity often consists of a generous impulse to give away something for which we have no further use. I have been a member of the Goodwill Industries Board for twenty years. Through those years, I have been made very much aware of the fact that one of our continuing problems has been the hauling away of "junk" left at pickup stations, which is of no redeemable value to anyone. It is cast-off material, the sleeves of a vest. And, would you believe there have been garments from which the buttons had been cut off? Can you imagine some thin and hungry recipient of that piece of clothing that could not be fastened!

> *I will not offer to the Lord, my God,*
> *that which costs me nothing.*

We cannot, however, sit in our glass house and cast the stone of judgment. There are so many within our churches who give a tip instead of a tithe. The sensitive Christian asks himself, "Is it I, Lord. Is it I?" If so, why is it that you and I and others are so easily satisfied to give God that which costs us nothing? The reasons are many. For one thing, we all have a tendency to accept the privileges of the church without bearing a fair share of responsibility. We have a way of distancing ourselves from the church's needs. We practice a deliberate "not knowing." We prefer a certain aloofness, feeling that what we do not know will not bother our consciences. At the same time, we want the church to be there when we need it.

I confess that I do not have as much scientific curiosity or "know-how" as I ought to have. Some people want to know how everything works and are always tinkering with materials to invent something new. The most notable in our country was Thomas Alva Edison. He always had thirty or forty ideas bouncing around in his head. Would you believe that before he died at the age of eighty-four, he had blitzkrieged the United States Patent Office with over one thousand patents. In the thirty-five years between the end of the Civil War and the end of the nineteenth century, the United States Patent Office granted more than half a million patents.

I envy those of you who do have scientific bent and skill. I have no insatiable hunger to know what the receiving arm is like inside the cassette recorder. I don't stay awake at night wondering how a car works. I like to turn the key and hear the purr of the motor. I don't begin to understand the miracle of television. I just like to turn the switch, watch the "big window" light up and see what mystery Quincy will unravel or rejoice in what the Boston Pops will be playing on Channel 9.

Some people are this way about the church. They don't care very much how it works on the inside. They would like to know that when they come on Sunday the building will be lighted and heated if it is wintertime; that there will be ushers on hand with bulletins to distribute; that the organ will be in good repair, and played by someone with ability; that the choir will be composed of good voices; and that the minister will have something to say instead of just having to say something. We like to feel that the announced weekly programs will click off satisfactorily. In short, we like to play it cool, but the only reason some of us can play it cool is because others are playing it hot. Many like to see this happening, even rejoice in it, but accept little, if any, responsibility for it, or have any real involvement in terms of physical presence or monetary support. Some would, by their actions, rewrite many of the old hymns of the church.

> *I love Thy church, O God*
> *Her walls before thee stand,*
> *But please excuse my absence, Lord,*
> *This bed is simply grand.*
>
> *A charge to keep I have,*
> *A God to glorify,*
> *But, Lord, no cash from me;*
> *Thy glory comes too high.*
>
> *Am I a soldier of the cross,*
> *A follower of the lamb?*
> *Yes, though I seldom pay or pray,*
> *I still insist I am.*
>
> *Must Jesus bear the cross alone*
> *And all the world go free?*
> *No, others, Lord, should do their part,*
> *But please don't count on me.*
>
> *Praise God from whom all blessings flow;*
> *Praise Him all creatures here below.*
> *O, Lord, my hymns of praise I bring*
> *Because it doesn't cost to sing.*[2]

Another reason why we tend to offer God what costs us nothing is that we bring to the area of stewardship the mind-set that we use in our business dealings in daily life. It is not much wonder why we are all made dizzy by it–revolving credit, spiraling prices and soaring taxes. Most of us grapple constantly with the problem of shrinking dollars and rising costs. Inflation cuts the dollar bill in half without destroying the paper. Costs of goods and services are continually escalating. People find themselves living in more expensive apartments without ever having moved. Salary increases are not always commensurate with inflation. One man wrote, "I wouldn't mind the spiral inflationary if my salary were not so stationary."

A war of nerves goes on relentlessly between us and those who would sell us their goods and services. Our aim is to get as much as we can for as little as possible. There is nothing wrong with this kind of thrift, bargain hunting and careful spending. It is commendable! But when such a procedure comes to the church, we are in serious trouble. When we approach an opportunity to give with bargain-mindedness–"How much can I get for how little?" or "How little can I give and still be respected and respectable?"–we are serving self rather than others.

I am afraid that some people spend twenty, thirty, forty and even fifty years in Christian churches around the world without getting their stewardship up from the minimal level. We often evaluate our gifts in the light of what they will mean to others, rather than in the light of what they actually cost us. You can tell more about a person by how much he has left after he gives rather than by how much he gives. But, the most important reasons why we fall into the pattern of giving to God what costs us nothing is that we are unable to recognize a growing capacity to give as our station in life improves. That's a fancy way of saying that affluence creeps up on us.

Very few people in our society are, by their own admission, well off. Many would say:

> *I don't want a lot of money;*
> *I'd be satisfied, I vow,*
> *If I could but afford to live*
> *The way I'm living now.*[3]

Affluence does creep up on us. We can rate our affluence by thinking about the various ways in which people approach the business of eating out. When we are really low on cash and wish to eat out, what we do is look at the menu posted in the window of the restaurant. If the arithmetic is on the high side, we keep moving. When we have a little money in our pocket, we don't stop to look at the menu in the window; it's too embarrassing. But, we go inside, we read the menu from right to left. When we are financially strong and perhaps have someone along we are trying to impress, we read the menu from left to right with hardly a thought of cost. The ultimate, of course, is to go to one of those exclusive fancy places where there are no prices on the menu. The assumption is that if you have to ask, you shouldn't be there in the first place. Probably the majority of us here are not studying the menus in the window. Let's be honest with ourselves here.

What happens, my friends, is that every time there is a bit of slack between our income and expenditures, the slack is immediately taken up by the purchase of the next item on our want list. These wants are the product of clever advertising and our own insatiable appetites. It's not always the high cost of living, but the cost of living too high.

I am convinced that many of us within the family of this church could do far more than we think we can because affluence has crept up on us so gradually that we do not fully realize our capacity to give.

I will not offer to the Lord, my God,
that which costs me nothing.

But, you may say, the church isn't God. The minister is trying to steal a base. It isn't right or fair to move from David's experience of offering something to God to a church's opportunity in stewardship. The church isn't God! But I dare to believe that the church *is* God's. However brokenly, we are his people, the sheep of his pasture, covenant partners with him in history, beneficiaries of his grace, and bearers of his mission in the world. A church that receives the consecrated gifts of its people has an enormous responsibility to exercise good stewardship. We tend to think of stewardship as belonging to the *giving* process. But stewardship is also very much involved in the *spending* process. It is an awesome experience to receive money from the people of God and feel the weight attached to a proper expenditure of these funds. Have you ever thought of it from that angle?

My experience has been that University Congregational Church is a zealous and wise overseer of its expenditures. It seems that every time we spend money, we have to clear it with everybody. That is as it should be. Every institution must have checks and balances. No one here has carte blanche–no layman, no minister that I know of, no board chairman or choir member. We scrupulously guard ourselves against unwise and unjustified expenditures. We owe this to you, and we feel our responsibility. If we level with God through this church and begin to think seriously about giving what costs us something, this church can promise in return that we all will be afforded contact with the needs of men and women everywhere. To use the language of Wall Street, the church is able to provide us with a "good investment spread."

Each of us has our own favorite special causes, but what is there like the church that touches so much of life in so many places? An ordinary offering plate can become an instrument by which the contributor can touch needs, not only near at hand, but in far places where we personally will never go. There is no such thing as a local church.

On an airplane flying from the West Coast to New York, a passenger suffered a heart attack. His hands began to quake, moisture formed on his brow and the color went from his cheeks. The cabin attendants gathered around him. Oxygen was administered. Eventually, the plane made an unscheduled landing in Omaha so that the stricken man could be admitted to a hospital. A man who happened to be in the same row as the man who became ill was moved to a back seat at the hour of the attack so that an oxygen tank could be put into place. In the renewal of the flight, one of the cabin attendants came by and asked him to sign a form as the closest eyewitness to the heart attack. The man adamantly refused, muttering something under his breath about not wanting to get involved. Once the cabin attendant gave up pleading with him, he reached into his briefcase and pulled out a newspaper and began to read about the world outside. When the ocean of the world's need rolled up on his little beach, he wanted no part of it. He preferred a safe, journalistic distance so that all the agonies, heart attacks and failures of life around him would seem like so much print.

We do try to keep in touch with reality here. Our antenna is out in sensitivity to need wherever we encounter it. We may not always *say* it right. We may not always *do* it right. But we are determined, in the name of the incarnate Christ, to be compassionate and relevant here, in the nation, and in the world. But, we need your help. An unlettered woman was asked to endorse a check that was given to her. She wrote on the back of it, "I heartily endorse this check." But, what they wanted was her name.

We set before you today a reachable goal. You and I are called to endorse the program with our name and dollar commitment to it. What will the figure represent to you and me? Will it show a willingness to accept a somewhat reduced standard of life? Will it represent a postponement of cherished consumption? Or, will it be something that we do with such ease that it costs us almost nothing–like giving away the sleeves of our vests?

> *I will not offer unto the Lord, my God,*
> *that which costs me nothing.*

Gift Suggestions

❧

The excitement of Advent accelerates with each passing day as we all look forward to Christmas, the day of days. The brightness of the season never dies even for those of us who are older in years, and we know that when we were young, Christmas Day could never come too soon.

> *Thirty days hath September,*
> *April, June and November.*
> *Then December doth arrive,*
> *And kids can't count past 25.[1]*

It will come as a startling statistic to some of you to hear that it was not until 1836 that Christmas became an official legal holiday in our country. And, it was not until 1890 that Christmas was recognized by all the then-existing states and territories. Now, it is celebrated in a countless host of ways. The custom of gift giving at Christmas time traces back to the story in the Gospels that tells of those who came bringing to the Christ child gifts of gold, frankincense and myrrh. Though we can give without loving, we cannot love without giving. So, we ask ourselves, "What can we give to those whom we love?"

Dr. Liston Pope, a former dean of Yale Divinity School, suggested two criteria in gift buying. "The perfect gift," he said, "should reflect the individuality of the giver and at the same time correspond to the wishes and needs of the recipient."[2] There are so many of you here who have hearts bigger than your pocketbooks. You would like nothing more than to be able to give expensive gifts to others, but financial limitation denies you this extravagance.

One man said, "Christmas is still many days away, and already my disposable income has been disposed of." At Christmas time, you don't have to have the holly, but you do need to have the berries.

But, all is not lost, for I come today bearing the good news that the gifts of greatest value can be given to others in spite of financial privations. Tangible gifts are a delight and welcomed by us all, but there are intangible gifts of great significance. What are these gifts? Kahlil Gibran answers that question in his essay on giving in this little book, *The Prophet*.

> *Then said a rich man, "Speak to us of giving."*
> *And he (the prophet) answered:*
>
> *You give but little when*
> *you give of your possessions.*
> *It is when you give of yourself*
> *that you truly give.*[3]

Ralph Waldo Emerson, the lofty idealist who, nevertheless, had a penetratingly practical knowledge of human nature, made an even stronger case when he wrote, "Rings and jewels are not gifts, but apologies for gifts. The only gift is a portion of thyself."[4] Well, we know that a tangible gift is a portion of ourselves, for it is an extension of our own personality–in the labor of hand and mind–that provided the money to make the gift possible.

What both Gibran and Emerson are saying is that there are intangible gifts that can be given which enrich the life of the recipient and the giver, gifts that require no money at all. In these minutes that are before us, I simply want to call to our minds what some of these gifts are. You will want to go beyond the gift suggestions I share and compile your own list. I would hope that on any such gift list that was prepared there would be the gift of physical presence. The fact that you are here in this church service, physically present, is a gift of your bodies and minds to the God who created us all. You have arisen early, prepared for this hour by washing, dressing, driving and parking, and you share now your physical presence with us all in giving the gift of your friendship.

The electronic ministries of radio and television are helpful to many who are shut in and unable to be physically present with others in worship. But, a radio and television ministry is no substitute for the physical presence of those who are well and able. No young man or woman in love would be satisfied with visiting only via phone. Each would want to be regularly in company with the other. Leigh Mitchell Hodges, the noted writer, was engaged in conversation with a prosperous businessman the day before Christmas. "Would you like to know," said the businessman, "what I'm giving my boy for Christmas?"

Expecting it to be some costly present, Hodges was surprised when the man handed him a paper on which was written:

To My Dear Son:
   I give you one hour each weekday, and two hours of my Sundays, to be used as you wish.
                                        Your Father[5]

Hodges smiled in surprise. He wondered how that boy would feel, and what he would think when on Christmas morning he read that slip of paper. If he was just an average boy, he would be much dissatisfied. If he was an unusual boy, he would realize that his father had given him something he could not repay. "Tell me," said Hodges, "how did you happen to hit upon the idea of giving such an unusual present?"[6]

The man answered, "The other day a young fellow, whom I had not seen since he was a lad about my boy's age, came to my office to 'make a touch.' His face and bearing carried the telltale marks of idleness and dissipation. He was simply a human derelict. 'Robert,' I exclaimed in amazement, 'I'm surprised to see you like this! And you with such a fine father.'

"The boy answered, 'Well, I've often heard Dad was a fine man. All his friends have told me so. I never knew him. He was so occupied with his business and his clubs that I only saw him occasionally at meal times. I never really knew him.' That made me think—and think furiously. And believe me, from now on I'm going to see to it that my son has a chance to know me, be it for good or for bad. I know now that the greatest gift a man can give—yet a gift every father owes to his son—is a little time."[7]

Harry Emerson Fosdick writes in his autobiography that the gift of physical presence was a gift his father made to him.

My father was more than a father; he was a companion and chum. There was a kind of fierce tribal loyalty in our home. We stood together, and we children knew that through thick and thin our parents were on our side. We read books and played games together. I recall especially euchre, checkers, cribbage. Father enjoyed the swimming hole as much as we did, and at last the great days came when he took me fishing with him in a rowboat on the Niagara River, where under the spell of comradeship in sport he got over to me more good sense than I would ever have taken in by way of command.[8]

The first gift for our list is physical presence.

The second is a gift of affirmation. In the giving of this gift, we affirm the worth of another. In a world that squeezes from us a sense of self-worth or significance, we desperately and definitely need to know that it matters that we live and that somebody cares.

The deepest need of the human spirit is to feel loved, needed and noticed. I shall not forget the conversation I had with a young man, a senior at the University of Washington. He was pointing out to me the difference between beauty and charm. "A beautiful woman," he said, "is one I notice. A charming woman is one who notices me."

With most people lovability is not absent; it is merely undiscovered. "Dig deep enough into anyone," observed St. Augustine, "and you will find something divine."[9] Have you not found that to be true? Often, beneath the most disheveled appearance–tousled hair, alcoholic breath, grimy face and unkempt attire–there beats the heart of one who is kindly and caring. Flip Wilson, the comedian, was asked why he selected a bulldog as a present for his children. He explained, "So that they would see that ugly face and discover all the love behind it and never take anything at face value in the future."[10]

Most people really don't know how beautiful they are or can be. They must be given hints. We are called to be enablers or encouragers. Would it not be a marvelous compliment if someone could ever say of us what one woman said to her friend? "I love you for the love you've given me, but even more for the love you've awakened in me and for the person you've helped me to become."

Goethe said, "If you treat an individual as he is, he will remain as he is. But if you treat him as if he were what he ought to be and could be, he will become what he ought to be and could be."[11]

But alas, so many of us are all too critical. We seem to have twenty-twenty vision when it comes to finding fault. Unfortunately, many of us fall into the trap of making sweeping judgments when we don't know what we are talking about. A case in point: At this season in hundreds, perhaps thousands of pulpits around the world, the innkeeper will again be maligned and criticized–called callous, cold and uncaring, one of the villains of the Christmas story. But, how do we know that? He could well have been a loving husband and a kindly father trying to do his work efficiently. All the evidence we have is that he simply said his inn was full. If there was no room, what would we have expected him to do–evict one of his tenants who was thoughtful enough to make a reservation? Did he not at least make some shelter available to Joseph and Mary, crude as a stable might seem? Some of us who have traveled through the night and have tried to find a vacancy sign or a motel would have given anything for even a makeshift shelter. Well, the innkeeper did that, and perhaps he did it for free. "You dear people," he might have said, "are terribly tired, and I will provide for you, but certainly won't charge for it." If we are inclined to blame, why the innkeeper? How about Joseph? Why did he not arrive earlier or dial a 1-800 toll free number and reserve a room?

To this day, the most memorable and to-the-point sermon I can recall is that of the Major League Baseball umpire who said it always amazed and dismayed him that a spectator three hundred feet up in the bleachers thinks he can call a ball or a strike more accurately than the umpire who is immediately behind the plate. Well, here we are two thousand years up in the stands, trying to make a judgment, and we could be very wrong. Maybe after all these centuries, we ought to say, "Let's hear it for the innkeeper!"

When the critical spirit dominates interpersonal relationships, it can make for a dismal situation for all involved. One woman said of her husband, "He seems always to be putting me down, hanging me up, putting me off or putting me on. He should have been a seismologist, for he has more ways of finding a fault than anyone I've ever known." It would seem to me that a perfect husband is one who doesn't expect a perfect wife and vice-versa. Another wife, whose experience was unlike the one to which I just referred, commended her husband for his willingness to overlook her frailties. "It's not what you see in me that makes you love me," she said, "it's what you refuse to see in me."

A mother, counseling her daughter prior to her wedding, said to her, "You picked him; now don't spend a lifetime picking on him." Marriage is not a reform school. There is no good point served in looking for the worm in the apple of your eye. "Be to his virtues very kind. Be to his faults a little blind."[12]

The gift of physical presence and the gift of affirmation, too, are marvelous gifts to others. I suggest one more gift for your list and mine, the gift of verbal praise. I am not speaking of palaver or flattery. When flatterers meet, the devil goes to dinner. I am speaking of genuine, heartfelt gratitude expressed with sincerity and integrity.

We are all leery of the glad-handing, back-slapping type, those who engage always only in sweet talk. Too much sugar is not good for the body or for conversation. Unfortunately, there are many who, for fear of being overly effusive, say nothing at all. One of the greatest injustices we perpetrate upon ourselves is to have a good impulse and then neglect or refuse to act on it.

> *A lovely deed was in my heart*
> *I never set it free.*
> *It died from lack of exercise*
> *And made its tomb in me.*[13]

We must do the good things we feel urged to do and speak the kind words we feel led to say. Speaking to a group of men years ago, Billy Sunday said, "Men, try praising your wife, even if it frightens her at first!"[14]

George Eliot, (Mary Ann Evans) said, "I want not only to be loved, but to be told I'm loved. The realm of silence is large enough beyond the grave."[15] She was a very prominent woman, and one might think she did not need that, but she did. No one ever outgrows the need for praise.

And, another man said, "I've yet to be bored by someone paying me a compliment."[16]

> *If you think that praise is due 'im,*
> *Now's the time to slip it to 'im.*
> *For he cannot read his tombstone*
> *When he's dead.*[17]

The summary of what I've been trying to say this morning is: You cannot buy the warm impulses of the human heart, and yet it is this gift above all others that the world so desperately needs today. At the Christmas season, humans are more human than at any other time of the year, and we see what joy and peace it brings to all. Spencer Michael Free has said it for us all.

> *'Tis the human touch in this world that counts,*
> *The touch of your hand and mine,*
> *Which means far more to an aching heart*
> *Than shelter and bread and wine;*
> *For shelter is gone when the night is o'er,*
> *And bread lasts only a day,*
> *But the touch of the hand and the sound of*
> *the voice*
> *Sing on in the soul alway.*[18]

Praise God for those who, in days gone by, wrapped arms of love around us and gave to us words of encouragement and hope. May He help us now, in our day, to be enablers, drawing forth from others the sleeping beauty that resides within all.

WAR AND PEACE

Networking for Peace

❧

A colleague of mine, one of the ministers of our Congregational Church back on the East Coast, told me that a woman in his church was thinking of withdrawing her membership because, as she said, "I would have hoped that the sanctuary of our church would be what the name implies—a sanctuary from the bombardment of all the problems 'out there.' I am looking," she continued, "for some peace of mind and am not in the mood on Sunday morning to be made painfully aware of still more anguish. I want peace, not challenge." You and I can relate to that. We are bombarded day after day by news headlines that beat us down and depress us with stories of war, murder and depravities of every kind.

It is true that a sanctuary should at times be just that—a sanctuary, a refuge from life's storms. Jesus did come to comfort the afflicted, but He also came to afflict the comfortable. My colleague's answer to his beleaguered parishioner was not without point. "My friend," he said, "I honor you for your forthright spirit, and if I deal with social action themes to the neglect of sermons that meet the need for comfort and solace, I apologize and will try to give more attention to that aspect of my preaching. However," he continued, "God knows we all want peace of mind, but I'm sure we all want honesty more. Better a tortured integrity than a phony peace."

My friend knew what I am sure we all know. These are serious times, and there are evils in the world that threaten our very existence. War, for instance, is the most deadly sickness known to humanity. Ten million people died in World War I; perhaps as many as forty million lost their lives in World War II; and twenty-five million have died as a result of war since 1945. A countless number of others have been permanently maimed, and millions suffer today from the loneliness that comes from the loss of loved ones claimed by war's madness. Sherman was right; war is hell!

Furthermore, the financial cost is staggering. The world is now spending more than five hundred billion dollars annually on armaments. Iran, for instance, spent thirty billion dollars on imported arms during the reign of the Shah. President Reagan is pushing forward now with his proposed 1.6 trillion-dollar defense program over the next five years. The making and purchasing of armaments is no longer limited to the great powers. The race for military equipment is occurring in the poorest sections of the world. This is money that Third World people can ill afford to spend. It takes food from the hungry and denies education and health care.

Nations traditionally seem to be incapable of dealing sensibly with insults or assaults. The tendency has been to respond with such severity that the offending nation will not be tempted to repeat the abuse. Each nation wants to teach the other nation a lesson, a lesson that is explosive and unproductive. In the orchestration of our world, each nation seems ready to beat the war drum, and no country wants to play second fiddle.

Whatever the worries of the citizen of the Revolutionary and Constitutional period of American history, the one problem they never had to worry about was human annihilation. Today, it is the central issue to which all others are subordinate. The means are now at hand for purging the earth of life in human form or, failing that, to lacerate it so severely that joy or meaning will be separated from the human heart. The individual who wants to do something feels cut off and paralyzed. Feelings of hopelessness and helplessness pervade our society, and we wring our hands in despair. We know that in the event of a nuclear war, the question will not be who is right, but who is left? General Omar Bradley was right: "The way to win an atomic war is to make certain it never starts."[1]

The very size of the problem creates a sense of remoteness from the individual. He feels connected to the danger, but not to the means of meeting it. Therefore, the mood of our times is one of discouragement and defeat. Recently, three newspaper columnists have pointed out that two out of three Americans, or sixty-eight percent, believe that there will be a major war in the next few years. We could ask: Is it possible to be an optimist in a world which has turned most if its organized brain power and energy and money into a systematic means of debasing life or mutilating it or scorching it or obliterating it? What basis is there for hope when the human future is increasingly in the hands of men who do not comprehend the meaning of the new power and who are, some of them, puny and fretful and prone to act out of frustration or false pride or mistaken notions of grandeur?

Mao Tse Tung said, "War can only be abolished through war."[2] Must we believe that? Are we so pugnacious by nature that we'll never find a moral alternative to war? There are millions who believe that our effort to stem the tide of another war is as futile as endeavoring to sweep back the ocean's waves with a broom. Could it be that, like Chicken Little, we are reacting before all of the research has been completed? I believe that we are. Edison said, "What man's mind can create, his character can control."[3] He said that before the day of atomic and nuclear power, but I believe it would be his conviction today. It is not unrealistic or naive to look for the promise as well as the problem.

Progress begins with the idea that progress is possible. Cynicism begins with the notion that retreat and defeat are inevitable.[4]

"I hate cynicism," said Robert Louis Stevenson, "a great deal worse than I do the devil; unless perhaps, the two were the same thing."[5]

We must be intelligent enough to be scared, but not so scared as to not be intelligent. We need to think like people of action and act like people of thought.[6] Thomas Paine reminded us that those who expect to reap the blessings of liberty must undergo the fatigue of supporting it.[7]

The first goal must be to do away with fear and distrust. This, we say, is easier said than done. How can we trust the Russians when we see what they have done in Afghanistan? "But," asks the Russian, "how can we trust the Americans when we see what they did in Vietnam?" It is so easy to engage in name-calling and make the mistake of comparing the best in one society to the worst in the other. I, with you, am wary of the Russians–as they are wary of us. My point is that we need to move toward understanding of each other. We need to remind ourselves of the truth made clear by Ralph Bunche when he said, "There are no warlike people, just warlike leaders."[8]

In time of war–or the threat of it–the first casualty is truth. We must not be hoodwinked by falsehood. We must keep steadily in mind that people the world over yearn and pray for peace.

Vivid in my mind is an experience that my wife Leone and I had in Leningrad several years ago. We attended a circus performance and were seated beside a Russian soldier. Though we were unable to communicate via language, we were able to convey our friendship to each other. We laughed together and slapped each other on the back when we watched aerial acts that required more than an "oh" or "ah." At intermission time, he left the arena, but returned when the performance was to begin again. He was bearing in his hands three ice cream cones, one for Leone, one for me and one for himself. Was he trying to impress? No! His spirit of friendliness was characteristic of people we met throughout our travels in the Soviet Union. How fallacious and evil it is to lump people together and condemn them en masse. People are people everywhere–some good, some bad, but all yearning for peace.

General Dwight D. Eisenhower said: "I think that people want peace so much that one of these days governments had better get out of their way and let them have it!"⁹ Amen! Leaders need to hear the citizen's cry for peace. We need more conference and less combat for the world will not be saved by bullets but by brains, not by missiles but by minds. We must begin, then, with a willingness to divest ourselves of prejudice and seek the truth as best we can discover it. There is a proverb worthy of our attention: When a little bird tells you, be sure the little bird wasn't a cuckoo.

We must seek to incarnate the best of ideas in our own lives. Camus said:

> *Great ideas come into the world as gently as doves. Perhaps then, if we listen attentively, we shall hear, amid the uproar of empires and nations, a faint flutter of wings, the gentle stirrings of life and hope. Some will say that this hope lies in a nation; others in a man. I believe rather that it is awakened, revived, nourished by millions of solitary individuals whose deeds and works every day negate frontiers and the crudest implications of history. As a result, there shines forth fleetingly the ever-threatened truth that each and every man (and woman), on the foundation of his suffering and joys, builds for all.*¹⁰

One of the most arresting comments that Einstein ever made was when he said that if two percent of our population should take a personal, resolute stand against the sanction and support of another war, that would end war.¹¹ Whether or not this estimate of Mr. Einstein's is as accurate as his cosmic mathematics, I presume no one of us can say for sure, but there is no doubt about the historical evidence on which the principle of his judgment rests.

I like the comment made by Bonaro Overstreet.

> *You say the little efforts that I make*
> *will do no good; they never will prevail*
> *to tip the hovering scale*
> *where Justice hangs in the balance.*
> > *I don't think*
> *I ever thought they would.*
> *But I am prejudiced beyond debate*
> *in favor of my right to choose which side*
> *shall feel the stubborn ounces of my weight.*[12]

When people, who are genuinely aroused in a deep human way about what is happening to them and their fellow human beings, act on their concerns, they can release tremendous power and energy that can change the course of history. For instance, consider the peace movement in Europe. It is growing extraordinarily because there is a deep sense that the arms race is going to bring about the destruction of everything the people have believed in and held dear. They are crying out to tell us that it is absolutely essential that we initiate a campaign to freeze the nuclear arms race at present levels. Enough is enough! They would hope that George Kennan's plea would encourage Russia and America to reduce arms by as much as fifty percent.

Would it not be possible now to have a revival in the churches of our country and around the world of a gospel message of love unlike anything ever seen before? Next spring at the United Nations, there is going to be another special session on disarmament. Would it be possible to have a million people in the streets of New York to demonstrate to the people who come there that the people of God and the people of the United States care about disarmament and the abolition of war?

Never before have there been so many churches and temples, and never before has the institution of man been in greater jeopardy. Christianity has not truly involved itself in the human situation. It has become strangely adjacent to the crisis of man, seemingly content with trying to create a moral and spiritual atmosphere instead of becoming a towering and dominant force in the shaping of a world congenial to man. It has become one of the values we fight for instead of a force in itself.

Let the great religions cease explaining their differences to each other and begin to chart the elements of basic unity that could serve as the building blocks for common action. If religions are the custodians for the spirit of man, and if that spirit is imperiled, then responsible action is possible and essential.

It was heartening to learn that nearly forty universities across the United States, including most Ivy League schools, have degree-granting programs in peace studies. Student interest is beginning to surge as it did in the 1960s when the mounting opposition of youth to the Vietnam War helped to bring about its end.

For many years Milton Mapes, Jr. has been director of the National Peace Academy, a non-partisan public interest organization headquartered in Washington, DC. This organization has been seeking to create an Academy of Peace and Conflict Resolution. And why not? We have four military academies and five war colleges devoted to maintaining peace by armed force. It is about time that we had at least one national institution dedicated to creating peace by affirmative means.

In 1980, a Congressional Peace Academy Commission, chaired by Senator Spark Matsunaga, Democrat from Hawaii, was formed to explore the feasibility of a national academy. Just last week, little publicized but happily true, the commission submitted a report to President Reagan and Congress recommending that a National Academy of Peace be established! Actually, the idea is not new. As far back as 1792, Dr. Benjamin Rush, a signer of the Declaration of Independence, lamented the fact that the United States did not have an office for promoting and preserving perpetual peace in our country. We have been more than slow in coming to this time of recognition for the need of a peace academy, but with the threat of total annihilation, we can no longer be dilatory.

The devil, in meeting with his henchmen in hell, expressed great concern because the quota of inductees into the lower region was far from what had been anticipated. "Let me go to Earth," said one of the imps, "and tell man there is no God."

"It will never work," said the devil. "They have seen too much of His love and goodness to believe it."

"Then," said another imp, "let me go and tell humans there is no devil."

"No," responded the devil, "they have seen too much of pain and suffering to believe that." Then the devil decreed a course of action that was his very own. "Go," he said to the imps, "go and tell the humans on earth that there is no hurry."

With that commission, the devil's helpers have come to move among us, whispering into the ears of all, "There is no hurry. There is no hurry." It could be that if our worst fears ever came to pass it would not so much be the bombs that would obliterate us. We would have really died before, victims of the odorless gas of apathy. Ah, Edward Everett Hale, your motto was one for us all.

> *I am only one,*
> *But still I am one.*
> *I can't do everything;*
> *But still I can do something;*
> *And because I cannot do everything*
> *I will not refuse to do the something that I can do.*[13]

May God, who hast made of one blood all nations, keep us from falling into moaning about how bad the world is and help us to work for the good it was intended to be. Comfort us when we are overcome by affliction, and afflict us with the pain of loving involvement when we are overcome by comfort, that we may be worthy disciples of the Prince of Peace, even Christ Jesus our Lord.

What the World Needs Now

❧

We are aware that the governor recently signed legislation banning music with spicy, erotic lyrics. Nevertheless, there is still much so-called secular music that could be shared inside the sanctuary. For instance, I think of music published in 1965 with lyrics by Hal David and a tune by Burt Bacharach. It could serve as an anthem sung by any choir. Though published twenty-seven years ago and first made popular by Dionne Warwick, we still hear the tune or sing the lyrics today.

> *What the world needs now*
> *Is love, sweet love.*
> *It's the only thing*
> *That there's just too little of.*
> *What the world needs now*
> *Is love, sweet love—*
> *No, not just for some*
> *But for everyone.*
>
> *Lord, we don't need another mountain;*

> *There are mountains and hillsides enough*
>   *to climb.*
> *There are oceans and rivers enough to cross,*
> *Enough to last 'til the end of time.*[1]

So, I want to talk about love this morning. It is apropos that I do so now–in the spring–when there is a surge in the urge to merge, when the thoughts of young men lightly turn to baseball and other kinds of pitching.

But, it is important and relevant, too, that we talk about love here in the church. Love is mentioned over eight hundred times in the Bible. It is the central word of the scriptures. Albert Schweitzer was asked which of the Ten Commandments is most important. He answered, "Christ gave only one commandment. And that was love."[2]

Dr. Richard Niebuhr, brother of the famed Reinhold Niebuhr, was also one of America's great teachers of the Christian religion. He said the purpose of the church and its ministry is for the increase of love. That's why we are here. Beyond these walls people will know we are Christians not by our race or nationality or sex; they will know we are Christians by our love.

Love has never lacked for testimonials. Teilhard de Chardin, the renowned French scientist and priest, said, "Someday after mastering the winds, the waves, the tides and gravity, we shall harness for God the energies of love, and then, for the second time in the history of the world, man will have discovered fire."[3] Emmet Fox, a spiritual leader who was born in Ireland in 1886 and had a long ministry in New York City, made an exceptionally strong statement of love's power. He wrote:

There is no difficulty that enough love will not conquer; no disease that enough love will not heal; no door that enough love will not open; no gulf that enough love will not bridge; no wall that enough love will not throw down; no sin that enough love will not redeem.

It makes no difference how deeply seated may be the trouble, how hopeless the outlook, how muddled the tangle, how great the mistake.

A sufficient realization of love will dissolve it all.

If only you could love enough, you would be the happiest and most powerful being in the world.[4]

Yet, not all are enamored of the word "love." Aldous Huxley wrote a strong indictment of the word love, saying:

"Of all the worn, smudged, dog-eared words in our vocabulary, love is surely the grubbiest, smelliest, slimiest. Bawled from a million pulpits, it has become an outrage to good taste and decent feeling, an obscenity that one hesitates to pronounce."[5]

We can understand Huxley's revulsion to the use of the word "love," for it has become so confused in our society. In the back seat of a parked automobile, a man may say to a woman, "I love you." But, is lust masquerading as love? Does he love her for the wholeness of her being or only for the sensual gratification of the moment?

Joseph Fletcher, an Episcopal writer and teacher, suggests that we substitute the word "justice" for "love" because it comes close to expressing love's true meaning. Justice is love in its working clothes. But, it seems to me unnecessary to discard the word "love" or to use a euphemism. The word needs proper definition. How would you define love? There are many definitions that come to mind.

Love is friendship set to music.[6]

Love is the shortest distance between two hearts.[7]

Love is the doorway through which we move from selfishness to service.[8]

Love is the only flower that blossoms and grows without the aid of the seasons.[9]

Love is when two people agree to overestimate one another.[10]

Love is six people in a small automobile for a journey of three thousand miles![11]

Erich Fromm, in his little book *The Art of Loving*, points out that love is sustained goodwill. It is non-demanding, non-manipulative and unconditional acceptance of another, regardless of race, nationality, goodness or badness or sexual preference. Love is open and affirming of all.[12]

When our church voted on the issue of becoming an open-and-affirming church, I was asked to write a statement in favor of it–which I was. But I said, "Why make it an issue?" Open and affirming is the very nature of the faith we proclaim. I was willing to write the column for the church paper, but I was embarrassed that we, a Christian church, must bother. Unfortunately, there are some Christian churches that are not open and affirming of gays or lesbians, and I am proud of our church for underlining its openness to all.

Love must begin with self. Self-love, a combination of self-esteem and self-development, is a basic duty of all conscientious people. One of the distinctive marks of religion at its best is that it encourages the believer to have a just estimate of self. Where the Bible proclaims healthy altruism, it always accompanies it with healthy egoism. "Thou shalt love they neighbor as thyself."[13] That is, care for yourself first so that you will be prepared to give a gift of more quality to others.

As long as humans are enslaved by wrong attitudes toward themselves, they cannot help express wrong attitudes toward others. If the self is not loved, how can the neighbor be loved as oneself? A religion that ends with self is no worthy religion at all, but a religion that does not begin with self is equally inadequate and distorted.

I have long appreciated and enjoyed Andy Rooney. He has a way of saying what is oft thought but ne'er so well expressed, a way of illuminating the commonplace. When Harry Reasoner, longtime participant on the CBS program "60 Minutes," died on August 6, 1991, a subsequent program devoted a block of time for a remembrance of Reasoner delivered by Rooney, a colleague and one of Reasoner's closest friends. I have the transcript from CBS. It was a marvelous tribute to a marvelous man. In his closing remarks, Rooney said:

> *I talked with Harry about death—his and mine—as recently as six weeks ago and know he had no intention of dying. Harry was the smartest correspondent that has ever been on television, but he did more dumb things than most of them, too. He would not have died at age 68 if this were not true. How does the smartest man I have ever known lose a lung*

> *to cancer and continue smoking two packs of cigarettes a day! I'm sad, but I am angry too, because Harry was so careless with our affection for him.*[14]

When someone invests love in us, we have an obligation not to injure that investment by bringing grief to the one who loves us. We must strive to live at our best, for we give to others not only what we have but what we are. We must not be careless with another's love.

Love reaches out to others, too, in specific ways. Ideas need landing wheels as well as wings.[15] Love is not simply to be *explained*; it is to be *applied*. How do we do this?

A young man wanted to prove his love for his girlfriend, so he swam the deepest ocean, crossed the widest desert and climbed the highest mountain to show her his love. But, she dropped him because he was never around. What we say we want and what we do to get it are often two different things.

Paul Tillich, the great theologian, said "the first duty of love is to listen."[16] When we listen, we affirm another. We say, "You are important," and we contribute to that person's self-esteem. But more than that, when we listen, we stand the chance of learning something. Knowledge has never been known to enter the head through an open mouth.[17]

President Reagan was known as the great communicator. Calvin Coolidge was the silent one. Though he was the class humorist at Amherst, he was quiet and reserved as a political leader. When word reached Dorothy Parker that Coolidge was dead, she asked, "How do they know?"[18] He might have been Silent Cal, but he listened, and he didn't apologize for his listening. "No one ever listened himself out of a job,"[19] he said.

A preacher worth his salt is grateful for those who listen with love and empathy. They encourage a preacher to be better than he would otherwise be. My seminary roommate, Ed Linn, was a national college champion in extemporaneous speech. He told me it was the animated help of a large woman who sat beneath the clock at the back of the auditorium that won it for him. "Every time," he said, "that I made a point her face would light up as if to say 'Yes, Ed, yes! Tell me more, and then what happened?' It was as though she and I were talking excitedly about something very important. I'll never know who that woman was," said Ed, "but I'll be eternally grateful to her."

Many of you here have helped me more than you will ever know, and I'll be eternally grateful. When you have listened as you have with love and affection, I have wished my spiritual perceptions were deeper and my understanding more broad that I could be more worthy of such kindly attention.

Love sees possibilities in others. "Love is blind" is one of the many proverbs that is only partly true. Love is the only reality that really sees. It calls into being what is hidden but nonetheless real. Goodness may only be in the embryonic stage, but love can bring it fully alive. Luther Burbank, America's great horticulturist, often said, "Every weed is a potential flower."[20]

Jesus believed every person was potentially good no matter how great the depravity, and he helped to bring that goodness alive. Jesus saw goodness in Zaccheus, the crooked tax collector, and he became honest. Who would believe in Mary, the woman of the streets? Jesus did, and she became pure. And who would believe in

Peter–volatile, tempestuous, impulsive, unpredictable Peter? Jesus did, and he became Peter, the rock, the symbol of stability.

We wish in some measure we could be a friend or have one such as Roy Croft describes:

> *I love you*
> *Not only for what you are*
> *But for what I am*
> *When I'm with you.*
>
> *I love you,*
> *Not only for what*
> *You have made of yourself,*
> *But for what*
> *You are making of me.*
>
> *I love you*
> *For the part of me*
> *That you bring out;*
> *I love you*
> *For putting your hand*
> *Into my heaped-up heart*
> *And passing over*
> *All the weak and foolish things*
> *That you can't help*
> *Dimly seeing there,*
> *And for drawing out*
> *Into the light*
> *All the beautiful belongings*
> *That no one else had looked*
> *Quite far enough to find.*

I love you because you
Are helping me to make
Of the lumber of my life
Not a tavern
But a temple:
Out of the works
Of my every day
Not a reproach
But a song.

I love you
Because you have done
More than a creed
Could have done
To make me happy
And more than any fate
Could have done
To make me happy.
You have done it
Without a touch,
Without a word
Without a sign.
You have done it
By being yourself.
Perhaps that's what
Being a friend means
After all.[21]

Love also gives space to others. Love does not dominate; it cultivates. A friend and pastor of a neighboring church tells of a member of his church who was extending a welcome to the congregation in a worship service several years ago. It was the fiftieth anniversary of that man's wedding. In the midst of the welcome, he said, "Some people ask the secret of our long marriage. I suppose if I could point to any single reason, it would be that we take time to go to a restaurant two times a week that includes a candlelight dinner, a glass of wine, soft music and a walk home. My wife goes out on Tuesdays, and I go on Fridays!" My friend said, "I think he was jesting, but maybe not." We need closeness and shared experiences in marriage or other close relationships, but we need time to be alone, too.

Kahlil Gibran, in his perceptive essay on marriage, writes:

> *Let there be spaces in your togetherness*
> *Sing and dance together and be joyous,*
> *but let each of you be alone,*
> *Even as the strings of a lute are alone*
> *though they quiver with the same music.*[22]

Goethe said, "A creation of importance can only be produced when its author isolates himself; it is the child of solitude."[23] Certain springs are tapped when we are alone. The artist knows he must be alone to create, the musician to compose, the religious person to pray, and the writer to work out thoughts. John Ruskin once asked his friends to consider him dead for a few months, for he wanted to work in isolation from others. One of the books on my library shelves has an inscription in the front, which reads, "Dedicated to my dear wife Helen, without whose absence this book could not have been written."

Sometimes, one of the best roles for a mother or dad is instant availability without continuous presence.

Adolescents need to create distance from their parents and from other adults to complete an important phase of the developing process.

Love finds little ways to express kindliness and caring. It may simply be a smile, a warm greeting or an unsolicited gift. It may be a letter–unexpected or un-required by a birthday or anniversary. Life will always have zest as long as there is a mailman. Nothing echoes like an empty mailbox, and there is an emotional difference between a first-class and a second-class letter. A phone call is beautiful, but a letter is a gift!

We do not have to go beyond this church or community to find people who are masters of life's little amenities. Today, we are particularly mindful that there was one who lived among us. Tomorrow, all that could die of her will be laid to rest at Acacia Cemetery. She always remembered birthdays, anniversaries and celebrations of all kinds, and made calls on people in need. She was a cheerful person. She didn't simply brighten the corner where she was. She illumined a whole room! There are those who when they walk into a room seem to say "Well, here I am," and others who seem to say, "Ah, there you are!" She was one of those "Ah, there you are" persons. She could have a good time just thinking about what a good time she would have if she were having it.

She was a great sports fan, particularly of the Washington Huskies. Her father took her to a game when she was fifteen, and she was hooked, missing only three home football games in sixty-three years! Last fall, she fell victim to cancer and was given only a few months to live. Coach Don James, learning of her devotion to the Huskies, gave her an autographed copy of his book *James* in which he inscribed, "To the Huskies' greatest fan. We couldn't have done it without you." That book was cherished to the very end.

People may not be greatly swayed by our thoughts, but they can be deeply moved by our thoughtfulness. Alas, we sometimes forget or neglect such kindnesses.

> *A lovely deed was in my heart.*
> *I never set it free.*
> *It died from lack of exercise*
> *And made its tomb in me.*[24]

It is important, too, to express verbally the love we feel. There is a shortage in our day of good old-fashioned, sincere appreciation. There are critics by the hundreds, but the person who takes the time and trouble to see and mention the commendable is all too rare.

G. K. Chesterton said our greatest fear is the fear of sentimentality.[25] See how often it robs life of its best. We laugh when we want to cry. We hide our tenderness under a cloak of sophistication. We live on the surface when all the time we want to think and feel from the heart deeply. It may well be that history will honor the poets and lovers longer than the scientists and the statesmen, for it is they who keep alive what is most human.

Fifteen years ago, I said in a sermon, "Express your affection and gratitude now. Act on your impulse. Don't wait." Today, we would say, "Just do it!"

A young man from the University of Washington went from that service to his room and called his mother and dad in Connecticut. His mother answered the phone. She was startled and wondered what was wrong. "Oh, there's no problem, Mom. I was calling to see how you and dad are and thank you again for opening the door for me to come to this great university. Every day gets better and better."

I know this happened, for fourteen days later the young man came to see me. "Mr. Turner," he said, "I came by to thank you for the sermon you preached suggesting that we express the love we feel. I went to my dorm and called my mom and dad and told them of my gratitude." Then there was a pause and tears came to the young man's face. "Mr. Turner, three days after I called, my mother was killed in an automobile accident. I have just returned from the funeral. My dad told me how much my call had meant to her, and she spoke of it several times. I want to thank you for that sermon. Otherwise, I would not have called."

"It was not my sermon," I said, "but your sensitivity that is to be commended. It is obvious that your mother and dad taught you a lot. I'm sure your mother will always be more to you than a memory. She will be a living presence."

Emerson said, "You can never do a kindness too soon for you never know how soon it will be too late."[26] "Nothing is more certain than death; nothing more uncertain than its hour."[27]

> *Gather ye rosebuds while ye may,*
> *Old time is still aflying*
> *And this same flower that smiles to-day,*
> *To-morrow will be dying.*[28]

And that is why we sing:

> *What the world needs now is love, sweet love;*
> *It's the only thing there's just too little of.*

| 155 |

What the world needs now is love, sweet love,
No, not just for some, but for everyone.[29]

One of my favorite poems reminds me of that truth.

Six humans trapped by happenstance
In dark and bitter cold–
Each one possessed a stick of wood
Or so the story's told.

Their dying fire in need of logs,
One woman held hers back,
For of the faces 'round the fire
She saw that one was black.

Another looking across the way
Saw one not of his church
And could not bring himself to give
The fire his stick of birch.

The third one sat in tattered clothes
And gave his coat a hitch.
"Why should my log be used
To aid the idle rich?"

The rich man just sat back and thought
Of the wealth he had in store
And how to keep what he had earned
From the lazy shiftless poor.

The black man's face bespoke revenge
As the fire passed from his sight.

For all he saw in his stick of wood
Was a chance to spite the white.

The last man in this forlorn group
Did naught except for gain.
Giving only to those who gave
Was how he played the game.

Six logs held fast in death's still hands
Gave proof of human sin.
They didn't die from the cold without.
They died from the cold within.[30]

As R. L. Sharpe has written:

Isn't it strange
That princes and kings,
And clowns that caper
In sawdust rings,
And common people
Like you and me
Are builders for eternity?

Each is given a bag of tools,
A shapeless mass,
And a book of rules;
And each must make,
Ere life is flown,
A stumbling-block
Or a stepping-stone.[31]

If love becomes central in your life and mine, our lives will never be stumbling blocks to ourselves or others.

They will be steppingstones to higher, finer, personal satisfaction and greater public usefulness. To that high end, we dedicate ourselves today.

❧

Creative Controversy

❧

S omeone has suggested that the well-known scripture verse in Matthew 18 should be revised to read, "Where two or three are gathered together in my name, there will be division among them." In a church and a world where there are thinking people, diverse opinions and controversy are inevitably present. The important thing is what controversy does to us and what we do with it.

As one who counsels couples prior to marriage, I try to point out that the manner in which conflicting opinions are resolved is of utmost importance in the solidarity and happiness of the union. There is a chapter in one book on marriage entitled "How to Quarrel Constructively." Though I do not encourage quarreling, there are situations where an open facing of a grievance at the risk of controversy might be the storm that clears the air and makes the marriage more meaningful to both.

Conscientious parents discover that in the training of children, there is a likelihood of controversy. In order to avoid unpleasantness or controversy, some parents are more permissive than they ought to be. By the time they put their foot down on a self-willed boy, he already has his on the accelerator, and their problems are compounded.

As we move out of home into community, there are inevitable clashes of opinion on a variety of issues. The sale of alcoholic beverages in the university district, capital punishment in the state and war in the world are but a few of the controversial problems that concern us all.

Some might say or believe that the church ought to be one refuge from disputes—a harbor into which we can sail, free from the storm of controversy. But this point of view or hope receives no support in the Hebrew-Christian tradition. The Old Testament prophets were continually stirring up controversy with their attacks on the injustices of their times. The vigorous pronouncements Jesus made on controversial matters sent him to the cross. Had he confined himself to Mickey Mouse morals, he would have lived out a normal life, and we would never have heard of him.

His church is commissioned to deal with vital issues today, and all vital issues are controversial. To avoid those issues is to be an irrelevant, innocuous institution that is always answering questions no one ever asks and does not grapple with the genuine concerns of people.

Obviously, there are risks involved in controversy, risks of misunderstanding, discord and alienation. But, happily, controversy can be creative, too. G. K. Chesterton said, "I believe in getting into hot water; it keeps you clean."[1] Creative controversy may result in personal satisfactions and improved social relationships. For example, without challenging the inequities and injustices of our society and the controversy that has ensued, it is unlikely that African Americans would have advanced as far as they have. But, there is no assurance that mere controversy will be constructive. There are conditions that must be met if controversy is to be creative.

Controversy is not creative if it degenerates into estrangement, vindictiveness and hatred. The purpose of life and the thrust of the church are to build community, or common unity. The church should unite rather than divide. In the face of conflicting opinions, one need not be cantankerous or arbitrary. Unfortunately, there are some who, although they hit the nail on the head, always seem to split the wood.

However, a person can be conscientious without being contentious; he can be determined without being dictatorial; and he can be dedicated without being demanding. The Apostle Paul made it clear that love is not arrogant or rude. It does not insist on its own way. I don't know why we should expect everyone to believe as we do; we don't demand that they look like us.

Creative controversy draws a distinction between an argument and a discussion. In argument, we set out to defend an already determined idea. In discussion, though we have ideas of our own, we do come with an open mind, ready to give a fair hearing to another point of view. Of course, it is not good that the mind be so open that everything falls out.

As G. K. Chesterton said:

> *The object of opening the mind, as of opening the mouth, is to shut it again on something solid.*[2]

In creative controversy, we look for the solid and substantial truth.

Naturally, each one of us does have his own opinion when any controversy begins, and as the poet Alexander Pope said:

> *'Tis with our judgments as with our watches; none*
> *Go just alike, yet each believes his own.*[3]

It is not easy to divest ourselves of those opinions. Yet, creative controversy says that no man has a right to his own opinion in the face of contradictory evidence, nor does any man have a right to an untested opinion.

The idea of free speech can be construed to include innuendo, slander, and guilt by implication and association. Free speech, as it has been historically developed in this country, assumes that a person accepts responsibility for what he says. While all of us have a right to an opinion, none of us can afford to hold it untested, or in the face of contradictory evidence.

The Biblical truth here is obvious. Jesus said, "You will know the truth, and it will make you free."[4] Hammering out the truth is a costly, painful and sometimes explosive project. Nevertheless, the controversy that always surrounds the pursuit of truth becomes creative when one is willing to test his data, and then has the courage to modify it in the face of new evidence. We must move from irresponsible opinion to responsible judgment.

We praise a man who has the courage of his convictions, but every bigot and fanatic has that. What is much harder and rarer is to have the courage to re-examine our convictions and reject them if they don't square with the facts. We need to be intelligent enough to recognize our ignorance.

Mark Twain described a man he knew by saying of him, "His ignorance covered the whole earth like a blanket, and there was hardly a hole in it anywhere."[5] There is a moral obligation to be as intelligent as we can be. Speaking straight from the shoulder is fine, provided it originated a little higher up.

In creative controversy, we do not impugn the motives of another, although we may disagree vigorously with his conclusions. In the liberal Christian tradition, of which we are a part, we strive for unity of spirit without insisting on or expecting uniformity of conclusion. When everyone thinks alike, no one thinks. Lovers of liberty must expect diversity.

Our responsibility in the context of our Christian faith is to square the position we hold with what we conceive to be God's will as revealed through Jesus Christ. God's will is the court before which our conclusions must be judged.

The directive of my ordination is not to preach views, but news, news of God's will. Sometimes, those of us in the ministry are not as inclined to be purveyors of God's news as we are to be propagators of our own views. We must be constantly on guard against this pitfall. I saw a cartoon in a church magazine that pictured a minister in the pulpit preaching. Someone had affixed a sign to the front of the pulpit that read, "The opinions expressed here are not necessarily those of the sponsor." It is God who is our "sponsor," and it is His will we try to learn and reveal.

I like to speak, but I hope I will always be more ready to listen; I like to teach, but I hope I will always be more ready to learn. The temptation to be continually talking is an occupational hazard in my work. The God who speaks to people through their pastors often struggles in vain to speak to pastors through their people. A minister honors those who differ with him on controversial issues, especially when they support their positions with their names.

The Reverend Henry Ward Beecher was involved in many controversial situations. One time, after he had taken sides in a particularly vexing controversial subject, he received a letter on which was inscribed only two words: "April fool." The next Sunday, Beecher took the letter with him to the pulpit and said, "I have received many a letter where a man forgot to sign his name; this is the first time I ever knew of a writer signing his name and forgetting to write a letter!"[6]

It is a curious, but revealing, fact that many of the critical letters that come are unsigned. They are, of course, quickly assigned to the circular file. Those who are so insecure in their own conclusions as to be unwilling to be associated with them are more to be pitied than censured.

Controversy becomes creative if one doesn't overplay one idea. There is a story told of a country fiddler who could play only one tune. It came out of the Spanish-American War and was entitled "There'll Be a Hot Time in the Old Town Tonight." The fiddler played it well in several keys and several tempos. He played it appropriately at family gatherings, weddings, square dances and so forth. He ran into real trouble one night, however, when he was invited to play at a wake!

The tendency to play one idea, without respect to the problem that arises, spoils the idea of problem solving and critical inquiry. For example, every student demonstration is not Communist-inspired, nor is every street looting incident a result of the black-white problem.

Creative controversy does not remain on dead center. It moves from discussion to decision, from talk to task. A commitment must be made in the light of the facts we do have. Most of the major commitments of life are made before everything can be known; therefore, a man does not wait to commit himself to a particular vocation until he knows all about it. He makes a commitment on the basis of information he does have about the nature of that vocation. Then, he grows in understanding once the commitment has been made. Must a man know all that is involved in marriage before he commits himself to it? How can this be? There are calculated risks in any important venture.

There is no merit in becoming a part of a significant venture if no risks are involved. Early in the Suffragette Movement, there was great opposition to women's right to vote. Women held parades of demonstration protesting this unequal treatment. One of the parades was held on Madison Avenue in New York City, and all men were asked to join the parade. However, only eighty-nine men showed up to join the women and face the catcalls and derision of those on the curbs.

Years later, when women's right to vote was recognized as an honorable and deserved right, a parade was again held in celebration of this victory of feminine equality. This parade on Madison Avenue also had a special section reserved for those who had marched years before. According to a major city newspaper, most of the same women were there, and they were joined by five hundred of the original eighty-nine men!

There is no doubt that, in the presence of great issues, the uncounted are the source of greatest weakness. We are responsible not only for what we do, but for what we don't do. Henry Ward Beecher said that the hottest corner of hell is reserved for those who, in a moral crisis, remain neutral.[7]

There is much to commend the action of Joseph of Arimathea who asked for the body of Christ for burial. But in our appreciation for his thoughtfulness and courage in that hour, there is, nevertheless, an element of sadness. Where was he when Jesus was alive, when the issue of Jesus' life was at stake? Perhaps a word from him, for he was a man of influence, might have turned the tide.

> *Mourn not the dead who in the cool earth lie–*
>
> *But mourn the apathetic throng–*
> *The silent and the meek–*
> *Who see the world's great anguish and its wrong*
> *And dare not speak.*[8]

It has been well said that certainly, in all controversy, our task is not to cast the stone of judgment or condemnation, but to offer the helping hand of reconciliation; not to assign blame for the past, but to accept responsibility for the present and plan for the future; not to proceed self-righteously and vindictively, but to walk humbly, repentantly, and searchingly toward the truth revealed through Jesus Christ, who alone can set men free. It is to this end we dedicate ourselves this day.

May God deliver us from the cowardice that shrinks from new truth, the laziness that is content with half-truths and the arrogance that thinks it knows all truth.

Probing Our Prejudices

❧

Today is Race Relations Sunday. Indeed, the whole month of February is Brotherhood Month, stemming in part from the fact that it is the month when we celebrate the birthday of Abraham Lincoln. Whenever we discuss race relations, there is one word that comes up more than any other word, and that is the word "prejudice." So, it is well today that we discover exactly what we are talking about when we use this word.

When we turn to *Webster's Unabridged Dictionary*, we discover that the word "prejudice" comes from two Latin words that mean "to judge beforehand." It means to judge in advance of having all of the facts before us, to make premature judgment, judgment therefore susceptible to error because all of the facts are not in. It means lumping people and classes together and rejecting them all, without recognizing the possibility of differences in individuals within the group.

However, the most definitive definition that I know came from the pen of one of America's great preachers,

Dr. Ralph Sockman. He wrote:

> *Prejudice is that blind unreason which shutters the mind against the light of logic and refuses to look the facts in the face. That is prejudice. Prejudice is that cold predisposition which closes the heart against the approaches of affection and judges before it hears the defense. That is prejudice. Prejudice is that vampire of the mind which flies about in the darkness of ignorance and sucks the blood of ruddy hopes and healthy enterprises. That is prejudice. Prejudice is the smoldering dislike of the different which can flame up in a rage of hatred against our pioneers, our saints and our saviors. That is prejudice Among the sins of men there are none which have brought more heartache and suffering or have hindered our progress more than prejudice.*[1]

In the first chapter of the Gospel of John, we read that Philip of Bethsaida had been called to be a disciple of Jesus, and he started immediately to win other followers to Christ. Soon, Philip found Nathaniel and began to tell him about Jesus. "We have found him of whom Moses in the law and the prophets did write–Jesus of Nazareth, the son of Joseph."

But Nathaniel was not impressed. He merely replied, "Nazareth? Can any good thing come out of Nazareth?" Nathaniel obviously had a prejudice against all Nazarenes. No longer thinking of the men and women of Nazareth as individual persons deserving to be judged on their own merits, he lumped them together and rejected them all. "Can any good thing come out of Nazareth?" However, when Jesus saw Nathaniel, he said, "Behold an Israelite in whom there is no guile."[2]

He was a respectable person all right, but the sin that lived within him was terrible.

Nathaniel has long since been dead, but the sin of prejudice is still very much alive. Tragically enough, it makes its home in some of the most fashionable churches and often resides with the most respectable men and women.

Prejudice is a sin of the mind, and sins of the mind are often more subtle than sins of the body. Sins of the body like sensuality, dissipation and intemperance usually leave their open marks on the body to produce a sense of shame and perhaps repentance and reformation. But, sins of the mind can sometimes lodge for years unrecognized or undetected by the person who has them. If we are honest with ourselves, we will admit that we all hold prejudices in our minds that are irrational and harmful. Many of them entered our lives before we were old enough to know how false and vicious they actually were. We are not born with prejudices; we acquire them, and we all have more prejudices than we probably suspect.

The child absorbs prejudices from his environment–from his parents, relatives, friends and the society in which he lives. We learn a great deal before we even go to school, and education is not always a formal process. We are constantly receiving impressions. Our formal education should not be underestimated, but it is by no means the whole of the matter. The attitude of the parents does much to affect the child.

We are not sure why Nathaniel was prejudiced against all Nazarenes. Maybe he had heard from his parents that Nazareth was a wicked city. Perhaps he had never even been there himself or met anyone who had, but if his parents had said so, it must be true. In fact, we can find little or no evidence to support the belief that Nazareth was more wicked than any other city.

Many parents, who would abhor the thought of poisoning the body of a child in any way, poison young minds without any qualms of conscience with ideas that harm or destroy and have no correlation to the truth. If parents hate Jews, Russians, Chinese, Catholics or African Americans, children catch that hatred. Prejudice is highly contagious. Even as we grow older and confront facts that reveal our conclusions to be illogical, we nevertheless find it difficult to put away prejudices, for they are often emotionally grounded in someone we love. To reject a prejudice often seems to be a rejection of the person from whom it was learned.

Spinoza said, "An affect (emotion) cannot be restrained or taken away except by an affect opposite to, and stronger than, the affect to be restrained."[3] We know that a prejudice that was not acquired by reason cannot easily be discarded by reason. Winston Churchill once observed that people "occasionally stumble over the truth, but most of them pick themselves up and hurry off as if nothing ever happened."[4] It is a mature person who can sit down before the facts and go where they lead.[5]

Fortunately, there are millions of conscientious parents who are trying to guide their children into intelligent channels of thinking. There is a woman in a New Jersey suburb who tells of her eight-year-old daughter's first manifestation of prejudice. The little girl came home from school one day dropping the remark that she did not like a certain playmate. The mother, being an alert person, sensed that perhaps this was the beginning of a prejudice because the disliked schoolmate had a Jewish name.

Figuring that she would nip the prejudice in the bud, she told her daughter that the Jewish people had just as much to be proud of as any other people. "Don't you know," she said, "that Jesus was a Jew?"

The tiny girl thought for a moment and then replied, "Well, anyway, God was an American."

Such confused thinking is humorous, understandable and, in some measure, excusable in a child. But, when prejudice persists in an adult, it is tragic and even dangerous. "The Jews?" said Hitler. "Can any good come out of that religion?" Moses, Isaiah, Jeremiah, Amos, Hosea, Jesus, Paul and subsequently hundreds of others ought to have made that crystal clear, but Hitler, unable to see this, lumped them all together. In rejecting them en masse, he destroyed millions of wonderfully fine people.

"China?" say some. "Can any good come out of China?" Unable to distinguish between the people and the government under which they live, they group Chinese people together and reject them all. In so doing, they build barriers between peoples and make peace less likely.

There are many in our society who say, "Catholicism? Can any good come out of that?" Lumping Catholics together, they reject them all. My father came out of Catholicism, and I loved him very much. How wrong I would have been had I been willing to believe that nothing good could come out of Catholicism. Many of our best friends are Catholics, and many people we admire are of that Christian persuasion. But, this does not mean that we are apologists for Catholicism.

There is a difference between conclusions that are gained by an analysis of facts and beliefs that are held without regard for the evidence that is available. The former can lead to convictions that deserve to be held and the latter to prejudices that must be called into question!

In spite of what I hope is my liberal and enlightened position on Catholicism, one of my friends once said to me, "Dale, you are prejudiced against Catholics."

To that person, I replied, "No, it is not against Catholics that I take a stand, but against some of the conclusions of Catholicism. If love of the democratic form of church government in contrast to the authoritarian government of Catholicism is prejudice, then I plead guilty to prejudice. If belief in planned parenthood is prejudice, then I am guilty. If the right of private judgment in interpreting the scriptures at all points is prejudice, then I am guilty as accused. If belief in the priesthood of all believers is prejudice, then I am prejudiced. If belief in the scriptures as final authority is prejudice, then I am guilty. You see, I have not lumped Catholics together to reject them all. Rather, I have studied Catholicism as best I know how and have rejected some of its conclusions. Is this prejudice?" No, it may be erroneous interpretation of facts or stubbornness, but it isn't prejudice.

There is nothing to indicate that when we assemble all the facts about any individual, group or ideology, we will automatically accept and love what we discover because we understand more fully. This is not necessarily true. Familiarity may even breed contempt. One man said, "We can't always trust first impressions. Sometimes they are wrong. For instance, I met a fellow who when I first met him irritated me a little. Later, I found out differently. When I got to know him, he irritated me a lot!"

The most pronounced and obvious prejudice in our society today is the white man's prejudice against African

Americans and African American prejudice against whites. Many white Americans do have a prejudice against African Americans. Lumping them together, they condemn them all. Can any good thing come out of that race? George Washington Carver, Booker T. Washington, Marian Anderson, Ralph Bunche, Thurgood Marshall and a host of others, known and unknown, have answered the question convincingly. But, many remain unconvinced.

In the Christian church, we do all we can to root out prejudice against African Americans. We believe that racial prejudice is as great a denial of the Christian God as is atheism, for race prejudice denies the universal Fatherhood of God and the brotherhood of man. These are central Christian affirmations. This is what we teach here and ought to teach in our homes. Yet, what we see in our society seems to counteract this teaching. We see segregation and discrimination in many ways. We see the black man in subordinate roles, denied privileges enjoyed by whites. An African American is paid less money than the white for the same job, and is subject to many other inequities. Seeing all of this, we conclude that the preacher was "just preaching," and these people with dark skins really are inferior.

And this visible evidence to support prejudice, irrational as it is, is reinforced by the language we use. We read that evil is black while white is virtuous. Angels who represent virtue are pictured as white. Did you ever see a black or dark-skinned angel? Black is a symbol of sorrow. White speaks of happiness and purity. We use such phrases as black sheep or black as sin. All of this subtly deepens prejudices against dark-skinned people.

So many white people have been brought up in this kind of segregated society that it would be a miracle if they had no prejudices. I confess that I have prejudices. I have been a victim of my society. Now intellectually, I am totally convinced that mankind is one. I know that brotherhood is not a hypothetical dogma but a biological and spiritual fact. Yet, there are vestiges of prejudice that reside in my emotions that I am continually working to discard.

Prejudice is an insidious sin because such reasoning is a distortion of human personality. It damages both the soul of the prejudiced and the one against whom the prejudice is directed. It gives the prejudiced a feeling of superiority and the victim a feeling of inferiority, neither of which is necessarily based on facts. It is difficult to know who is damaged more–the prejudiced or the one against whom the prejudice is directed. Benjamin Mays, a great African American leader, points out that millions of African Americans now alive will never be cured of the disease of inferiority.[6] Many have come to really believe that they are inferior or that the cards are so stacked against them that it is useless for them to try to achieve the highest and best. Segregate a race for hundreds of years, tell that race in books, in law, in courts, in education, in church and school, in employment, in transportation, in restaurants, hotels, motels, and in government that it is inferior, and it is bound to leave its damaging mark upon the souls and minds of the segregator and the segregated.

Because of the white man's discrimination against the African American for so many years, the African American has prejudices against the whites. Many African Americans believe that all whites are phonies, long on talk but short on practice of brotherhood. It is unfair of the African American to lump us together and condemn us all, for there are countless individuals within the white society who work and sacrifice on behalf of the African American.

But, the opportunities for African Americans to know us, and the opportunities for knowing African Americans are limited by the geographical boundaries of housing. This separation provides fertile soil for misunderstanding and prejudice. It affects our schools and churches. Busing students in and out of the central district is a temporary expedient at best; it is merely a stopgap measure, a putting of salve on a cancer.

Our church is affected by housing restrictions. Although ours is a highly mobile society, many tend to go to a church nearby, and here there are few, if any, African Americans nearby. What we are teaching our children by indirection and by exposing them to an all-white environment here does not demonstrate the brotherhood we profess, nor does it prepare them for the multi-racial society in which they are to live.

It is to our shame that there is more Jim Crowism at eleven o'clock on Sunday morning than at any other time. According to a recent estimate, only one-tenth of one per cent of all African American Protestant Christians in the United States are in "white" churches. Dr. Benjamin E. Mays, to whom I have alluded, said that he would tremble for the Christian cause if fifty African Americans were to enter an average local church on Sunday morning and ask to become members.[7] It is a well-established fact in social science that the average churchgoers in our country harbor more social, ethnic and religious prejudice than do non-churchgoers. What a sad commentary to have to make.

We want all to feel welcome here. There are two African Americans now on our church staff, and we would be pleased to have a competent African American as our Minister of Administration if we can find one who would want to work with us and would meet the job requirements. African Americans are in administrative roles in government, industry, education, athletics and many other areas of community life. We are not seeking African American leadership just to reveal our freedom from prejudice, but if a capable African American helper applied, he would be given every consideration given anyone else. We would agree with James E. K. Aggrey, a great African American Christian, who said:

> *You can play some kind of tune on the white notes alone. You can play some kind of tune on the black notes alone. But for real music with full, rich harmony, you must play both the white and black keys.*[8]

The conscientious Christian feels deeply his responsibility toward all people. He reads, "Love your neighbor as you love yourself,"[9] and he believes his neighbor is any man. If he really loves him, he will desire every opportunity for others that he desires for himself. The Christian, then, is deeply concerned about the prejudices and inequities in his church and society. He wants to do more than lament it or talk about it. He wants to do something not because he is a radical or an extremist, but because he is a Christian, and every man is his brother.

This could be more than just a service where we have talked about freedom from prejudice. For each of us, it could be the beginning of a new dedication and concern for equal treatment for all. Our methods may differ, but we can all do something. Each one can say:

I am only one,
But still I am one.
I cannot do everything,
But still I can do something;
And because I cannot do everything,
I will not refuse to do the something
That I can do.[10]

When a man joins hands with that plan, he becomes one of the pioneers of a new day of brotherhood, which is sure to come.

⚮

Amnesty

❧

We are all well aware that the question of amnesty is a difficult and delicate one, highly charged with emotion and deep feelings. One of my colleagues in the ministry does not tackle controversial issues such as this in sermons, for he reasons that the problem will not receive a totally fair and honest hearing when opportunity for dialogue, rebuttal and questioning are ruled out by social propriety.[1] And, of course, his point is well taken. This is one of the risks that are involved in bringing the subject to the pulpit.

But there is a risk, too, in saying nothing and in acting as though there are no problems. The speaker, therefore, is under obligation to be as fair as he knows how to be. I see no reason why we cannot agree to disagree agreeably, if we must. It is, you know, possible and acceptable to disagree with your minister without being irreligious.

It is also possible and acceptable to disagree with your political leaders without being unpatriotic. Governor Evans[2] disagrees with President Nixon's ideas relating to capital punishment. This does not mean that our governor is subversive or that he does not respect President Nixon. I disagree with Governor Evans's[2] conclusions about lowering the drinking age to nineteen, but that does not mean that I am subversive or that I do not have respect for our governor.

Hopefully, we all pray for one another and are supportive of one another in every way that in good conscience we can be, yet feel free to disagree when a position taken by another does not seem to us to be the wisest or most loving policy. Lovers of liberty must expect and welcome diversity. When "everyone thinks alike, no one thinks at all."[3] I suspect Milton was right: "God prefers the lush and many-tinted profusion of springtime to the frozen conformity of winter."[4] In this context of love, openness and acceptance of one another, we look together at our theme of the morning.

During the Vietnam War, thousands of young men left our country and went to Canada, Sweden, Switzerland and elsewhere as political exiles. Thousands more deserted the armed services and went underground to avoid military service. Others openly refused induction and accepted the penalty of the law. Now, we are trying to decide whether, when or how, and under what conditions to bring these men back into the life of the community. The policy our nation chooses could be an important element in re-uniting our society, or it could further divide us. This is one of the reasons why it is important for us to consider the question of amnesty here.

Amnesty comes from the Greek word "amnestia," which means "not remembering," or "overlooking." It does not mean forgiveness. Forgiveness implies a pardon given to a guilty person. Amnesty is reconciliation with people who feel no guilt because their actions were ethically motivated.

We cannot assume that all of the young men who fled to other countries are looking longingly across national borders, eager to come back to the United States. Most, I suspect, are desiring to return, but not all. Some are now permanently and happily situated elsewhere, but would welcome the opportunity to visit family and friends here without being brought to trial.

Senator Charles H. Percy, an Illinois Republican, suggested that self-exiled draft dodgers and those in hiding might consider voluntary surrender rather than wait years for an uncertain amnesty. He pointed out that only one third of those prosecuted on charges of draft evasion are convicted and nearly three quarters of the convicted are put on probation.

Probably those of us here could be classified in any one of three categories. Some of you would say no amnesty. Others would agree with a conditional amnesty–that is, that amnesty should be conditional upon fulfillment of some generously defined and appropriately limited alternative service. And, there are those here who would affirm the rightness of blanket or general amnesty–wiping the slate clean, forgetting what has transpired and starting anew.

Those who believe that there should be no amnesty usually list at least five reasons for their position. One is tradition. There has never, following an American war, been a general amnesty for draft dodgers. Since President George Washington pardoned participants in the Whiskey Rebellion in 1795, there have been thirty-seven separate incidents of amnesty in American history, but no general amnesty. In other countries, yes, but not here. A review of American history brings to light several instances of amnesty of one kind or another for deserters, most of which occurred in connection with the War of 1812 or the Civil War. But, amnesties for those violating the draft laws have been few indeed.

Secondly, national unity forbids it. The most recent Gallup poll reveals that two out of three in America are against general forgiveness. The country, it is argued, would be divided, not united, by such a policy.

In the third place, justice demands that those who fled abroad or went underground be brought to trial. For every individual who deserted, hundreds served. Fifty thousand who served paid with their lives, not to mention the thousands more who are permanent cripples. Is it fair to the dead, wounded, hospitalized–fair to their families–that the runaways could come home scot-free?

In the fourth place, the rule of law must prevail. If a man can decide which law he will heed and which one he will break, then there will be anarchy.

And last of all, national security is at stake. Exoneration of draft dodgers and deserters would set a precedent that might convince young men in future emergencies that they risk little or nothing in ducking the country's call. The impact would be dramatic and adverse upon the men in the services who either volunteered or answered the call of duty.

Perhaps the most widely accepted of the three responses to amnesty is that of conditional amnesty, some generously defined and appropriately limited alternative service. Robert Taft, senator from Ohio, drafted a bill granting amnesty to draft resisters and deserters if they agreed to work for three years at subsistence pay at hospitals, or in the Peace Corps or Vista programs, or if they were willing to sign up for a four-year hitch in the peacetime armed services. Other such documents and bills have been suggested.

But, the American Legion objects to conditional amnesty. Its spokesmen point out that alternative service in a government agency such as a veterans' hospital would take jobs away from people who need them–for instance, from unemployed veterans of the Vietnam War. Moreover, they say that the quality of service in VA hospitals and other agencies would deteriorate if these were staffed by men who viewed government service as a sort of punishment.

The World Without War Issues Center, housed in Berkeley, CA, recommends conditional amnesty. They say:

> *It is false to assume that men who left this country or deserted are traitors or cowards. It is just as false to assume that they are all moral heroes whose just reward is unconditional amnesty. These men acted in a wide variety of ways for a wide variety of reasons. Equity for those who served and for those who resisted openly and accepted the legal penalty for their acts dictates that those who chose to leave the country or the military perform an alternate service assignment as a condition for amnesty.[5]*

Membership in a political community involves obligations as well as rights. One of those obligations is to obey the law or submit to its authority if conscientious refusal to obey is indicated. Unconditional amnesty would tend to undermine respect for law in our country and our world. Both need law, if we are to move away from war and violence. An editorial in a major New York newspaper points out that Socrates, Thoreau and Gandhi did not seek amnesty. They accepted the penalty of violation.

Then, there are those who espouse general amnesty–this is, forgetting what has happened, wiping the slate clean and beginning anew with no questions asked, and no penalties exacted. They contend it would be fair, more fair than to select a few scapegoats to bear the brunt of justice for all. Why pick on only the draft evaders, resisters or those who went underground?

Major Clement St. Martin is a Vietnam veteran now retired, who in retirement commanded the Newark, New Jersey, Induction Center, the fifth largest induction center in America. He says that for every draft evader who fled to Canada, a thousand legally evaded the draft through political influence, claims of homosexuality and submission of false documents, thus remaining in the United States. In the interests of equal justice, these, too, should be brought to trial. Others bought their way out of military service by going to college, but they are not labeled as draft dodgers, nor are they going to be punished.

In addition, many contend that the war itself was illegal. Congress did not declare the war though it continued to authorize funds and personnel for it. The small group in Washington who, in defiance of public opinion, made the decision to enter and escalate the war, broke both the moral and constitutional law. Yet, no note of humility or any intimation of wrongdoing has been sounded in Washington, regardless of which political party was in control. In fact, accusations continue to be heard.

In a recent speech before the Veterans of Foreign Wars, Vice President Spiro Agnew said that the nation must be unyielding in punishing deserters and draft evaders because they have not admitted they were wrong. Is it just for a stronger body to coerce a weaker one to confess to a wrong that he sincerely believes was not a wrong? This is to force a person into hypocrisy and a lie. A majority of the Americans are now convinced that our involvement in Vietnam was a blunder, but what government official is apologizing for that?

David Harris, former student body president at Stanford, points out that any type of amnesty, especially conditional amnesty, would force those who spent time wasting in American jails (where Harris spent twenty months for refusing the draft) to admit they had done something wrong. The only crime of those who fled to Canada, Sweden or elsewhere was to recognize with foresight what a majority of Americans did in hindsight: that the war was a mistake. They would be punished for premature wisdom. "We exiles," said Harris, "shouldn't accept a pardon or amnesty. We should accept an apology."[6]

He has a point. If the war was a mistake, as most believe, is it just to punish those who helped to dramatize that mistake at whatever cost? If their insights were ahead of public opinion and government policy, shouldn't it be easy to forget their error?

There are those who contend that the draft dodgers have failed in their duty to their country. But are there not other ways to serve a country than to fight for it? Is there not a contribution that a sensitive conscience can make? Must we always be in accord with our nation's political philosophy? Is it our country, right or wrong? What should have been the stance of sensitive youth in Germany at the time of Hitler?

If I see a friend whom I dearly love running toward a cliff of destruction, what course of action am I to take? Am I to run willingly along with my friend and die with him, no questions asked, or am I to shout warnings and try in every way I know to halt his progress or divert his direction? To witness his fatal course and sit by silently when something might have been done is a betrayal of friendship.

If I see the country I dearly love moving in a direction that seems suicidal to me, what am I to do? Is it unpatriotic to want to do something? How can I divert it from its headlong plunge? To flee to Canada may not be cowardice or rejection of country at all, but one way to vote for a new national policy and direction. There is no doubt that the thousands of men who did flee helped to sensitize the American conscience to the wrongness of our involvement. Is not the exodus of so many a warning to our government not to involve itself where it does not belong? There are some passages in the Bible, such as Romans 13, which was read today, that suggest that Christians should always be working with the powers that be. But, of course, there are ten passages to one asking them to seek a kingdom that goes beyond the kingdoms of this world.

Whatever one's opinion of the Nuremburg trials, in which the victors judged the vanquished, they resulted in wide acceptance of the idea that obedience to illegal or immoral orders is not the highest or even a valid form of service to country. General amnesty would restore to useful citizenship those whose disobedience to law helped their fellow Americans discern the true nature of the Vietnam War. If the civil rights of these men–men who refused to condone the massive violence in Vietnam–were restored by general amnesty, they would tend to be a leaven of good influence in our country against violence and a repetition of wars like the one we have just experienced.

The Seventh General Synod of the United Church of Christ, meeting in Boston in the summer of 1969, recognized the plight of these men when it urged the President to grant, at the earliest possible opportunity, amnesty and pardon for those who, for actions witnessing to their beliefs, have been incarcerated, deprived of the rights of citizenship, or led by their conscience into exile. The Synod statement continued:

> *We urge these bold actions because this nation needs, and is strong enough to embrace, both those who have engaged in the Vietnam conflict and those who have opposed it.*[7]

Pronouncements at our Synod meetings are not binding on any church or individual, but I find myself in agreement with the Synod statement and the political position of general amnesty. I am not unaware of the risks and the seeming inconsistencies in such a position, but the risks of love, generosity and forgetfulness would be worth taking. It seems to me that the policy of magnanimity is wiser and more far-sighted than the radical policy of punishment and revenge. Punishment inflicted on people who do not feel guilt or admit it has no value to them. It simply reinforces the unhealthy attitudes of hatred and revenge against the punishers, and therefore leads to deeper alienation instead of reconciliation. I do not see what worthwhile purpose would be served by a refusal to grant general amnesty, except to exhibit further the desire to punish and be vindictive.

There is joy in forgiveness and forgetfulness, and relief, too. There is pleasure and pride in magnanimity and bigness of soul, and we need the spirit of charity and goodwill today. The time has come again to bind up our nation's wounds and bring the healing touch of love and acceptance of one another.

I am only one. You, too, must decide. What you believe does make a difference. Public opinion is but the composite of the individuals who comprise society. May God grant wisdom as each one of us seeks to be part of the answer and not part of the problem.

∞

DIFFICULT EMOTIONS

Loneliness

❧

There are Sundays in this church and others, when we feel like the theme of the morning is irrelevant to our concerns or needs. It would be difficult to believe that that could be so today, for when the preacher talks about loneliness it includes us all. To be a human is to experience periods of loneliness.

Billy Graham was asked, "What is the one problem that plagues more people these days than any other?" His instant response was an answer that surprised many who were in the circle of questioners. "Loneliness," he said, "from the letters I get."[1]

In a poll of psychiatric patients, more than eighty percent of those interviewed admitted that loneliness was the principal reason they sought help. Depth studies of those attempting or succeeding in suicide–whose numbers may run as high as half a million in America each year–have revealed that it was loneliness that triggered the majority into their extreme action. Members of Alcoholics Anonymous testify how loneliness drove them to excessive drinking until alcohol became the central problem; a drinking habit that was at first a thread only, became a seemingly unbreakable cable.

Loneliness strikes without regard for age, place, sex, color or nationality. There is the loneliness of small children whose parents have too little time for them or have few, if any friends. A lonely child, wanting companions, said once to his mother, "Mother, I wish that I were two little puppies, so that I could play together." There is the loneliness of teenagers who feel edged out among peer groups, who feel alienated and misunderstood. There is the loneliness of the single person who longs for someone with whom to share. One young lady said, "I don't want to be liberated until I know what it is to be captured."

There is the loneliness of the marriage bond where many couples feel estranged from their partners even while living together. They exist only as ships that pass in the night. It is a desolating feeling to be alone in a room with another person.

There is the loneliness of one who has lost a loved one. There is the longing for the touch of a vanished hand and the sound of a voice that is still. Old or young, rich or poor, male or female, loneliness can assail us at any time, and often for no apparent reason. "It doesn't happen just on dark days," points out popular novelist Faith Baldwin, "It can pierce you like a knife on a spring morning or a golden summer afternoon, no matter where you are or what you are doing."[2]

The ravages of loneliness being what they are, I think it is not too much to say that a basic art of living consists of finding ways to conquer this most universal problem. We must understand what loneliness is and what it isn't, how it comes and how it can be dispelled. I do distinguish between loneliness and aloneness. They are far from being the same. Aloneness can bring on loneliness and often does. But it need not. Some of the most radiant and productive people I know are those who by necessity are alone much of their time, but who have learned to use their time creatively. In fact, we all need periods of aloneness from which we generate the physical and spiritual reinvigoration for our crowded days.

This is what the Psalmist meant when he wrote, "He leadeth me beside the quiet or still waters. He restoreth my soul."[3]

"A creation of importance can only be produced when its author isolates himself," said Goethe. "It is the child of solitude."[4] We must learn to pause or nothing worthwhile can catch up with us.

There are positive possibilities in loneliness. The experience of loneliness can teach us to appreciate more fully the family and friends we do have. It is occasional deprivation that enhances so many of the goods we might easily take for granted. Dag Hammarskjold wrote in his book *Markings*:

> *Pray that your loneliness*
> *May spur you into finding*
> *Something to live for*
> *Great enough to die for.*[5]

That something to live for, great enough to die for, is love. The deepest need of the human spirit is to love and be loved. When this need goes unfulfilled we are lonely. Dr. Reinhold Niebuhr said:

> *To love ourselves is our greatest hope*
> *To have another love us is our greatest joy*
> *To love another is our greatest fulfillment.*[6]

We are born to love, to reach out to others and be receptive as others reach out to us. We are lonely because we build walls instead of bridges. We isolate and insulate ourselves, and in that apartness we experience loneliness. Emerson, in his poem "Each and All" writes, "All are needed by each one. Nothing is good or fair alone."[7]

Love is the doorway through which the human soul passes from selfishness to service, from solitude and loneliness to kinship with all humankind. A Latin proverb says, "One man is no man at all." That is true. No one of us is complete in himself or herself; our families and friends are the rest of us. We were made by God to be at one with others. That's what the theological word atonement means, *at-one-ment.* It is important for emotional, spiritual and physical reasons that we establish the unity or community that we were created to know.

Perhaps you are familiar with the work of James Lynch, a specialist in psychosomatic medicine at the University of Maryland. His book, appropriately named *The Broken Heart: Medical Consequences of Loneliness,* probes the physical consequences of lack of human contact. He evidences that such can cause disease and cardiac problems. His conclusion speaks loudly to our culture: "Medical practitioners must make people aware that their family and social life are every bit as important to health as dieting and exercising."[8] Sometimes, in family or community groupings, one or more are shy and need others to reach out to them to establish the at-one-ness for which we long. Sometimes, people who may seem to us unfriendly and cold are merely shy and would want more than anything a friendly relationship that they find hard to initiate. Indeed, psychologists tell us that shyness is our most common psychological problem.

A woman told me that her son desperately wanted to help others. He had a beautiful sensitivity to people and their problems, but he was shy. He chose, therefore, to be a doctor. Among the many reasons for his choice was that it was a profession where those in need reached out to him. Most of us who have some measure of shyness reach out falteringly in some way or another in our effort to know community and experience at-one-ness with others.

Mrs. Corinne Wills tells of a time when she and her husband were lured to a stop by a roadside sign which read, "Antiques." Walking onto the porch they were met by two old ladies who ushered Corinne and her husband into the living room where they were served tea. When they asked to see the antiques one of the elderly women responded hesitantly, "We are the antiques." Then they told about their loneliness.

"We needed friends," one explained, "but how were we to make them? That's when we thought of the antiques sign. Only nice people appreciate nice things. But remember, our sign does not say 'Antiques for Sale.'" We've made so many beautiful and lasting friendships. We even correspond with many. We believe God isn't angry with us for this little trick, and we hope you aren't. Would you care for more tea or a crumpet?"

Rupert Brooke, a talented young poet who died when he was only twenty-eight years old, told of the time he was leaving England to come to the United States. There was no one at Liverpool to see him off on the ship, not a single person. So he looked around and found a half-clad, dirty-faced urchin and gave him sixpence to stand on the dock and wave to him until the ship was half a mile out. Mr. Brooke was desperately lonely in the crowd and said he would forever cherish the memory of the mercenary friendship of that urchin who was paid to wave his dirty handkerchief until the ship sailed out of sight.[9]

The problem of developing community is complicated in our day because we live in such a highly mobile society. Here in America the average human being moves fourteen times in his or her lifetime. A full fifty-five percent of our adults live over five hundred miles from the place of their childhood roots.

A further complication is present because of the high crime rate, certainly in most every major American city. Ours is a strange world of hostility, conditioning the extent of our hospitality. We feel we must build protective devices against the invasion of others into our lives. We hide our money, lock our doors, chain our bicycles, protect our apartments with dogs, and our roads with "No Hitchhiking" signs, and our airports with safety devices. We are participants in a culture that encounters hostility in so many ways, but perhaps the remedy of isolation and self-protectiveness is far worse than its disease.

Our responsibility and quest here is a twofold one. We seek an awareness of God and a commitment of loving relationship to others. Ours is a humanizing task. We come here week after week not just to fulfill a duty of physical presence, but to nurture friendships which are valuable to us all, relationships that transform God's lonely people into God's lovely people. It is good not to be lonely. It is good for us to be together in this place, not as a collection of individuals but as a community of love and concern.

We try to create here in our church conditions wherein bonds of affection can be fashioned in the midst of emotional, social and existential loneliness. The moment of greeting in the midst of our worship is not an interruption of worship flow, but a reaching out, fleeting and inadequate though we know it to be. The coffee hour is not a concession to our physical hungers. Indeed, most of us had coffee before we left home, or could have secured it en route. Rather, the coffee hour is a well-conceived plan, here and in other churches, to contribute to our emotional and social needs–a form of communion rescuing us from the isolation that is loneliness.

The minister stands at the door at the close of the service, not to receive congratulatory comments for the excellence of his sermon. To be sure, there are plenty of times when the preacher would like nothing better than to slink hurriedly to the privacy of his study when the service is concluded, for he knows all too well that he has had little to set before the faithful who have come. He remembers what one woman said of her minister, "He had nothing to say and he said it!" When the minister stands at the exit of the sanctuary, he sees his presence there as a part of the network of relationships that we all need as humans–clergy and laity alike.

The choir members share their talents with us, leading in our worship. But, of equal importance is the fact that the members of the choir minister to one another through the friendship bonds that are fashioned. I have encouraged others to become part of this choir, not only for the musical skills they will develop and share, but because it will afford them opportunity to come to know the choir director and be lifted in spirit by his friendly and positive spirit. There are so many wonderful human beings in this choir that I am eager to have new people welcomed into their circle of friendship and to be warmed by it.

A radio ministry, helpful though we hope it is to some, has its limitations. It offers the ministry of voice but denies the ministry of physical presence, the friendly hand and the kindly smile. It is, as the high school boy said, the difference between telephoning his girlfriend and being physically present with her.

> *'Tis the human touch in the world that counts,*
> *The touch of your hand and mine,*
> *Which means far more to an aching heart*
> *Than shelter and bread and wine;*
> *For shelter is gone when the night is o'er,*
> *And bread lasts only a day,*
> *But the touch of the hand and the sound of*
> *the voice*
> *Sing on in the soul alway.*[10]

There is an additional dimension still, invisible but equally real and important. It is at-one-ness not only with other human beings, but with God that we seek. Only that relationship can ultimately rescue us from our loneliness. St. Augustine stated it well and accurately in his well-known prayer: "Oh God, Thou hast created us for Thyself and our hearts are restless 'til they find rest in Thee."[11] We all yearn, aspire, and reach out to know the God who created us. In prayer, meditation, reflection and the searching of the scriptures we seek Him and find Him.

The greatest promises of the Bible are those that assure God's children of His presence among them.

> *Be not afraid, neither be dismayed: for the Lord, thy God, is with thee, whithersoever thou goest.*[12]

> *When thou passest through the waters, I will be with Thee.*[13]

> *God is our refuge and strength, a very present help in trouble. Therefore, will we not fear though the earth be removed and the mountains shaken into the heart of the seas.*[14]

> *My God, who is rich in loving kindness, will meet me at every corner."*[15]

> *The eternal God is thy refuge and underneath are the everlasting arms.*[16]

> *Yea though I walk through the valley of the shadow of death, I will fear no evil; for thou art with me.*[17]

When we respond to the divine bidding, we come to know as a never-failing companion, the Christ who told His followers, "I call you not servants, but friends.[18] I will never leave thee or forsake thee."[19] In all of literature there is surely no more comforting assurance than Christ's word: "Lo, I am with you alway, even unto the end of the world."[20]

With such a presence we find our strength and are lifted above the desolation of loneliness and despair, and know the peace that passes all human understanding.

❦

Conquering Fear

There is an old story of a young fellow who read his doctor's thesis in history before a group of history professors. He started out, "Caesar is dead. Napoleon is dead. Cromwell is dead. And I don't feel so well myself."

Strange, isn't it, how fear can grip us? Memory takes wings and words come haltingly, if at all. We have a fantastic number of fears. Psychologists tell us that we are born with only two: the fear of loud noises and the fear of falling. But it is not long before we acquire a countless number and variety of fears: fear of the dark, fear of the unexpected, fear of open places, or closed places, fear of self, fear of other people, fear of water, fear of change, fear of insecurity, fear of the future, fear of the past, fear of failure, fear of loneliness, fear of growing old, fear of sickness and fear of death. Fears, too, have their symbols: black cats, Friday the 13th, ladders, broken mirrors, and so on.

We sometimes erroneously believe that all fear is bad. Nothing could be farther from the truth. Humanity could not long have survived without it. As Martin Luther King said, "Fear is the elemental alarm system of the human organism."[1] Fear warns of threats to our security. We are keyed by fear to snap into readiness for fight or flight. Natural fear is one of the sentinels of life. The great advances of civilization have had fear as part of their motivation. It is the fear of failure that prods us to study; the fear of disease builds medical schools; fear of poverty develops industry; and fear of nature built cathedrals, for primitive religion was grounded in fear. The fear of being socially ostracized makes us more law-abiding. It is the fear of death that makes men drive more carefully.

Shakespeare has Laertes say to Ophelia that "safety lies in fear."[2] Airlines, knowing that their business prosperity is based on their ability to allay man's fear of death, advertise the number of millions of passenger miles without accident. It is the fear of ignorance that has built colleges. Founders of Harvard, fearing a time when there would be no ministers, began the college, as the records say, "To provide against the time when the present ministers will lie in the dust."[3]

Fear, then, is our ally. Only fools are not afraid. "Education," says Angelo Patri, "consists in being afraid at the right time."[4] But fear, like fire or water when uncontrolled, can be not our ally or friend, but our enemy. It is a great servant, but it can be a ruinous master. Excessive fear can become panic, terror and chronic anxiety. In the hour of crisis, fear motivates activity in the adrenal glands. Epinephrine is sent into the bloodstream, supplying additional strength and reserve for the immediate need. Inordinate, unnecessary fear continually calls out for the flow of adrenalin, and what was intended to be a stimulant becomes a chronic poison. Excessive fear is a continual ringing of the fire alarm when there is no fire, a crying of "wolf, wolf" when there is no real danger to be met. Obviously, this is not a healthy situation, but one that describes the plight of many.

As one man put it, "Even when my body is idle, my mental motor continues to roar. I'm nervous so much of the time that when I'm not nervous, then I get nervous." So, much fear is good, useful, stimulating, and protective. Like salt in food, it must be in the right proportion. It is with the unnecessary, excessive fear that leads to anxiety, worry, fretfulness and phobias that we must deal if life is to be lived with any degree of happiness and usefulness.

What shall we do with these chronic, neurotic fears that plague us? Fortunately, we can do something. Goethe, the great German writer, was afraid of high places, one of our commonest fears—traceable, I suppose, to our fear of falling. In an effort to overcome his fear, he practiced climbing high towers until his fear left him. That is rare courage and illustrates one direct method of attack on needless fear. But many fears are not so obvious. They lie deep within the subconscious—furtive fears within the mind, not clearly defined nor understood. Another approach to these fears that poison life is to drive them out of the closets, caves of the mind, subject them to the light of faith and reason, and see them for what they really are. It is when they remain mysterious that they do their greatest damage, draining away nervous energy.

Dr. Harry Emerson Fosdick tells of a young boy whose rest was disturbed nightly by a terrifying nightmare that a tiger was chasing him. He would awake startled and upset. The counselor who met with the boy told him that the next time he was pursued by a tiger, he should stretch out his hand and pet it. Sure enough, at the next appearance of the tiger, it took only the outstretched arm to convince the boy that it was only an imaginary tiger. His rest thereafter was undisturbed. If we would pet the tigers of fear that plague us, many of them would be revealed as harmless.[5]

One fearing loneliness can well realize that the fear comes partly out of the unwillingness to give completely of himself. He who would have friends must show himself friendly. Of course, there is a loneliness that comes to those who have lost a companion of many years, for whom no glib solutions to loneliness will suffice. There is that longing for the touch of a vanished hand and for the sound of a voice that is still. Yet, to lose ourselves in a cause greater than ourselves has healing for the fear of loneliness.

It is recorded in the book of John that the Greeks came to one of the Jewish feasts and requested to see Jesus. We do not know all that he said to them, but one thing he did say is memorable: "Except a grain of wheat fall upon the earth and dies it abides alone; but if it dies it bears much fruit."[6] Loneliness is the price to be paid for the unwillingness to die to self. Jesus pointed out this truth on many occasions. He who would save his life must lose it, and the recognition of this truth is to take a step away from the fear of loneliness.

There are those who suffer all that the Ancient Mariner of Coleridge's poem endured after he had slain the albatross:

> *Like one, that on a lonesome road*
> *Doth walk in fear and dread*

And having once turned round walks on
And turns no more his head
Because he knows, a frightful fiend
Doth close behind him tread.[7]

There are those who fear consequences of misdeeds of
the past–a violated trust, a friend betrayed, outraged inner
standards of conduct, or perhaps an infidelity long repented
of never again to be repeated. The finer a person is the
more he is disturbed. Here the Christian religion teaches
the need of confession–confession to God, confession in
some cases to the offended, to a trusted friend, counselor
or minister so that this burden of fear might be lifted. An
amazing number of people have fears of the past, most of
which are unnecessary, ill-founded fears.

Many fear that their destiny has already been fashioned by inheritance. "He will always be a weakling, just
like his father." Caught in the grip of habit, they feel they
are victims of inheritance. When we bring such a fear out
into the light and place it beside the facts, we see no evidence for saying that the tendency toward alcoholism or
other moral excesses are inherited. It is impossible to find
any trait of character that can be directly traced to inheritance. Nothing is more misleading than to say, "He has
criminal tendencies because his father is in jail." True,
much can be attributed to environment, but a man can rise
above that. Karl Menninger says that inheritance is probably confined to physical structures, including patterns.

The happiest, best integrated people are those who
have felt God's forgiveness, whose secret closets of the
mind have been cleaned, and whose life is lived openly
and aboveboard. There is nothing that must be hidden,

no ghost of the past to ruin the present. An honest confession is good for the soul.

As some fear the past, so others fear the future for a crisis it may bring–a depression, recession, sickness or personal tragedy. It is good to have a reasoned concern for the future, but inviting trouble or crossing bridges before we come to them is needless worry. Man, through the gift of imagination, foresees many hardships and disasters. Some have a difficulty for every solution. Most people would agree that the words of Addison are true:

> *Were a man's sorrows and disquietudes summed up at the end of his life, it would generally be found that he had suffered more from the apprehension of such evils as never happened to him, than from those evils which had really befallen him.*[8]

On his way to the Celestial City, Pilgrim heard the roar of lions in the distance, and he was frightened. When he got to the place where they were, he saw that they were chained and a safe distance from the road. They were quite powerless to harm him.[9]

Most of us experience the fear of failure. It is true that fear of failure can drive man to worthwhile achievement, but an overdose of the same fear can lead to distraction and misery. It can make tyrants or nervous wrecks out of those who fear failure too greatly. We must see it for what it is and not be too disturbed when failure comes. We are in good company. Everyone carries in his body the scars of many a lost battle. Doctors will admit they have had patients for whom their help was in vain. A professor friend of mine has written an article entitled "Students with Whom I Have Failed." Every housewife can look back on a burned meal, and usually when guests were present. What preacher cannot look back on far too many sermons that never came close to the point, failing miserably to get his ideas expressed logically and helpfully? Babe Ruth hit more home runs than any other baseball player, but he also struck out more than any other player of his day. Edison numbered hundreds of failures to each success. But, failure is a symbol of effort.

We need to reevaluate our failures. Perhaps we take ourselves too seriously. Mark Twain sat trembling in his chair prior to an after-dinner speech that he was about to give. He was consoled by one who sat next to him, who said, "It's all right, Mr. Clemens. Remember, they don't expect much."[10] I suppose we wouldn't worry what other people think about us if we knew how seldom they do. "It is better to fail at a cause that will ultimately succeed than to succeed at a cause which will ultimately fail."[11]

All of us experience at one time or another the fear of growing old. Physical powers of which we were once so proud begin to wane; spring is gone from the step, and games in which we used to contend, we now observe. And, time goes so very fast. "My little child," wrote one man, "tumbles out of my arms on his way to school and returns bringing me my shawl."[12]

When the fear of growing old is placed beside the facts, it is not as discouraging as it would at first seem. There are consolations, compensations in growing older that are not to be discounted. More mature judgment can come, more loyal friends, appreciation of life, a mellowness and peace not known to youth. And, one can always stay young at heart. It was said of James Whitcomb Riley that he never grew up in his heart. Even those who are infirm can minister greatly to those who take care of them, through the gift of gratitude, good cheer, and the spirit of optimism and joy.

A poll was taken at a church forum in Florida some time ago. Those present were asked to check the happiest period of life–childhood, teens, twenties, thirties, forties, fifties, sixties, seventies or older. Perhaps it would be surprising to teenagers to know that the sixties received the most checks. Since most of those marking the poll were in their sixties, it can be inferred that to them the age at which they were then living was the best.

Listen to Julia Ward Howe at ninety-two saying, "The deeper I drink the cup, the sweeter it tastes; all the sugar is at the bottom."[13] Or, note the words of Robert Browning.

> *Grow old along with me!*
> *The best is yet to be,*
> *The last of life for which the first was made:*
> *Our times are in His hand*
> *Who saith, "A whole I planned,*
> *Youth shows but half; trust God: see all, nor be afraid."[14]*

There are many who fear death. As Shakespeare's Hamlet said when he was contemplating suicide:

> *But that the dread of something after death,*
> *The undiscovered country, from whose bourn*
> *No traveler returns, does puzzle the will*
> *And makes us rather bear those ills we have,*
> *Than fly to others we know not of?[15]*

We tend to fear the unknown. So many like "Ol' Man

River" are "tired of livin' and skeered of dyin'."[16] In focusing the light of faith and reason on this experience in life, we take courage. The hope of immortality seems a logical belief. Surely, the human spirit is not snuffed out like a candle. We refuse to believe that at the hour of death, we will cease to love a person and begin to love only a memory.

Ultimately, even with all the logic we can assemble, we are driven to faith. It is faith in the goodness and love of God that dispels fear. "Fear knocked at the door. Faith answered, and there was no one there."[17] We must learn to say with Robert Louis Stevenson, "I believe in an ultimate decency of things: ay, and if I woke in hell, should still believe it."[18] Paul writes, "God has not given us the spirit of fear, but of power and of love and of a sound mind."[19]

A poem by Elizabeth Cheney describes a bird resting on a frail branch of a tree that is swaying in the tempest, threatening to break with every gust and to hurl the little creature into the void. Yet amid it all the little bird sits on the limb and sings, knowing it has wings–resources, unfailing, upon which he depends. Much of our fear not only of death, but of life, is based on unwillingness or indifference in the practice of faith and trust.

> *Said the Robin to the Sparrow:*
> *"I should really like to know*
> *Why these anxious human beings*
> *Rush about and worry so."*

> *Said the Sparrow to the Robin:*
> *"Friend, I think that it must be*
> *That they have no heavenly Father*
> *Such as cares for you and me."*[20]

And, in the words of M. L. Haskins:

> *I said to the man that stood at the gate of the year:*
> *"Give me a light, that I may tread safely into the*
>   *unknown!"*
> *And he replied:*
> *"Go out into the darkness and put your hand into the Hand*
>   *of God.*
> *That shall be to you better than a light and safer than a*
>   *known way."[21]*

It is this faith and this trust that makes us more than conquerors over the fears that would defeat us.

❧

Dealing with Irritability
and Depression

Depression, irritability and discouragement deaden our hopes, kill our enthusiasms and hinder us in our achievement of worthwhile goals. Depression, disillusionment and discouragement are the devil's favorite tools.

We must learn to take depression for granted. We all have our "ups and downs." No life always runs on an even kccl. Furthermore, we would be lacking in spiritual depth if we could look at our situation in the world and not be depressed. Any person who is sensitive to human need should feel his heart deeply ploughed by the events of our day. The more sensitive we are, the more deeply we feel, and the higher we rise or the lower we sink.

> *It's being such an optimist*
> *That makes me feel so low*
> *Because my hopes rise higher*
> *Than my earthbound fcct can go.*[1]

I constantly marvel how Charles M. Schulz, the writer of the "Peanuts" comic strip, gets so much out of nothing. In one of the sequence of cartoons, Lucy addresses Charlie Brown, "Well, you certainly look cheerful today, Charlie Brown."

"Oh yes, I'm not always depressed, you know.... Every now and then I have a good day," he responds. Then, in the last frame, his face reflects the darkest gloom, and he says, "It's between those nows and thens where I have all my trouble."[2]

Granted, we all have periodic blue days, but we are "not always depressed, you know." Experiencing some depression, blue days, discouragement and irritability is normal. However, if the distance between those nows and thens widens to too great an extent, we get worried about it–and rightly so.

Abraham Lincoln suffered deep depression for a full year. He was at one time the prisoner of gloom to the extent that his closest friends wondered if he would ever escape from it. He never did escape entirely. Although never losing his sense of humor and proper perspective, he was always a melancholy man. Look closely at his portrait, or visit the Lincoln Memorial and take a long look at the face of the greatest of all Americans. The sadness of all humanity is evident in the lines of his face. It is for this reason that we feel a kinship with him, and whether we understand it fully or not, it is for this reason that he wins his way into the heart of each succeeding generation. Out of his familiarity with grief and tragedy was born a tenderness, compassion, and yet, a firmness. We understand why it was that Tolstoy called Lincoln "a Christ in miniature."[3]

There are moods of depression and irritability which move in over our lives like a heavy fog to darken our days, and we can't understand from whence they came or why. We know that the cause of some despondency has its roots in physical reasons. Glandular irregularities can poison the system and induce moods of melancholy and irritability. In the role of amateur psychiatrists, we can sometimes do more harm than we realize by telling our friends to "buck up" or "try harder." Where overstrain or chronic fatigue has brought on nervous prostration, it is not wise advice to tell a person to try harder. It could be the worst possible kind of therapy.

While in seminary at Yale Divinity School, I also attended classes at the Yale Medical School where seminarians were instructed in psychiatry. The intent of this training program was not to make of us full-fledged psychiatrists, but to make us aware of how very involved some problems can actually become. The hope of our instructor was that our knowledge of the complications that can be present in mental illness would rescue us from glibness and ready willingness to have all of the answers for problems that we could not possibly understand. For this brief sojourn into the realm of psychiatry, many of us have been, and are, truly grateful.

While we do all that we can to bring the insights of Christian faith to bear in all counseling situations, it is often that we refer people to other counselors or psychiatrists who are able to bring other resources to aid in the healing process. The ideal is not to fall into blue moods and then crawl out of them; the ideal is to not fall into them. Careful attention to all that goes into healthful living may be a helpful precaution.

Plenty of exercise helps to induce physical tiredness and subsequent rest. An insurance company's survey reveals that Americans are not walking as much as they did years ago. The daily average in this country is now down to five miles a day. Many years ago, it was seven. We have largely given up walking, but there is still hope, for one must by some means get to the garage.

We need to avail ourselves of the fine uses of play as a means of relaxation. James Fisher, in an autobiography entitled *A Few Buttons Missing*, says that there is more healing in playing five minutes a day with a dog or cat than in taking a vacation trip around the world.[4]

I think it would also be a service to the dog and cat. It has been my observation that many household pets are hungry for evidences of love and affection. We house them and feed them but seldom talk to them. Too often they are disregarded altogether.

> *He prayeth best who loveth best*
> *All things both great and small;*
> *For the dear God who loveth us,*
> *He made and loveth all.*[5]

Many times we become moody and irritable because we have been too busy. We are exhausted and on edge because we have tried to do too much. We have taken too little time to trim the lamp of friendship or become acquainted with our own families. A boy's best friend is his father, and all too often, if the boy gets up early enough and stays up late enough, he may even get to see him.

We can be lifted out of despondency and despair by remembering better days. This is one of the high uses of the memory God has given us. If we are now in the valley, we can recall our mountain top experiences. If today is cloudy, we can remember the days that were fair. If some have uttered words that cut us deeply, others have spoken words to heal. If some have been unjust, others have been more than fair. If there are those who have despised us, there are others whose love has been constant and unfailing. This thought is the theme of one of Shakespeare's great sonnets.

> *When in disgrace with fortune and men's eyes*
> *I all alone beweep my outcast state,*
> *And trouble deaf heaven with my bootless cries,*
> *And look upon myself and curse my fate,*
> *Wishing me like to one more rich in hope,*
> *Featured like him, like him with friends possessed,*
> *Desiring this man's art and that man's scope,*
> *With what I most enjoy contented least;*
> *Yet in these thoughts myself almost despising,*
> *Haply I think on thee—and then my state,*
> *Like to the lark at break of day arising*
> *From sullen earth, sings hymns at heaven's gate;*
> *For thy sweet love remembered, such wealth brings*
> *That then I scorn to change my state with kings.*[6]

God has given us foresight to look ahead. We ought to think optimistically and not cross bridges of despair before we get to them. In John Bunyan's *Pilgrim's Progress*, Pilgrim, who was on his way to the Celestial City, heard the roar of lions ahead, and it frightened and discouraged him. When he arrived at the place where they were, he discovered they were chained a safe distance from the road, powerless to harm him.[7] So much of the trouble we borrow from the future never comes to pass.

We help to overcome despondency when we tackle the self and do not blame circumstances. We don't have to revel in our gloom or make of it an emotional indulgence. We don't have to wait until something happens to lift us out of the abyss of gloom. We can tackle ourselves, and not blame circumstances. We can be masters and not slaves, if we will. It is no disgrace to be down. The disgrace lies in not trying to get up. It has been well said that a man is like a tea bag; his real worth is revealed when he gets in hot water.[8] Difficulties need not depress us because they can become a stimulus and prod to finer achievement. No one would have blamed Columbus if he had become depressed and turned back, but no one would have remembered him either. We who live in this great country are grateful for the adventurous spirit that encouraged him to sail on, and on.

Some things are so important, they must be done whether we feel like it or not—and in loyalty to a task we forget our despondency. Some years ago, a student at one of our great universities was carried across the platform on the shoulders of his classmates to receive his college diploma. Four years before when his name was first called, the professor said, "Stand up!"

"I wish that I could, sir," was the reply, "but I have been unable to stand since I was four years old." On that graduation day, he received an ovation unlike any heard to that hour. The temptation to despondency plagued him, but some things were so important, he worked right through to accomplishment.

Remember, too, there are others in this world besides ourselves. We have some responsibility to them. We are our brother's keeper. Our spirit can pervade a whole room for good or ill. Some people make others happy by walking into a room, and others by walking out. A morose and sullen spirit can infect a whole household. How strange the punishment of evil.

A man can steal only a small quantity of goods, and he is imprisoned for many years. But, he can be irritable, morose, sullen and depressed, and steal away the happiness and good spirit of a whole home. He can rob the twinkle from a little child's eyes and go absolutely free. How tragic to live with one whose quarrelsome, cantankerous spirit steals away the joy of life itself. One wonders why such a person is not imprisoned but remains free to visit his affliction upon others.

Good cheer is one of the finest contributions we can make to life. We can make life pleasant for others while we are with them. It was said of Will Rogers that he never made anyone unhappy until he went away. If we have no great skills, we can at least brighten the corner where we are.

> *The thing that goes the farthest*
> *Toward making life worthwhile*
> *That costs the least and does the most*
> *Is just a pleasant smile.*[9]

May God grant to each of us the ability to shield ourselves from the melancholy and the morose that seeks to invade our life, choosing instead the radiant life.

Grief

G rief is part of the bundle of emotions involved in what it means to be human. As soon as we are capable of feeling any emotion–love, joy or hate, we discover what it means to "come to grief." Among the dictionary meanings of the word "grieve" are these: "To suffer emotionally" and "be in mental pain because of an evil or sorrow." It was not premature or irrational to speak to children as I did in the sermonette of misery, grief and sorrow. Children soon experience grief. Their grief reasons seem small by our adult measurements, but their hurts are very real to them. Last week, Leone and I were back again at Seabeck where I was lecturer for the YMCA family camp. I recall the pained look on a four-year-old face when that child showed me the "owie" on her finger. That was very real and painful to her.

Mark Twain, in his autobiography, remembered his seven-year-old daughter crying her heart out over a broken toy and a picnic cancelled because of the rain. With some impatience, her mother told her not to cry over "little things," and the little girl responded, "Mama, what is little things?"[1] Francis Thompson was getting at the same truth when he wrote, "Children's griefs are little, certainly, but so is the child."[2] Grief is a matter of relativity; the source should be estimated by its proportion to the sorrower. A gash is as painful to one as an amputation is to another. Some of us here can remember childhood griefs–someone close to us dying, losing a favorite pet by accident, or some other disappointment that we experienced at an earlier time.

As parents, we have the instinct to shelter and shield our children from grief experiences. Some of you were here when the Reverend James Gillion came to speak several weeks ago. Jim told us of the time when his young son wore glasses for the first time. He was fearful that those at school would kid him, so he rose that morning filled with fear and apprehension, grieving that it was his lot to suffer rebuff by his peers–maybe even rejection. Jim and his wife Donna would have gladly shielded him from that pain, but they watched him walk through the yard, out to the sidewalk, pause a moment, then throw his shoulders back and head for school. He returned that evening reporting that it was not as bad as he had feared. In fact, it was not bad at all.

All through life, we are confronted with grief in its many forms. There are "Gethsemanes" in all our lives. We all pass through the garden in the midst of night. In most lives, Gethsemane is harder than the cross. Mental grief and anguish exceeds physical pain. We come to grief or it comes to us in our rejections, remorse, illnesses and losses. We move from a familiar setting to a strange place, and we feel grief. We say goodbye to a child bound for college, or a friend or loved one from whom we will long be separated, and we feel a particular kind of hurting. We run into snags resulting from our work, health, goals or relationships with people, and we can be hurt deeply. Some suffer marital dissolution–a form of death–with grief pangs of guilt or sorrow. So, sooner or later, grief comes to us all. Therefore, it is imperative that we learn how to handle it wisely and constructively.

There are many ways in which we experience grief, but the particular form on which I want to center today is the grief associated with the death of one very near and dear to us–the death of a parent, son, daughter, sister, brother, or another relative with whom we have known affinity, such as a partner or close friend. We go through certain fairly well-defined stages in resolving or dealing with this form of grief. Many studies of grief suggest that there are at least three stages we are likely to experience: shock, suffering and recovery.

The first stage, experienced in the immediacy of grief, is shock, and it generally lasts from one day to a month or more. It is characterized as a feeling of lost-ness, a state of unreality, or a difficulty in making deci-sions. Sometimes, a person will accurately diagnose it herself when she says, "I don't think it has really hit me yet." It is this numbness that sometimes helps to explain the composure of many mourners as they walk through those difficult days following the death of a loved one. I have thought that it was a part of God's grace, this state of numbness and shock that is a kind of anesthesia against the deeper realization of grief.

The second stage is suffering or, as one observer terms it, recoil. It is the most painful stretch, and it can last upwards of a year. Unfortunately, some people never get beyond this stage, and it becomes a permanent state. In this stage, the numbness has been lifted, and the ability to feel has returned. Loneliness, anxiety, self-pity, quiet bitterness and remorse can be involved in our response to the loss. Anger, too, is sometimes there, and sometimes even an ambivalent anger toward the loved one who has died, for leaving such a legacy of sorrow. It is a time of difficult, mixed emotions when a person is working through her grief, and it hurts.

Ironically, this is the time when a person is most alone. The family and friends who flocked around in grief's immediacy have returned to their work and their ways. For all but the most intimate survivors, it is back to business as usual. That part of our response to a friend's grief is worth thinking about. We do so much for a person in the state of numbness–a gift of food, flowers, a call, card or letter–and surely those are sorely needed then, and the memory of them is a comfort. Yet, often, we neglect the friend when the anesthesia of numbness is worn off, and the hurt is intense. A friend, truly, is one who walks in when the rest of the world walks out,[3] a friend who remembers grief's progression. In this little book, *The View from a Hearse*, we read of a doctor in Boston who sends a plant to a patient's daughter each year on the anniversary of the death of her mother.[4]

Then, hopefully, there is the third stage–recovery. Its onset varies with individuals, of course, but often, it becomes evident from three months onward. It is not always uninterrupted, but gradually, it involves a letting go of the past and the building of a new life. It may mean learning to be alone, finding ways to be useful, growing out of self-pity to self-giving, finding a certain peaceful perspective on life, and in general responding to light at the end of the tunnel. Many of us can think of people who beautifully illustrate this third stage, people whose wounds of grief have largely healed, and while the scars are there, they nonetheless live lives of purpose, service and joy.

Shock, suffering, and recovery–we do well to remember these three stages, both for ourselves and others for whom we care. Against the background of these three stages or in the context of them, I suggest ways in which we can grieve creatively and rightly.

First, we can grieve naturally. We can shed tears, God's provision in our hour of grief to lift the agony from the soul. We sometimes extol the courage and strength of an individual who moves through bereavement without a trace of a tear, yet we know that repressed grief often reappears in negative forms at a later day. Thus, we are to move toward some mastery over our emotions, rather than let our emotions master us. But tears are a vehicle for expressing grief, just as laughter is a vehicle for expressing joy, and we need not be ashamed to use them. "The soul would have no rainbow had the eye no tears."[5]

The author of Ecclesiastes spoke for us all when he said, "There is a time to weep and a time to laugh."[6] Moreover, we help others grieve naturally when we ourselves can naturally express our feelings in the presence of another's grief. It may be a sympathizing tear, a firm handclasp, an arm around the shoulder, an embrace, or a deed of caring. These may convey sympathy more than any well-chosen words. Sometimes, our greatest eloquence is revealed in silence. The highest joy and deepest grief cannot be verbalized. But, to be physically present is the highest service we can render. I have, in the nature of my work, encountered death and grieving perhaps more than most of you, and if it is any consolation to you, I often do not know what to say either.

Charles Reynolds Brown was a great dean at Yale University Divinity School a generation ago. He said over and over again to young students frightened by the prospect of being called to a home at the hour of death—unprepared for what to say and fearful of fumbling and doing more harm than good. "The first thing to do," he said, "is to get there. What to do when you get there will be given to you at that hour."[7] It is my experience that what is really required when death strikes us is not more talk—God knows we have enough of that—but a willingness to practice what might be called "the ministry of standing by." Just being there can help. Just saying "yes" when the bereaved wife offers more coffee, just entering into some of the light conversation that is generated to crowd out the awful dimensions of loss.

Thursday, I conducted a memorial service in Everett for a congregant. This woman's husband, a dentist, died of a heart attack last year, leaving her with three sons. She was killed a little more than a week ago in an accident on Aurora Avenue. The three sons are now without mother or dad. I was most impressed at the service held at the First Presbyterian Church in Everett, to see the oldest son Charles, age twenty, stand at the door, thanking the many who came for what they did to enrich the life of his mother, and expressing gratitude for himself and his brothers for those who stood by them in their hour of grief. I was impressed by the young men who came by, and gave only a tearful embrace to their friend and buddy. Though in many instances no words were spoken, the action was beautifully eloquent.

It is not always easy in our society to know where the grieving and afflicted are. One of the sad aspects of modern day city life is that people can die and be buried without the rest of us being aware. In the area where I lived as a boy in the Midwest, it was customary for the family who suffered a loss to place a wreath or a bouquet of flowers on the doorpost of the main entrance into the building. As youngsters, when we saw those flowers, we showed our concern and respect by not playing in front of that house for a few days, and we were quiet in that area. It was the community's way, however poorly, of acknowledging that the bells had tolled for us. Flowers are no longer posted on the doors of homes where death has come, but hearts are still in need of the kind of comfort that a friend may bring.

But, there also comes a time when the grieving process does afford good reason to talk naturally about the person who has died. As friends, we are sometimes wary of that, out of what we think is consideration for the survivor's feelings. It becomes what Granger Westberg calls "a quiet conspiracy of silence." In his little book, he writes:

A typical illustration of this is a widow, whose husband died a year or so ago, who is with a group of friends who knew her husband. As they are talking together, one of them recalls a very humorous story about her husband. He is about to tell it and then he thinks to himself, "Oh no, I must not reopen the wound. I must be considerate of her." Consequently, he carefully steers away from any conversation about her husband, as does everyone else. Actually, if he had told this story, she doubtlessly would have laughed heartily and been most pleased. He might have seen a tear or two in her eyes. If he had said, "I'm sorry. I should not have told that story," her response in all probability would have been, "Don't say that. You are the first person in weeks who has even mentioned my husband. No one ever talks about him anymore. It is a wonderful feeling that someone remembers him."[8]

Comfort does not come in forgetting the happy past. People bring others well-meant, but miserable, consolation when they tell us what time will do to our grief. We do not want to lose our grief, for it is bound up with our love. And, we could not cease to mourn without being robbed of our affection.

But now comes a second step. As Christians, we not only grieve naturally, but we can come to grieve usefully. One of Charlie Brown's favorite expressions is "Good grief!" And happily, even grief can be good, contributing to a positive end. Grief sensitizes us to others in similar plight. How often we have seen it happen–that the people who convey the greatest strength to a hurting person in time of sorrow are those who have experienced a similar sorrow. Remember the line in one of Thornton Wilder's plays, "In Love's service only the wounded soldiers can serve."[9]

Grief, like trouble, is never welcome. It is not something we would seek, but once it comes, it can be transmuted into service and sympathy, understanding and under-girding of others. As noted by Robert Browning Hamilton, God can work for good in all things.

I walked a mile with Pleasure,
She chattered all the way,
And left me none the wiser
For all she had to say.

I walked a mile with Sorrow
And ne'er a word said she;
But, oh, the things I learned from her
When Sorrow walked with me.[10]

In another parish, one of the closest friends our family had was a man who for many years was the Bursar of the University of Kansas. He had lost an arm as a boy in an accident, but it did not seem to deter him in any way. If I were to describe him to you, the probability is that I would talk at length about his personality and only incidentally tell you of his infirmity. His positive spirit, love, kindness, optimism, and love of sports is what I most remember. Indeed, it was the handling of his infirmity in such positive ways that made him a helpful counselor to others who had the same misfortune. He could console one who had suffered a similar loss with more authority than I or anyone else who had not experienced the same.

And in this parish, too, there are so many of you who have ministered helpfully to the rest of us by meeting grief and adversity in such a way as to give us all hope. You have taken the pieces of a broken heart and fashioned them into an altar, bringing you, and us, ever closer to God. It was for such as you that Sarah Bolten wrote these familiar lines.

I like the man who faces what he must,
With step triumphant and a heart of cheer;

> *Who fights the daily battle without fear;*
> *Sees his hopes fail, yet keeps unfaltering trust*
> *That God is God–that somehow, true and just*
>   *His plans work out for mortals; not a tear*
>   *Is shed when fortune, which the world holds dear,*
> *Falls from his grasp–better, with love, a crust*
>   *Than living in dishonor: envies not,*
> *Nor loses faith in man; but does his best,*
>   *Nor ever murmurs at his humbler lot;*
> *But, with a smile and words of hope, gives zest*
>   *To every toiler: he alone is great*
>   *Who by a life heroic conquers fate.*[11]

When the Apostle Paul wrote the scripture that was read this morning the Christians were being persecuted–killed throughout the land–and grief was great in the loss of loved ones and in the ever-present threat of death. Against this background, the Apostle Paul wrote to the Romans:

> *What then shall we say to these things? If God be for us, who can be against us? Who shall separate us from the love of Christ? Shall tribulation or distress, or persecution, or famine, or nakedness, or peril, or sword? Nay, in all these things, we are more than conquerors through him that loved us. For I am persuaded (sure) that neither death nor life, nor angels, nor principalities, nor powers, nor things present nor things to come, nor height, nor depth, nor any other creature, shall be able to separate us from the love of God which is in Christ Jesus, Our Lord.*[12]

This, then, is our faith. Thank God for the assurance that enables us to walk even through the valley of the shadow of death without fear, for we are ever in God's care.

❦

Suicide

◈

Dorothy Day has a fine passage in her autobiography in which she suggests that no preacher ever goes into the pulpit without promulgating heresy.[1] What she means is that the truth is so pure, so holy and so vast that we never see it whole. We always understate some parts of it in order to make another part plain. I recognize the truth of that today. Who could ever fathom the intricacies of life that lead to self-destruction? But, we do not learn to swim by lingering on the shore. We must get into water over our heads. If we do not know all of the answers, we must at least try to ask the right questions.

This subject should be of particular interest to those of us who live in Seattle and in a university area. Suicide is the second most usual cause of death for young people between the ages of fifteen and nineteen, and the major cause of death for young people between the ages of twenty to twenty-four. Seattle has consistently been among the cities where self-destruction has been most prevalent. Did not a recent news release tell us that last month there were more suicides in Seattle than in any month on record? Here on the West Coast, we are second only to San Francisco, which is the suicide capital of America. Los Angeles is also gaining in this dubious distinction. Suicide has ranked among the first ten causes of death in America for most of the past half century.

Suicide is a major cause of wasted lives and family disruption, causing indescribable family upset and deep feelings of guilt. We usually feel some measure of guilt when a loved one dies, but that guilt is accentuated when one close to us takes his or her own life. We experience self-recrimination, feeling that perhaps we could have done something to forestall or prevent the death.

It is imperative that we think as clearly as possible about such an important human concern. There is much falsehood, myth and misinformation associated with suicide. Josh Billings, a homespun philosopher of another day observed, "It isn't that folks don't know, it's that they know so much that ain't so."[2]

Everyone has a right to his own opinion, but no one has a right to be wrong in the facts. For instance, some believe that Seattle is consistently among the cities where self-destruction is most prevalent because the rainy, gray days provoke feelings of depression and despair. But, the fact is that trained researchers will not agree to this. They say that it is impossible to establish a definite relationship between suicide and the weather. Such a relationship is only speculation since Denver and Los Angeles, with climatic conditions far different from Seattle's, also are consistently in the top echelons on suicide charts.

One might think that the celebrative seasons of the year would bring the greatest happiness. For many this is true, but for others it is not. The happiness of others makes their own despair more real. The greatest number of suicides occur at Christmas time and in the spring of the year. T. S. Eliot has a line of poetry in which he calls April the cruelest of months.[3] For many people the beauty of the world without accentuates the despair they feel within.

Some believe that those who intend self-destruction don't tell others of their thoughts in this regard, but this is not true. The fact is that eight of every ten persons who kill themselves have given definite warnings of their suicidal intentions.

Some believe that suicidal persons are fully intent on dying, but the fact is that most suicidal people are undecided about living or dying, and they gamble with death, leaving it to others to save them. Almost no one commits suicide without letting others know how he or she is feeling. It may be in code or seemingly facetious remarks. For example, "My family would be better off without me," "I'm going to end it all. I can't stand life any more," "I won't be around much longer for you to put up with," or "I don't want to be a burden." Sometimes, it is nonverbal–the buying of a gun or giving things away.

Some believe that suicide is inherited, or it runs in a family. True, Ernest Hemingway shot himself to death in 1961, and his father had done the same thirty-three years before, but the fact is that suicide does not run in families. It is an individual matter and can be prevented.

Some believe that all suicidal individuals are mentally ill, and suicide is always the act of a psychotic person. But, the fact is that studies of hundreds of genuine suicide notes indicate that although the person is extremely unhappy, he is not necessarily mentally ill. The overpowering unhappiness may result from a temporary emotional upset, a long and painful illness or a complete loss of hope, but the person is not necessarily psychotic.

Some believe that once a person is suicidal he or she is suicidal forever, but the fact is that individuals who wish to kill themselves are suicidal only for a limited period of time. If they are saved from self-destruction, they can go on to live happy, useful lives. The probability is that most everyone here or listening via radio has at one time had a fleeting suicidal thought. If so, we go in company with many of the greats.

Tolstoy, when young, was utterly disheartened and had decided to kill himself. Happily, the attempt failed. Mark Twain put a loaded revolver to his head but lacked the courage to pull the trigger. William James, in his dispirited youth, almost took his own life.

Dr. Harry Emerson Fosdick tells in his autobiography that when he was a young man, he suffered a nervous breakdown and would have killed himself had not his father intervened by calling, "Harry! Harry!"[4] Out of that desolating experience, Dr. Fosdick wrote the book *The Meaning of Prayer,* which has been continuously in print since 1917.

Some believe that suicide strikes more often among the rich, or conversely it occurs more frequently among the poor. The fact is that it is neither the rich man's disease nor the poor man's curse. Suicide is represented proportionately among all levels of society. However, there are conclusions, verified by statistics, that more men than women take their own lives, though more women try and fail to achieve self-destruction. With increasing equality among the sexes, the differential between male and female suicides is less and less.

The act occurs most frequently at the beginning of the week, especially on Monday or Tuesday and in early morning or evening. Fewer suicides occur during wars. The rate rises in days of unemployment and depression. Professional men are more vulnerable than artisans or laborers, and leaders are particularly susceptible. These would include army officers, actors, political leaders, physicians and particularly psychiatrists. The lowest rate is among miners and ministers. Anyone for the ministry?

The rate among whites is four times greater than among blacks. Because of the white man's insidious prejudices and distortions of truth, the black man came to have a low expectation for himself. But, as doors of opportunity are opening to the African American, the rate of suicide among them is increasing rapidly.

The larger the city is, the higher the rate of suicide. The greatest number of suicides occur in the congested or lodging house areas. Widows and widowers commit suicide more frequently than do members of an existing marital partnership. Single men and women destroy themselves more frequently than do married people, and divorced individuals show the highest rate of all. In fact, self-destruction occurs most frequently in people who have the weakest ties to social groups such as family, church or community.

How shall we see this in the context of our Christian faith? What is the ultimate destiny of the soul of the deceased who has taken his own life? Surprisingly, the Bible does not offer any precise statement on the morality of suicide; it neither condemns the simple morality nor sanctions the complex morality. The Bible does not make suicide the crime of crimes or the shame of shames. Implicit though, in the Bible, is the sacredness of life.

In the early days of the Christian faith, suicide was condoned and often encouraged. Martyrdom was glorified. For a man to end life, even by his own hand, was to open the door for the Christian to move into heaven.

St. Augustine was the first to denounce self-destruction as sinful. His thinking shaped the conclusions of the church and encouraged it to say that there is never a justifiable violation of the commandment, "Thou shalt not kill."[5] By the fifth century, suicide was condemned by the church. Thomas Aquinas called it an unspeakable offense, a crime. To kill self, he said, would mean that there was no time for repentance.[6]

The end of life, like the beginning of life, is widely regarded as the prerogative of the Deity. As late as the nineteenth century, suicides were refused Christian burial in many parts of Europe. Some societies imposed severe penalties on the families of suicides in the hope that the individual bent on self-destruction might be deterred by the stigma his act would inflict on his loved ones.

In the Middle Ages, indignities were practiced on the bodies of those who committed suicide. The bodies were often dragged through the streets, burned secretly in out-of-the-way places, and, of course, there would be no Christian funeral. John Wesley, founder of Methodism, said that every female who committed suicide should have her dead body dragged through the streets naked, and this would appeal to women's vanity and prevent them from taking their own lives. Twenty years later, when Wesley had experienced his own depression and despair, he wished his earlier statement could have been recalled. It did not mean he condoned or favored suicide, but his critical attitude was tempered.[7]

In lieu of clear-cut biblical statements in regard to suicide, we have witnessed many different attitudes and interpretations evolving in regard to it. We must strive to correlate our conclusions with what we believe is consistent with the will of the loving, heavenly Father in whom we believe. Implicit in the Bible is the affirmation that life is sacred. God wills that we live. No matter how desolating or agonizing our experiences are, there is still something we can do to contribute constructively to the world around us. It takes more courage to live than to die, and suicide is often the cowardly response to life. The Bible's word to those considering self-destruction would seem to us to be, "No, there is still something positive you can do. Your life is a sacred trust. Use it in the service of others. Do not die by your own hand, leaving behind grief and pain in the lives of those who love you. You can yet be a useful person."

What shall we believe is the destiny beyond the grave of those who do take their own lives? Are they lost forever? The Koran, for instance, teaches that suicide is a greater sin than the murder of another. But, what of Christianity? Well, who of us can be absolutely sure? My own assessment is that God, who is a loving Father, draws those who are physically ill, depressed, emotionally disturbed or hurting in any other way ever closer to Himself as I believe we who are earthly fathers would do. We do not reject our children or cast them out in their hours of deepest need. It may well be that in the world beyond this one those who were plagued by problems in this life will find new liberty, power and fulfillment in a measure they seldom, if ever, knew here. I do not believe we are knowledgeable enough, nor is it our prerogative, to determine the destinies of those who go before us. Let us leave that issue in the hands of the merciful God, and trust that those whom we have loved continue in His care.

The prevalence of suicide in our society, or the inclination that humans often have in that direction, should encourage us to be more sensitive and understanding of others. "Be kind," said Ian McClaren, "everyone you meet is carrying a heavy burden."[8] The consciousness of our kinship with all people should encourage us to be less inclined to point the finger of judgment and more inclined to extend the hand of friendship, the arms of love and the sympathetic ear. Sometimes, we learn the hard way.

Martin Buber, the brilliant Jewish theologian who has given so many insights about how people can relate to one another, got that way in part because of an experience he had early in his professional life. He was a professor and one day a student wished to see him. Buber allowed the young man in, but he was not really present for that student. He was thinking about papers he had to grade and articles he had to write. The student sensed this and apologized for his intrusion and soon left. Shortly after, the young man killed himself. Buber determined that thenceforth when another human being wished to be listened to, he would be totally present to listen, and if need be, to speak.[9]

In defense of Buber, we do know that often it is not easy to discern the depth of another's hurt. If someone breaks a leg, it is placed in a cast. We see this, so we are kindly toward that person and make no extra demands of him. We know that a time for healing is needed. But, when another is broken or bruised mentally or emotionally, his condition is not always easily discerned. There is no cast, and our expectations concerning that person are not altered or diminished, nor is our sympathy accelerated. Their outward demeanor may not suggest in any way that they might well be walking with a limp or are crippled in any way. The best actors and actresses are not in Hollywood. Those who really deserve the Oscars might well be nearby, in our own families or our own circle of friends. Louisa Driscoll's words alert us to this reality.

God pity all the brave who go
The common way, and wear
No ribboned medals on their breasts,
No laurel in their hair.

God pity all the lonely folk
With Griefs they do not tell
Women waking in the night
And men dissembling well.

In common courage of the street
The crushed grape is the wine,
Wheat in the mill is daily bread
And given for a sign.

And who but God shall pity those
Who go so quietly
And smile upon us when we meet
And greet so pleasantly.[10]

We give evidence of compassion and sensitivity when we strive to see beneath the masks that others wear to hide themselves from us. It is important to remind ourselves how widespread loneliness, despair, and depression are. "The mass of men," said Thoreau, "lead lives of quiet desperation."[11] What better service, then, could you and I bring to others than to be a messenger of light and hope in a world that for so many people is dark and distressing? Emily Dickinson's aspiration for her own life could well be adopted as our own. She writes:

> *If I can stop one heart from breaking*
> *I shall not live in vain;*
> *If I can ease one life the aching*
> *Or cool one pain,*
>
> *Or help one fainting robin*
> *Unto his nest again,*
> *I shall not live in vain.*[12]

May God grant us the ability to set aside despair, finding sacredness and joy in the life that we have been given.

AN ENLIGHTENED
RESPONSE

Finding Our Way
Through a Sexual Wilderness

O f all of the stories about Albert Einstein, the one I like best is about the time he was invited to be guest of honor and speaker at a banquet, where distinguished intellectuals were in attendance. When he was called upon to speak, he rose slowly from his chair amidst generous applause, moved to the speaker's podium and said quietly, "Ladies and gentlemen, I'm sorry, but I have nothing to say." He paused while a silence of surprise from the audience greeted him, and then added, "But, when I do I'll come back." Six months later, he did come back to that audience and made an important speech.[1]

Just think what would happen if our politicians, radio and television newscasters and commentators, and even preachers emulated this example. There might be a refreshing silence settling over the land! But, sometimes silence may not be refreshing. Silence may be a "cop-out," an unwillingness to wrestle with a complicated theme. We are under no illusions. Anything we think about today will be only introductory to what I hope will be a continuing discussion in your home. It is a bewildering maze of ideas through which we must find our way.

There are, however, some things that are clear to each one of us. We know at an early hour in our lives that sex is a strong drive, second only to the drive for food and water. Every thoughtful person is rightly concerned with how to understand, evaluate and direct his or her own sexuality in the most constructive ways so as to enable him or her to find greatest personal fulfillment and contribute most helpfully to society's good.

The erosion of traditional values and the disappearance of some formerly accepted modes of behavior have left humans free but rudderless. Young people today face more moral dilemmas in twenty years than our grandfathers did in a lifetime. Our journey through the sexual wilderness today is made more confusing by the fact that the introduction of the pill and liberalized abortion have opened the door to a new day of permissiveness.

This has also been fanned by the deluge of pornography and sensuous ads that old-timers would never have dreamed could become a part of our culture. There was a time when the saltiest thing in the theater was the popcorn. No more! The movie marquee tells us what might be expected inside. One such sign above a movie house read, "Now Showing–Everything." It's hard to believe that some of the movies "now showing" were released. They must have escaped!

We must face up to some of the confusion, ambiguities, failures and successes of our traditional Christian attitudes and behavior in the realm of sex, and honestly ask what it is that we should believe, maintain and defend.

Have new occasions actually taught us new duties? Has time made ancient good uncouth?[2]

In earlier centuries, the church, state and respectable society spoke in one voice on questions of morality. There was a more cohesive attitude toward sexual behavior. It was not that everyone behaved accordingly, but they at least knew what the rules were. The strong stand on premarital chastity, monogamy and marital fidelity that was taken by family and church was undergirded by society as a whole. In a real sense, it was easier to live up to standards in making choices. But now, everything that was once nailed down seems to be coming loose. Traditional ideas are being questioned or flaunted altogether.

It would seem that home is the most logical setting for any such discussion, as indeed it ought to be. The church is a supplement to the home and not an institution to supplant it. It is great if a parent or parents can and will visit constructively with their children on this theme, but many feel inadequate. Sexuality, we know, involves modesty both for parent and child. Feelings of constraint in this area are built into the human race as a basic part of its nature. At times it is solacing, and at other times frightening, to know that children get their basic feelings about what it means to be a man or a woman, and the relationships between them, from the way parents treat one another. Example is important. "Not the cry, but the flight of the wild duck, leads the flock to fly and follow."[3]

In some instances, the earliest recognition of sexual difference came by virtue of the normal, healthy, curiosity of little girls or boys as they learn about the bodies of the opposite sex. Some have been introduced to sexual language by way of graffiti that they saw scribbled on restroom walls, and others have been informed or misinformed by their peers. I suppose that for me something of all of these were a part of my growing up process. But, aside from what I learned in the home, one of the most memorable impressions came when I was fifteen years old. I was among those at a YMCA meeting who had the privilege of listening to an informed, wise and articulate doctor. He told us to thank God for our sexual desires; they were God-given and were not base, low or evil. He compared the sexual drive to fire and water, which are neither good nor bad per se. Their value is determined by the purposes they serve.

Fire controlled heats our homes, warms our bodies, cooks our meals and serves many other worthwhile purposes. But, uncontrolled fire burns our houses, destroys our lives and causes millions of dollars in damage. Water, purified and channeled, quenches thirst, cleanses the body without and within. It waters the crops, giving nourishment to the soil that provides food for our bodies. But water, un-harnessed and uncurbed, runs rampant, flooding our fields, destroying our crops and even drowning our bodies. So the sexual drive, he said, when controlled, guided, restrained and directed aright, can be a powerful force for usefulness. But, left undisciplined it can be most destructive.

The YMCA and the YWCA are arms of the church, and their ministries are the church in action. But so often, the church itself has not lifted a clear witness in this matter we are discussing today. First Corinthians 14:8 says, "If the trumpeter sound an uncertain note, how shall we know when to charge?" The church has sounded a trumpet, all right, but the sound it emits often seems muffled or reminds us of nothing so much as a sturdy boy's first attempt to blow a horn, "an awful alternation between unbelievable silence and unbearable sound."

In Protestantism, the Bible is our authority; we look to it for light and guidance. Unfortunately, it is not always as specific in counsel as we might wish it were. We do not use proof texts to substantiate our conclusions in our liberal tradition. Rather, we find in the Bible attitudes and principles to be applied to each situation in each succeeding generation. The Old Testament and the New Testament generally regard sex as wholesome. There is guidance for our sexuality, and there are warnings against its abuse. The seventh commandment enjoins against adultery, a rule that for centuries has been interpreted as a prohibition against all sexual experience outside of matrimony.

Jesus upheld the letter of the law and went even further, linking adultery not only with the physical act but also with the individual's thinking.

Whosoever looketh on a woman to lust after her has committed adultery with her already in his heart.[4]

The Apostle Paul upholds the practice of chastity before marriage, extols sex within marriage, but attacks promiscuity and infidelity.

The Christian faith does not teach that human nature is evil, especially in regard to its physical manifestations. If we did believe this, then it would make the body the chief source of evil and would interpret as good only what is non-material or spiritual. Sex, which belongs to the biological side of our human existence, would be something that had the taint of evil upon it. But, this conclusion cannot be reconciled to Christian teachings that say that the human body is not condemned as the source of wickedness, but is regarded as the dwelling place of the Divine Spirit. Physical pleasures are not necessarily evil, and sex is not a degrading necessity of human beings. The Bible teaches that God created our sexuality with deliberate intent and blessed it. Sex must be understood as a good gift from God. Gratitude for the gift is revealed in the manner in which it is treated.

The question is: Are these Biblical concepts of chastity, monogamy and fidelity defensible or relevant today? There is no virtue in conforming to a pattern because it is traditional or customary, but neither is there any point in breaking with custom just to be different. The intelligent response is to honestly evaluate new truth that comes and weigh it carefully. Get all the facts, from all the sides, analyze, compare, decide and then act.

A young man in a fraternity where I spoke some weeks ago tried to convince me that the regulations and conventions articulated in the scriptures were arbitrarily, as he said, "laid upon us by religionists of another day and are nothing more than faulty conceptions and superstitions of a past generation which are no longer, if ever, valid or wise to live by."

I appreciated his comments because some Biblical directives were local and parochial and were never intended for all time. But, as far as directives for sexual expression were concerned, I did try to point out that those conclusions were derived largely from the experiences of people before they were attributed to be the will of God. It was not until the Hebrews saw that polygamy and infidelity were detrimental to their own state that they attributed their opposition to them to be the will of God. They found the ideal relationship and then ascribed it to the will of God.

This is not simply the dogmatic pronouncement of theologians and religionists, but sociologists and psychologists as well. All, of course, do not support chastity, monogamy and fidelity. But, many do–and for what seems to me good reason. The human being is not merely a body. She is mind and spirit, too. The key question is: What are the essential requirements for full realization of total personality? The body is not the whole, but it is a symbol of the whole. The reverence and respect that we have for a person is indicated in the way we treat the body. For this reason, there are certain intimacies that lose their spiritual significance when they become cheap and common. For instance, the kiss under certain circumstances may have important meaning, but the meaning is lost when the kiss is given too freely or given to persons who mean nothing to us.

If we follow the principle that one human life is as valuable as another, then the welfare of one cannot be sacrificed for the gratification of the other. This is why the church has been historically opposed to prostitution. The insidious evil of prostitution is that one person is used by another–the man for money, the woman for physical gratification of man. The total personality is discounted. This is a tragic evil and deserves to be exposed for what it is–pure, unadulterated and hedonistic selfishness. The Christian does not see others as being for him. The Christian is a person for others. Freedom in matters of sex, without the responsibilities that are entailed, is a monstrous evil. "The monstrosity of sexual intercourse outside of marriage," wrote C. S. Lewis, the late English scholar, "is that those who indulge in it are trying to isolate one kind of union from all other kinds of union which were intended to go along with it to make up the total union."[5] Physical relations outside of marriage express more than either party intends or is able to fulfill, so it is a false symbol. It prompts feelings of guilt. When our gestures belie our inner intentions, personality disintegration begins.

There is a false notion held by many that it is unwise, even dangerous and harmful, to suppress sexual desires. This could not be more wrong. Restraint, inhibition and self-control are positive words. Without restraints this would be a more chaotic world. Not self-indulgence, but self-discipline is called for if we are to enjoy the integrated, whole life.

Character is not a gift; it is an achievement. The kingdom of character always lies upstream. It is never reached by drifting. It is only negotiated by those who battle the currents and headwinds of temptation.

There are those who are governed by their senses alone. They consider the existence of desire all the justification that is needed for its gratification. The mature person learns to live not for the feeding and perishable ecstasy of the moment, but for the eternal and abiding values, which alone are the sources of self-respect and peace of mind. Spinoza once said:

If the way I have shown to lead to these things (peace of mind) now seems very hard, still, it can be found. And of course, what is found so rarely must be hard. For if salvation were at hand, and could be found without great effort, how could nearly everyone neglect it? But all things excellent are as difficult as they are rare.[6]

It appears to be the congenital nature of people who play free and loose in sexual matters to have interpersonal problems. Suspicions are bred that militate against domestic tranquility. This is not simply the pious preachment of a parson. The conclusions of countless counselors confirm the fact that promiscuity and infidelity can open a Pandora's box. Philanderers can often date the beginning of their roamings within marriage to promiscuity prior to it. The best way to break a bad habit is to be sure it never begins.

It would be an oversimplification to say that premarital chastity or marital fidelity are all that is needed to assure a happy marriage. Building a life together is a complicated venture, and no one factor guarantees the health of the whole. Even so, some factors of behavior prior to and during marriage condition to a great extent the happiness that is achieved in the relationship. Loyalty to the ideals of chastity, monogamy and fidelity belong to this group.

Many years ago, I visited with a young woman who had voluntarily quit her job with no prospect of another because she was involved at work with a married man. She was wise enough to see that it was a dead end street, maybe even a cliff of total destruction for her, for him and for everyone else in the family circle. She did not feel strong enough to withstand the temptation if she stayed at that job in the office where she was employed. I commended her for her wisdom and courage. Retreat is often the better part of valor.

We do not meet here week after week as self-righteous prigs professing to have no sins or indiscretions ourselves. Indeed, one of the conditions of church membership is the recognition that we are sinners in need of God's grace. No one of us is in a position to cast the first stone at anyone. We have not come to the temple to thank God that we are not as other men, but we have come as the publican, saying, "Lord, be merciful to me, a sinner."[7] The church, as Henry Ward Beecher observed, "is not a gallery for the exhibition of eminent Christians, but a school for the training of imperfect ones."[8] We do not claim to have arrived, but we do want to be on the way. Keeping sexual drives within bounds is not just a challenge to the young, but persists through the years. We recognize our vulnerability, and we pray for power to restrain any illegitimate expressions of sexuality.

Sensual desire was a plaguing problem for Augustine, one of the most brilliant men who ever lived. He aspired to the good life, but he could not attain it. His prayer is both humorous and sad. "Lord," he prayed, "make me pure, but not yet." Walking one day in a garden, he heard a voice within him say, "Take up and read." There was a Bible on a bench before him. He turned to Romans 13:14 and read the words, "Put ye on the Lord Jesus Christ and make not provision for the flesh to fulfill the lusts thereof."[9] He closed the book and then and there the issue was really decided. He gave his life to Christ, totally, and with the indwelling presence of Christ that followed, he found the power that enabled him to suppress his desires and win a victory over that which could have destroyed him.[10]

In a church this size, it is safe to assume that there is someone here who needs to make that decision today. If that person persists in the current pattern and practice, only sorrow and disaster can result for self and others. In every indiscretion, somebody pays.

This could be a monumental moment for someone, if seeing his or her own struggles mirrored in what has been said, that person flees like the young woman from irresistible temptation. Or, better yet, commits his or her life to Christ. That commitment could enable that man or woman to prevail over what threatens to destroy. For someone here, habit has not yet become master, but tomorrow may be too late. Character can be amended and improved, but not just anytime. The soul, like the soil, has its seasons. Jesus never said tomorrow, but today. "Now is the day of salvation."[11]

May God forgive us for the easy way in which we have rationalized our pleasures and allowed the world to squeeze us into its mold. May He help us become good stewards of our affections and wise in the distribution of the secrets of the heart.

Genetic Experimentation

◈

Ｗe are in waters today that are deep, and our ability to swim is not all that we wish it were. But, one does not learn to swim if he remains on the beach or only in shallow waters. One of the current issues we deal with is genetic experimentation. Is this a threat or a threshold to something more wonderful than anything we've known? Genetic experimentation, or recombinant DNA, is a system of splicing together large blocks of genes from the same or diverse organisms. Recombinant means "crossing over." It is the transfer of genes from one organism to another. It is a revolutionary technique that permits genetic information to cross species barriers, opening the door to the rearrangement of the genetic heritage of millions of years of evolution. This technology appears to offer the power to transform living organisms comparable to the power of nuclear fission to transform matter. DNA technology is probably the most significant advance in microbiology since the invention of the microscope.

It is not within the scope of my knowledge or the limitations of our time to deal with the intricacies of this experimentation. Our intention today is only to encourage further reading and listening by all of us and to respond with an informed and intelligent attitude toward it. A Major League Baseball umpire preached one of the best sermons I ever heard. He said he often wondered how a spectator seated three hundred feet up in the bleachers felt that he could call a ball or strike more accurately than one who was immediately behind the plate. We are varying degrees removed from the home plate of experimentation, and we do not, like Chicken Little, want to react before all of the research is in. There are some people who get so uptight in controversial situations that they twang in a strong wind.

But a question that might be legitimately asked is: Why do we deal with this scientific theme here, in a church service? There are, we know, religions that ignore developments that are made in the world of science and technology, but Christianity is not one of them. I know there are some Christians who understand the faith solely in spiritual or personal terms, and who think of Christians as the guardians of eternal truths and timeless values in a world of change and decay. The intrinsic earthiness of biblical faith, with its insistence that God has always been and remains constantly involved with matter through the creation, preservation and redemption of all things, has moved Christianity again and again into the center of public policy concerns. These concerns arise from new information and new methods relating to our stewardship of the earth and the life it supports. It ought to come as a surprise to no one, therefore, that from the time of the first splitting of the atom down through the destruction of Hiroshima and Nagasaki, to current controversies about nuclear weapons, power plants and Trident submarines, Christian people have been involved individually and corporately at every level of the debate–not incidentally, but specifically because of their Christian commitment. There was no way for the church to be the church without somehow being involved in these crucial issues. And, the same is to be true now as public interest shifts from nuclear physics to molecular biology, from the splitting of atoms to the splicing of genes.

Arthur Compton, Nobel Prize winner in atomic physics, said, "Science has created a world in which Christianity is a necessity."[1] Science has often found in religion not an ally but an obstacle. Scientists have often been opposed by religionists, who have supposed they were doing God's will by suppressing scientific research. The long struggle is described in all its gory detail in a book by Andrew Dickson White entitled *A History of the Warfare of Science with Theology in Christendom.* It was published in 1896 and tells the story of Cornell University, founded in 1868 by White and Ezra Cornell in order to provide a place for the free pursuit of truth unhampered by the prejudices of religion.

But science is not to be permitted to steamroller its discoveries without having an hour of accountability. The dropping of the atomic bomb and the killing of bird life by DDT revealed clearly that what happens in the laboratory has repercussions far beyond. Science needs religion and religion needs science. As Albert Einstein said, "Science without religion is lame; religion without science is blind."[2]

In a commencement address at the University of
Michigan in 1977, Joseph Califano, Secretary of Health,
Education and Welfare, pointed out that science has
become too important to be left solely to the scientists.
With specific reference to recombinant DNA research, he
noted that policy deliberations in this area must be conducted with concern and deliberation. He explained:

> *This is the slowest way, the most inconvenient way, and*
> *in democracy the only way to make such decisions.*
> *Decision makers in science and medicine must learn the*
> *hard lesson that decision making behind closed doors*
> *breeds distrust, even if what happens behind those doors*
> *is perfectly legitimate.*

The questions we ask are: What are the risks and what
are the benefits anticipated from such experimentation?

There is always the possibility that pathogenic bacteri-
um will be produced in a laboratory that will escape, say,
in the intestine of the laboratory worker, thus bringing on
an uncontrollable, perhaps irreversible bio-disaster.
Another fear is that newly created life forms could be
Frankensteins in our midst or that terrorists could learn
the technique and devise biological warfare attacks. The
problem of mishandled power is not new. Leonardo
DaVinci invented a submarine and then tore up the plans
for fear of what men would do with it. Alfred Nobel
invented dynamite, never thinking that so dreadful an
explosive would ever be used for war. Then, with the
profits from dynamite, he established the Nobel Peace
Prize to make his hopes for a peaceful world come true.
One of our present day scientists, J. Robert Oppenheimer,

did not want the first nuclear bomb to be dropped on Hiroshima. He and others wanted it dropped on a small, uninhabited island off the coast of Japan to exhibit its great powers without killing anyone.

On the other hand, the anticipated benefits of recombinant DNA research are mind-boggling. The rat insulin gene has already been cloned (or replicated by means of DNA technology) by a group of researchers at the University of California, San Francisco. It is theoretically possible to design bacteria that will manufacture hormones, or blood-clotting factors for hemophiliacs, or highly specific antibiotics. It might even be possible by recombinant DNA technology to develop vaccines that will attack viruses. And the list of possibilities goes on. It may be possible to create nitrogen-fixing bacteria that would enable crops to make use of nitrogen from the air and thus virtually wipe out the need for artificial fertilizers. Do you see what this could do for the alleviation of hunger in our world?

We may be able to design a strain of bacteria that would use sunlight to split the water molecule into hydrogen and oxygen, providing an unlimited source of energy. Or, to develop bacteria that, as decay agents, could transform wood and straw into sugar, or hydrocarbon molecules into protein, or mop up oil spills, or break down plastics. DNA techniques will produce insulin, the rare substance vital in the treatment of diabetes.

Even those who work with the calculation of consequences, however, know that the facts are never all in, and that calculations have to be made with less than adequate evidence. Costs, risks and benefits are so largely theoretical that it is difficult to move with certainty. The wise course would impose some restraints without so stymieing the effort as to work to the detriment of enlarging our understanding.

Wise and cautious people are governing this research. A conference was called at Asilomar, California, in 1975, and it urged federal guidelines over DNA research. The following year, the officials at the National Institutes of Health announced that all federally supported DNA research must have their approval. Every scientist must file a memorandum describing his experiment and conform to containment regulations.

Industry researchers are not, however, covered by these rules. It is readily agreed that some regulating should be done, but who is to do it? Some believe that genetic engineering ranks with nuclear power in its dangers and ought to be kept under careful federal control. But, should political leaders be judge and jury? What is the expertise that should grant them such authority? Should government prohibit free expression of new ideas or procedures? Totalitarian governments do so, but should it be so here in the United States?

There are DNA committees across America that meet to pass judgment on an experimenter's plan. These committees are comprised of a cross section of our citizenry. For nearly two years, I have been on the committee at the University of Washington, supposedly to ask the ethical questions. I have observed what I have long known–that clergy are no more concerned with ethical questions than are the scientists who are involved. I have the highest respect for the integrity, sensitivity and good common sense of those with whom I serve. Given the scarcity of hard data on which to calculate probable costs and benefits, how can responsible decisions be made in the midst of this uncertainty?

This is a complicated question and no one of us wants to be the fool that rushes in where angels fear to tread, but how can we really know what the costs and benefits are until the research is under way or completed? Recombinant DNA research is, of course, not the only area in which uncertain conditions prevail. It is equally true with regard to nuclear power, delicate diplomatic relations, fragile economic balances and environmental concerns. How can you be sure on any investment you make? You can't. The element of risk is there. You can never get to second base by keeping one foot on first.

Jacob Bronowski says in the *Ascent of Man* that the ascent of man is always teetering in the balance. When man lifts a foot for the next step, is it really going to come down pointing ahead? Uncertainty is inescapable.

It is impossible to imagine a society in which no research of any kind could be done until the researcher had demonstrated beyond reasonable doubt to a judge, jury or committee that it should be done. The entire scientific enterprise would grind to a halt. It could well be that society has overreacted to potential hazards and has erected obstacles to research that have either drawn it to a halt or circumvented it with so many restrictions that it has deterred progress in many crucial and important areas of research.

Nobel Prize winner James Watson was the co-discoverer of DNA, along with Sir Francis Crick. He once said researchers were being blocked from studying the viruses that cause leukemia or breast cancer. If fact, two of them had to locate in London to isolate DNA from a common human virus.

Scientific research has never been amenable to rigorous cost-benefit accounting in advance. Nor, for that matter, has exploration of any sort. But, if we have learned one lesson, it is that research and exploration have a remarkable way of paying off quite apart from the fact that they demonstrate that humans are alive and insatiably curious. And, who of us would want to stay the hand of progress because of dangers inherent in advance?

I, with I suspect most of you, am optimistic and hopeful in the presence of DNA research. New and marvelous possibilities are open to us. Humankind has revealed ingenuity, resourcefulness and adaptability in the past, and there is no reason to believe it cannot be true in the future.

Often, we read about what was once feared that has now become a boon. In 1829, Martin Van Buren, then governor of New York and later president of the United States, wrote a letter to Andrew Jackson who was president at the time. In the letter, he was protesting the spread of a "new form of transportation known as railroads." With the benefit of a certain local bias of upper New York State, he wrote:

> *The Government should create an Interstate Commerce Commission to protect the American people from the evils of railroads and to preserve the canals for posterity. As you may know, Mr. President, railroad carriages are pulled at an enormous speed of 15 miles an hour by engines, which, in addition to endangering life and limb of passengers, roar and snort their way through countryside, setting fire to crops, scaring the livestock, frightening women and children. The Almighty certainly never intended that people should travel at such break-neck speed.*[3]

It was a needless fear for railroads became an asset to us, uniting our nation with lines of steel. They are still important to our economy and transportation today, but additional modes of travel have made that fifteen miles an hour seem like a dead stop.

When it has been true to itself and its mission, the Church has promoted literacy, encouraged learning, established universities, and founded libraries and scientific laboratories. Its darkest hours have been those times when it has lost touch with its origins and turned against those who sought or found new information about the world or human life. Can we believe that God who gave us minds could have made certain areas of life inviolate from the mind's intrusion? The Christian ought never to fear new information about anything. He lives with hopeful attitude. He does believe that in all things God works for good with those who love Him.[4] Our discoveries can be turned to productive and useful purposes.

God did not give us minds with the intention that we should place them on shelves and refuse to use them. When we stop searching we are dead. I cannot conceive of God putting us in a world and giving us dominion over it and then hiding some things in it that were never intended to be found. We do not create God's laws; we discover them and so order our lives as to use those laws and direct them to worthwhile ends.

Thomas Jefferson said, "There is no truth on earth that I fear to be known."[5] He also felt that it was more dangerous to live in ignorance than to live with knowledge. I believe we would agree. I sometimes wonder which is worse: a child who is afraid of the dark, or an adult who is afraid of the light?

The writer of this verse expresses in homely style the philosophy to which many of us subscribe:

> *If youth had been willing to listen*
> *To the tales their grandfathers told,*
> *If the gray-bearded sage by the weight of his age*
> *Had been able attention to hold,*
> *We'd be reading by candles and heating with wood,*
> *And where we were then we'd have certainly stood.*
>
> *If youth had been willing to listen*
> *To the warnings and hints of the wise,*
> *Had it taken as true all the best which they knew,*
> *And believed that no higher we'd rise,*
> *The windows of sick rooms would still be kept shut*
> *And we'd still use a cobweb to bandage a cut.*
>
> *If youth had been willing to listen,*
> *Had it clung to the best of the past,*
> *With oxen right now we'd be struggling to plough*
> *And thinking a horse travels fast.*
> *We'd have stood where we were beyond question or doubt*
> *If some pestilent germ hadn't wiped us all out.*
>
> *So, although I am grey at the temples,*
> *And settled and fixed in my ways,*
> *I wouldn't hold youth to the limits of truth*
> *That I learned in my brief yesterdays*
> *And I say to myself as they come and they go;*
> *"Those kids may find something this age doesn't know."*[6]

Thomas Edison offered another hopeful note when he said, "What man's mind can create, man's character can control."[7] I believe that! And, to this high end of Creation and to intelligent and loving control I call us all to dedicate ourselves this day.

∞

Obscenity

❦

Throughout my ministry, I have always been interested in words, and I suppose understandably so. They have been my tools. They have been at the same time my joy and my despair. They are my joy, for they are conveyors of ideas I would impart, but my despair too, for the necessity of their use has confronted me with potential pitfalls. It is somewhat unsettling when I see on my library shelf the little book *7000 Words Frequently Mispronounced*. It is a disconcerting thought to know that every time I stand to speak I have at least seven thousand distinct possibilities of making myself ridiculous. It's almost enough to encourage me to take a vow of perpetual silence!

Getting the words together in a manner that does not violate rules of grammar is an ever-present challenge. I know that a speaker's sentence structure should be one of the things of which he is proudest. Therefore, there is the continual challenge to find the apt word to convey the thought intended. Mark Twain said that the difference between the right word and the almost-right word is the difference between the lightning and the lightning bug.[1]

But as interested as I have been in individual words, I think I have been even more interested in definitions, for they are more encompassing and illuminating. For instance, there is a word that appears with some regularity in our newspapers and magazines, a word that deserves a closer look and broader understanding. It is the word "obscenity." The *American Heritage Dictionary*, which is always at arm's length in my study, defines obscenity in these words: "Obscenity is that which is lewd, loathsome and offensive to accepted standards of behavior, expression or appearance."

There is a much smaller book on my library shelf–less than one hundred pages–but it comes to grip with the meaning of obscenity in a far deeper manner. The book is titled *Include Me Out: The Confessions of an Ecclesiastical Coward.* It was written by Dr. Colin Morris, an English Methodist parson who has served most of his ministry in Africa, where for a time he served as president of the United Church of Zambia. It is a fresh, frank discussion of what it means to be a Christian and a church person in these times. It is both a fascinating and disturbing book. Though it deals with several themes beyond obscenity, it did set my mind to thinking about some larger and deeper meanings than those delineated in the *American Heritage Dictionary*.

In the book, Dr. Morris quotes Lenny Bruce, a strange, or at least a different kind of a comedian, who committed suicide many years ago. Steve Allen, in his book assessing comedians, gives Bruce a high rating as one of the creative comics of our time. In spite of his skills, Lenny Bruce was denied performance in many nightclubs because of his profanity, off-color and even dirty stories. Perhaps he should have been invited to speak in our churches, for though what he had to say might have been delivered in a crude and offensive manner, it was nevertheless something we needed to hear.

From among the many things that Lenny Bruce had said, Colin Morris singled out some very biting and incisive judgments. Said Bruce:

> *I know in my heart by pure logic, that any man who claims to be a leader in the church is a hustler if he has two suits in a world in which most people have none.*[2]

Commenting on that biting epigram, Dr. Morris writes, "Anyone in the house care to argue about that?"[3]

Colin Morris goes on to talk about clergy in particular. He writes:

> *Obscenity is a strong word, but I know of no other so apt. Obscenity is the jeweled ring on a bishop's finger. Obscenity is the flash of my gold wristwatch from under the sleeve of my cassock as I throw dirt on the coffin of a man who died of starvation, murmuring the while the most asinine words in the English language: "Since it has pleased Almighty God to take to Himself our brother." Obscenity is the religious leader who cries "murder" when a woman aborts a piece of bloody tissue, who keeps silence or indeed gives a blessing while thousands of fully formed sons and daughters of women are incinerated in war.*[4]

Maybe the words of the comedian and clergyman alike are overdone and overstated. I confess that I do have two suits of clothes and a wristwatch, and am not yet under enough conviction of sin to renounce the other suit and the wristwatch. Nevertheless, the point that the preacher was making does get through to me loud and clear and in convincing fashion. Simply put, there are deeper meanings to obscenity than the common connotations of pornography and profanity, and he indicates that Christ's kind of language unearths those deeper meanings.

Now, before anyone begins to interpret this sermon as an indirect sanction of freedom and the filth that flows so freely in so much modern language and literature, stage and screen, let me try to set the thermostat at the beginning of the sermon. We are here concerned about all obscenity, and that includes speech, stage and books. If this morning we succeed in proving the "deep" meanings of the word obscenity, let it not be at the expense of a concern for the common meaning of the word.

You would expect a preacher to take a dim view of such obscenity, but listen to these words from *Time*, a so-called secular magazine.

> *A nation gets the kind of art and entertainment it wants and will pay for. Thus, to many serious critics, they are by no means all bluenoses. The explosion of salacious material in cinema, theater and bookrack is disturbing. Esthetically, pop sex may well reflect a stunting of imagination, a dilution of artistic values and a cultish attempt to substitute sensation for thought. Morally and psychologically, it may signal a deeper unease connected with a crisis of values. On any level of creative intent, it is hard to defend the bulk of salacious literature being churned out today. Most of it is perverse, narcissistic, brutal, irrational and boring.[5]*

This is not *A.D.*, our church magazine, but *Time*. So much is profane and obscene in our society today that even the most naive and sheltered of individuals must be aware of it. So much of perversity, nudity, and sadistic, crude material from the pen of writers finds its way into books and ultimately onto stage and screen. Not since Manhattan Island sold for twenty-four dollars has so much dirt been sold so cheap. But, it is what seems to appeal to so many. Of one author it was said, "His sins were scarlet, but his books were read."[6] At one time the saltiest thing in the movie house was the popcorn. No more. One marquee said it all, "Now Showing: Everything."

All of this saddens some of the old timers. Several years ago, the American Film Institute honored James Cagney with the Life Achievement Award. Mr. Cagney, a very private man, agreed somewhat reluctantly to all of the festivities surrounding the one hundred twenty-five dollar plate dinner, but took part because the fifteen hundred present, in paying such a price, would be underwriting scholarships for young, aspiring filmmakers. "Maybe," said Mr. Cagney, "they could put through a constructive program and improve the quality of pictures. Get rid of nudity and the language, the pornographic thing. It is," he said, "very disheartening."[7]

Jesus, as I understand him from the Gospels, was no prim and prudish figure, conveniently looking away or turning away from the dark and sometimes dirty realities of life in his day. He went home to eat with the sinners, made himself at home with the rough and tough fishermen, stopped to talk with the harlots on the street and was finally sentenced to die on a rugged cross between two thieves at the town's garbage dump. He saw life in all its rawest, crudest fashion, but he never adopted the language or the manners of the gutters. He kept insisting that human beings were so much more than the animal, that there was more to life than the dark cellars in which so many lived. He drew people up without being drawn down himself.

But now, come back to this sermon's beginning. Consider that those of us who are concerned about obscenity in the traditional meaning of the word may be just those who need to see that there is much more to the matter than that. Malcolm Boyd, in one of his books, was getting at this truth.

> *Obscenity cuts much deeper than words. It involves actions and attitudes. Dirty words are apparently a greater shock to many people than the dirty realities we have been conditioned to ignore–the dirty things we do to each other each day, often in the name of high sounding words like patriotism, duty and religion. Why is it that so many people who campaign most fervently for "decency" are often reluctant to call so many realities by their names: racism, napalm, sex, death?*[8]

And when you stop to think about it, isn't this just exactly the problem Jesus faced in his dealings with the Pharisees? Here were people who lived by the book, followed rules, and kept the letter of the law in speech and in deed. They were people who regarded themselves as clean and others as unclean. Certainly, Jesus did not argue with them in regard to a code of decency. It was the same code by which he had been raised and by which he lived. But again and again, he kept making the point that something was missing in their understanding of the dimensions of righteousness. It was so largely external and did not go deeply enough to reach their hearts and shape their lives.

So the word pictures that Jesus drew of the Pharisees are pretty sharp and scathing–nowhere more so than when he told them that they were like whitewashed tombs, beautiful on the outside–perfectly proper and neat–but on the inside filled with all manner of uncleanness.[9] In a sense, he was telling people who despised obscenity that they had missed some deeper obscenities in their own lives.

Go through the Gospels and think of some of the obscenities that Jesus described and decried.

> *The Priest and the Levite walking along the Jericho Road and ignoring the victim of the thieves.*[10]

> *The Pharisee in the church who prayed, "I thank thee God, that I am not as other men are," offering this prayer while looking down his nose at the Publican nearby.*[11]

> *The money changers in the temple, exploiting the pilgrims, and, as Jesus said, making the house of prayer into a den of thieves.*[12]

> *The crowd, ready to stone to death a sinful woman, blind to their own transgressions.*[13]

> *The Scribes, who as Jesus said, devour widows' houses and for a pretense make long prayers.*[14]

The irony is that so many of these were the so-called "solid" citizens of their day, people who went to church, paid their bills and obeyed the law.

"Ah," said Jesus, "these ought you to have done without neglecting the weightier matters of justice, love and faith."[15]

Come across the centuries to our own day. What if Jesus were physically present in our country and culture? What are the deeper obscenities that he would point to now? What would he say to the publisher or advertising men who grow fat from falsehoods? Or, to the farmer who exploits the migrant workers, or to the migrant workers who rip off the farmers? Or, to the politician who wheels and deals? What would he say to the young and old who are eager for violence and strife and are callous to the value of human life? What would he say to those who run to drugs or alcohol as an escape from life's responsibilities? Or, to those who get behind the wheel of a car when they are intoxicated?

What would he say to the eighty-nine percent of Americans who never support any political party financially, and yet continuously gripe about their government? Or, to those who fail to vote in an election? What would he say to adults who reason that public schools are not their concern for they have no children or young people, or their children are now grown? Or, to those who have children and hold out no time to be with them? What would he say to those who impugn the motives of others—who write people off because of the length of the hair, manner of dress, color of skin or nationality? What would he say to those who share rumors with others without checking the accuracy of the story? What would he say to those who accept a call to a board or a committee and then seldom show up at a meeting? Or, to people who say they'll do something, then don't?

What would be his judgment of the nations of the world that pour billions of dollars into instruments of destruction? It is incredible, but true; the nations of the world spend one million dollars per minute for the development and production of arms, while millions of hungry, distressed human beings wander about looking for a crust of bread to sustain their bodies. What a terrible obscenity we are witnessing in the arms race. How ironic it is that in this season as we prepare to celebrate the birth of the Prince of Peace we should announce plans for a multi-billion dollar missile and, obscenity of obscenities, suggest for it the name "Peacemaker."

There is a book published some years ago entitled *North Toward Home*. It was the odyssey of a man who came north to live, but one incident in that book that impressed me the most had nothing to do with geography. One day the author was on a train in route to New York City. He said that as they crossed into the Bronx, the train unexpectedly slowed down for a few miles as they witnessed the aftermath of a recent accident in which a boy had been severely hurt. This is what the author wrote.

In the orange glow of the late afternoon, the policeman, the crowd, the traffic for a moment were immobile, motionless, a small tableaux of violence and death in the city. Behind me, in the next row of seats there was a game of bridge in progress. I heard one of the four men say as he looked out at the sight, "God, that's horrible." Another said in a whisper,

"Terrible, terrible!" There was a momentary silence, punctuated only by the clicking of the wheels on the track. Then after a pause I heard the first man say, "Two hearts"... I know, what could a person do on a fast moving train? What can anyone do for anyone who is hurt from the fast moving train of his life and his work?[16]

The only thing is that I thought I detected some obscenity in that account–not when the man said, "My God, that's horrible," but later when he casually resumed bidding "two hearts." And, the most uncomfortable part of it all is that I can so readily see myself related to that man.

Maybe it was this kind of obscenity that Jesus was crying out against when he said:

I was hungry and you gave me no food, I was thirsty and you gave me no drink, I was a stranger and you did not welcome me, naked and you did not clothe me, sick and in prison, and you did not visit me. Inasmuch as ye did it not to the least of these, you did it not for me.[17]

The curtain of this sermon could go down in a gray gloom and guilt, but it really does not need to. The Gospel makes it pretty clear that something very hopeful and exciting can happen when a person begins with himself or herself and honestly says, "God, be merciful to me, a sinner."[18] At any rate, there is quite a club of those whose honest-to-God goodness began and continued with that kind of humility–Peter, Paul, Mary Magdalene, Augustine, Francis of Assisi, John Wesley, William Booth, Lincoln, Luther, Pope John XXIII, Andrew the Disciple, and all his anonymous one-talent successors. The good news of the Gospel is that the club is still open to member-ship. It is not a private, exclusive group. "Whosoever will may come."[19]

Our prayer is not for any less vision to see the evils about us that are so blatant, but rather for more vision to see the sins within us that are so stealthy and subtle. May we gather strength from our worship this morning, that by being disturbed by Christ's judgment, we may find our hope in new obedience to His lordship of our lives.

∞

Drinking

⁂

It is with some trepidation that I tackle this subject. Vivid in my memory is the pastor of a church in the community where I went to college. He was violently opposed to the drinking of alcoholic beverages, and he managed to bring his views into nearly every sermon, regardless of the morning's theme. He railed against drinking so much that many came to believe that they had really missed something if they had not tried an alcoholic beverage. He created, inadvertently, more "men of distinction" than he ever suspected. However, those of us in a more liberal tradition may perhaps err in that we do not confront the subject often enough.

There is a story that has gone the rounds concerning another minister, one in a more liberal tradition, who was equally vigorous in his opposition to the use of alcohol. He, too, took every opportunity to make his views known. It was also his practice to always acknowledge publicly any gift given to him by his parishioners. One of his close friends, revealing a sense of humor, sent him a quart of blackberry wine and dared him to acknowledge that. The pastor was equal to the challenge. The next Sunday, he began, "The minister wishes to thank Mr. Jones for the gift of fruit and for the spirit in which it was given!"

The important thing about this sermon will be "the spirit in which it is given." The spirit in which we approach this theme is not one of arrogance or dogmatism. It is an honest, earnest effort to evaluate the important issue of drinking as objectively as we know how in the context of the Christian faith we profess. There are no simple answers to this perplexing question as it relates to conduct. The Germans, French, Italians, Spanish and others regard wine and beer as articles of food. It is the Islamic faith that is the teetotal religion; no alcohol is to be drunk in any form by its adherents. The Mormons, Seventh Day Adventists and others are also strongly opposed to drinking. Protestant denominations vary in their teachings concerning the use of alcohol. At one time, the Methodist and Presbyterian denominations were unequivocally opposed to the use of alcohol by their members, but those strict regulations have now been eased and altered.

The Congregationalists invite the enlightened mind and conscience of each member to determine what his attitude will be toward the use of alcohol. It is to be expected, then, in this congregation, that there will be varying conclusions concerning this matter. Each of us will contend for the view he holds without being contentious, and we will agree to disagree agreeably.

It is an appropriate beginning for the Protestant, who takes the Bible as his guide in conduct, to see if an answer is in the scriptures. You will have noted in the reading of the scriptures that the guidance is nebulous and contradictory:

> *Wine is a mocker, strong drink is raging;*
> *Whosoever is deceived thereby is not wise.*[1]

> *Drink no more water, but take a little wine for thy*
> *stomach's sake.*[2]

However, if an answer is not explicit in the scriptures, it is nevertheless implicit in Jesus' teachings. Jesus was not a legalist, and we who are his followers do not find our directives in proof texts nor in isolated instances or incidents. We try to discover the principles and attitudes that are advocated. The tenor of Jesus' teachings makes clear the dignity and worth of each individual, the sacredness of human life, and the responsibility that we have for ourselves and for the welfare of others. The things that influence the self and others are religious problems. Alcohol does affect the lives of people, so it is, therefore, a legitimate concern for us. The Bible does encourage us to seek the truth, for it is the truth that shall set us free. We are to sit down before the facts and determine where they lead us.

Taking this biblical counsel seriously, we therefore call in those who are best prepared to set the facts before us–the educators, sociologists, law enforcement officers, social workers, psychiatrists, medical doctors, religious leaders and others whose training has prepared them to shed light on our quest. We can, of course, reject their conclusions if we choose, but the burden of proof will then be upon us to summon our own counsel and verify their reliability.

Doctors and scientists tell us that alcohol, even in small amounts, impairs reason. Alcohol is not a stimulant, but a narcotic, a sedative, a "domesticated drug" that relaxes controls of intelligence and will. We are reasoning creatures, and our welfare and the welfare of others we meet and live with are conditioned by our ability to remember, plan, think and act. The brain is a sacred trust. To misuse it or limit its effectiveness purposely has little defense. "I have better use for my brain than to poison it with alcohol,"[3] said Thomas Edison.

Shakespeare, who was not a reformer or a puritan, puts words on the lips of Cassio in the play *Othello* after Cassio has committed a blunder while under the influence of alcohol: "O God, that men should put an enemy in their mouth to steal away their brains."[4]

"Clear heads choose what?" reads an old Calvert's ad. If the head is to remain clear, it will make a great deal of difference what is chosen.

It has long been said that there are three parties in Washington, DC–the Republican Party, the Democratic Party and the Cocktail Party. One wonders how many critical decisions have been made in our capital city by those who were not fully recovered from the influence of alcohol.

Furthermore, alcohol weakens self-control and encourages and permits the drinker to do things he would not do if in full control of his faculties. Penal authorities tell us that alcohol is involved in fully two-thirds of all major crimes. Year after year, the FBI comes up with just about the same figure–some sixty percent of all arrests are alcohol-related. Three out of five!

Chemist Floyd Shupe of Columbus, Ohio, found through a long study that, of persons arrested for stabbing, eleven out of twelve were under the influence of alcohol, while in the case of assaults, ten out of eleven were under alcoholic influence. A survey revealed that 1,215 out of 1,720 men in the Virginia State Prison said that liquor was a factor in the anti-social conduct that led to their incarceration. Under the influence of alcohol, they lost their self-control and did what they would have otherwise left undone.

For many years, I carried with me a billfold that was made in prison by a friend who is serving a life sentence for killing his wife. At the time it happened, he was so inebriated that he does not remember his crime at all, but that fact did not alter his sentence. He was, and is, an intelligent man, but that indiscretion of over-drink robbed him of his intelligence, his wife whom he dearly loved, and his freedom to realize the life of usefulness that could have been.

The presence of alcohol in the body distorts judgment. There is a story about a mouse who was standing alongside a keg of wine. He took a sip of the drippings and felt his muscles tighten. After the second sip, he reared back and exclaimed, "Bring on that cat!" He believed himself to have equipment for battle he did not possess.

What looks one way when a person is drinking may look altogether different when he is not. It was Ogden Nash who wrote:

> *Glances that over cocktails seem so sweet*
> *May be less charming over shredded wheat.*[5]

The presence of alcohol in the system affects physical skills. Even after one drink, typesetters make more mistakes, and the rifleman falls off his marksmanship. The acuteness of the sense of sight and touch are lessened, and our reflexes are slowed up. Pilots of commercial airliners are not permitted to drink any alcoholic beverages in the twenty-four-hour period immediately before they take charge of a flight.

One drink in the body of the driver of a car can be deadly to himself and others. In the second of time required to perform the simple muscular response of taking one's foot off the accelerator and putting it on the brake, an auto running at a legitimate speed will travel from sixty to one hundred thirty feet. Now, if even one bottle of beer should slow the driver's reaction one fifth of a second (a contingency that psychological tests have shown to be entirely possible), consider what would be the difference in the opportunities for avoiding an intersecting machine or in the chances of missing a little child who has darted out into the street from behind a parked car while in pursuit of a ball.

The one-or-two-drink driver is more of a menace than the one who is highly inebriated. For the one who is drunk will soon fall asleep and hit a pole or not be allowed by his companion to drive at all, but those who drink only a little take chances and assume skills they don't really have. We are not talking here about hypothetical possibilities. Unfortunately, what I am saying is demonstrated all too often on our highways and reported graphically on television and in our newspapers. Last year, some fifty-four thousand died in highway accidents in our country, and thousands more were permanently crippled. In half of those accidents, one of the drivers had been drinking a short time before the accident.

I once heard a comedian say that there are three kinds of drivers to look out for: "the urban, suburban and bourbon." But how can you know when this "bourbon" driver is approaching?

Those who talk about the horrors of war–and I am one of them–might well include in their concern the fact that more Americans have been killed by autos in the hands of drinking drivers than have been killed in all of the wars in the entire history of our country.

Will Rogers died in a plane crash long before there were the 113 million autos on the highways that are now present. He warned against undue alcoholic consumption at the Fourth of July season. He pointed out that we have killed more men on the highways celebrating our independence than were killed on the battlefields winning it.[6]

I can recall a safety council that sought slogans for the Fourth of July season that would hopefully deter the carnage on the highway. One that was submitted, though not accepted, was catchy enough to be remembered: "He who goes forth with a fifth on the Fourth, may not go forth on the fifth."

Drinking is supposed to be the mark of good sociability. This idea has been so thoroughly sold that a great many fine people are convinced that they can't entertain without liquor. In a day and a country where more people are educated than ever, it astonishes me that the wells of communication must be primed to make rapport between adult guests. Often, the consideration a host or hostess reveals does not extend to the non-drinker who must on occasion endure the tasteless or offensive humor, the interminable soliloquies and the occasional aggressiveness of those who are imbibing overmuch. Some alcoholics want to do anything other than make themselves anonymous. And, I have spoken at banquets following "happy hours" when I was not sure that many were aware of what was going on at the podium.

I read advice columnists with some degree of regularity, and most of their answers seem to me to make good sense. One column included a letter from a distressed wife. She informed the columnist that her husband was an alcoholic. He had stopped drinking completely, but years of excessive drinking had damaged his health and caused them financial difficulties. She described how when they attended events their so-called "friends" constantly offered him drinks though they knew of his previous problems.

Unfortunately, after several years of being dry, the man succumbed to an invitation to drink. It started him down the nightmarish road of alcoholism again for about a year. The woman begged the columnist to tell readers that liquor to some people was deadly, and it was no act of friendship to force it on someone who said, "No, thank you."

The enlightened or correct host or hostess always sees that there are alternative drinks on the tray, as though it was to be expected that there would be some who wouldn't care for an alcoholic beverage. Such hospitality reflects good manners, and good manners are simply concern for the feelings and convictions of others.

Alcoholism begins, of course, with drinking in moderation. Dr. Andrew Ivy of the University of Illinois contends that of every seven people who take a drink, one will become an alcoholic or pre-alcoholic. Then, what kind of Russian roulette do I play as a host if I offer drinks to seven people in the knowledge that for one of them the chamber is "loaded"?

There are two stages in the life of a drunk: (1) when he could stop if he would, (2) when he would stop if he could. And, obviously, many are stopped only by death. There are now approximately eighty-five thousand alcoholics in the state of Washington. Thirty-eight thousand of them are in King County receiving treatment, and less than five percent of these are skid row indigents. There are nine million alcoholics in the country, and we are increasing that total by fifty every hour or twelve hundred every twenty-four hours. That includes an alarming increase of young people fifteen to twenty years of age who are having problems relating to alcohol!

There is legislation now pending in our state to lower the legal age at which young people can purchase alcoholic beverages. We know the familiar arguments: If they are old enough to vote at eighteen, make contracts, die at war, then they are old enough to make this decision. I am for maximum privilege for young people, but I am not convinced that such a vote would be the best expression of my love for them. I would be handing them a Pandora's box, and the problems traceable to drink in our society would be increased.

To say it is already being done–young people are getting liquor so why not legalize it–seems to me a stupid reason. Jaywalking, bank robbery, murder are already being done; therefore, why not legalize them? I definitely oppose the legislation that would make it legal for those eighteen years of age to purchase intoxicating beverages. And again I repeat, I take this stand not because I want to limit the freedom of the young, but because I believe it is the best expression of my love for them.

Statistics from Michigan, a state that lowered the legal age for the purchase of liquor to eighteen years of age effective January 1, 1972, would give support to the stand of opposition. The Michigan state police report that for the first nine months of '72 compared to the first nine months of '71, the number of persons killed on the highways increased forty-one percent, (thirty-four lives); the number of persons injured increased ninety-nine percent, 91,963 persons); and the number of persons arrested increased one hundred thirty-two percent for males and three hundred thirty-two percent for females or 1,302 more arrests.

We talk about alcoholism being the third greatest health problem in America, harder by far to cure than cancer, yet we go on filling our TV screens, our magazines and newspapers with the most persuasive possible advertisements for drinking. They have lifted some of our most beautiful words to further sales: "Your key to hospitality," "reputation unequaled," "partners in popularity," "symbol of gracious living," "distinctive," "smooth," "mellow" and "refreshing." I shed no tears when *Life* magazine died several months ago. All too vivid in my memory was a December 16 issue years ago that carried thirty-two and a half pages of alcoholic beverage advertising to bring "Christmas cheer."

Now, I did not expect a secular magazine like *Life* to be our voice in propagating the gospel, but I did think we had the right to expect it to show a moral responsibility for people's sobriety. When a magazine going into millions of homes at Christmas time devotes nearly one-third of its space to liquor ads, it defaults its public responsibility in pursuit of the almighty dollar.

The sponsorship of athletic events by liquor interests gives a wrong correlation between drinking and sports. They take full advantage of our native love for athletics, commercializing a habit which, when it fosters itself upon people, knows neither sportsmanship, fair play nor respect for human personality in any way, shape or form. Gratefully, Mark Spitz is advertising milk and not alcohol.

The advertisements for liquor do not even hint at the fact that some forty million adults in America do not drink at all, nor do they tell that alcohol has instigated the flow of more tears, snapped more wedding rings, ruined more homes, broken more hearts, caused more accidents, taken more lives, filled more prisons, and ruined more potentially great men and women than any other one thing. I think of one of my uncles–a fine, gracious, fun-loving, kindly person, and a bright young man, too–graduating at the top of his class and titling his valedictory address "All that Glitters Is Not Gold." But, alas, succumbing to the lure of alcohol, he found himself chained to the bottle and died an alcoholic. Certainly, all that glittered was not gold.

Ah, John Barleycorn, you are a cagey individual, but a phony most of all. You cannot always fool us in spite of your claims to be our friend. You package your ware beautifully and wrap them attractively with ribbons and bows, but they are full of evil spirits. You make drink seductive by the clink of glasses, the lilt of song and good fellowship, but you are a demon in disguise. We unmask you now and see you for what you really are, an enemy to be avoided.

We are all aware that the Church must get at some of the ills that make drinking seem necessary to so many–the loneliness, frustration, sorrow, deep-seated personality problems and discouragements which plague so many. We must dedicate ourselves to the alleviation of those ills that drive people to drink and strike at the root of the problem. We must be sympathetic and hold out the hand of help-fulness, rather than pointing the finger of condemnation.

Each one of us must make some stand on this issue. I admire the courage of the president of one of our leading universities who said, "I cannot propose to control the total life of this university, but never in my own home or in any function of the university for which I have respon-sibility will liquor be served."

There is nothing pious or holier-than-thou in that statement, no pointing of the finger of condemnation. It is just a firm, resolute stand, a statement of conviction on a vital issue.

What would you have said if you had stood where I stand today? What are your conclusions on the matter? These are searching and important questions because the answer you give could well be life or death to you or a fel-low human being.

May God grant us wisdom to make those decisions, which are most in keeping with His will and enable us with the mind He has given us to discover that truth which shall surely set us free.

The Christian Faith
and Homosexuality

Two boys, walking home from school together, fell into a vigorous discussion as to which one was the better athlete. "It's true," said one, "that you can kick a football farther and throw a baseball harder than I, but I can run faster than you."

"Oh," said his friend, "how fast can you run?"

"I can run one hundred yards in 9.7 seconds."

"I could do that, too," replied the boy, "but for two reasons. There's so little time and so much ground to cover." In confronting a subject such as homosexuality, we could easily say the same this morning, "So much ground to cover and so little time."

Robert Schuller, whose television ministry has gained such a wide viewing, does not tackle controversial issues in his sermons because he says that such a short period of time as is allotted for a sermon cannot possibly give a fair hearing to all sides.[1] Dr. Schuller deals with volatile themes in seminars, classes, forums and discussion groups. I salute him for his earnest desire to be impartial. There are risks of distortion when, as here, there is no opportunity for rebuttal. I am aware, too, that it can be a "no win" situation for the preacher. I think of the political candidate who was warned by his supporters to remain silent in public address on a critical, controversial tax issue. One night, when speaking before a large audience, he said, "Now, my friends, concerning this troublesome tax issue..." His supporters, startled by his failure to heed their counsel, began to signal for his silence, but he continued. "Concerning this proposed tax issue. Some of my friends are for it, and some of my friends are against it, and I want you to know that I am for my friends!" Another, with equal political savvy, when asked his favorite color said, "Plaid."

Obviously, there are risks in controversy–risks of misunderstanding, discord and alienation–but happily it can be creative, too. G. K. Chesterton said, "I believe in getting into hot water; it keeps you clean."[2] There are risks, too, in silence and non-involvement, risks of innocuous, dull, drab, irrelevant nothingness.

Dealing as we are with such a highly charged, emotional theme makes it incumbent upon us to be as loving and as intelligent as possible. Speaking straight from the shoulder is all right provided it originates a little higher up. Above all, it is our directive in this place to consider homosexuality in the context of the faith we profess as Christians. Those who have not committed themselves to our faith have no obligation to consider it by our standards; but we do, or our faith becomes a mockery, merely ornamental and irrelevant.

"But," someone may protest, "why do you deal with it here? There are other concerns more important that deserve to engage our attention. There are so many people around the world whose fundamental rights are endangered, so many hungry people whose needs must be met. There are those who are grieving and need solace and comfort. Why, therefore, in a church service should we focus on sexual preferences and bedroom habits? Why this, here?"

I can empathize with this. Not many years ago, it would have been improbable that such a subject would be discussed in this place. But what was once an untouchable subject is now unavoidable. It affects more people than we might suspect. Dr. Paul Gebhard, head of the Kinsey Institute for Sex Research, asserted that when one speaks of homosexuality, one is talking about millions of United States citizens.[3] *Newsweek* states that there are at least twenty million or more in the United States.[4] According to another news magazine, there are one hundred twenty thousand in San Francisco, a city of six hundred eighty thousand. Officials reckon that twenty-eight percent of the city's voters are homosexual.

Estimates of Seattle's gay community center around thirty thousand, but who can say? Based on research, the best estimates suggest that in America five of every one hundred persons are exclusively homosexual throughout life, and that one person in every three has had some homosexual experience. Sheer numbers alone would warrant our consideration of the issue.

Furthermore, Christian theology and our attitudes and practices in the church have helped to foster the conditions of oppression that lesbians and homosexuals face each day. Generally, we in the Christian churches have proclaimed that homosexual acts are by definition perverse, repugnant and sinful; that homosexuality is a distortion. Whatever its source or cause, and regardless of the power it may exert, this belief must be resisted and, if possible, rooted out. This teaching both reflects and confirms the thinking of the heterosexual majority, whose attitudes, in turn, create the context in which homosexuals live their lives. It should not surprise us, therefore, that gay people do not look to the church for solace or support.

Because this rejection prevails, homosexuals are frequently abused, ridiculed or caricatured, and subjected constantly to social exclusion and disdain. They are sometimes refused acceptance by their own families; often, they are frozen out of religious fellowship and denied pastoral care. They are denied equal protection of their civil rights and equal access to vocational opportunities.

Witness James M. Gaylord, a teacher at Wilson High School in Tacoma, who even though he had been an excellent teacher–in fact, a superior one for twelve years–was fired from his job when it became known that he was a homosexual. This seems to some of us an injustice with which church people should be concerned. Sexual preference, like race, gender, creed and national origin, should not be determinative in a person's ability to perform as a professional in any given field.

In my own experience, I have had homosexual teachers who have inspired me and heterosexual teachers who have bored me. I have had homosexual teachers who bored me and heterosexual teachers who inspired me. But most of all, regardless of warm, human qualities and achievements, homosexuals and lesbians are denied personal respect and suffer all manner of oppression. Fearing reprisals if known to be homosexuals, the majority remain closeted, often suffering lives of loneliness and despair.

The Christian Faith and Homosexuality

Since we who are related to the church and involved in its mission have contributed to the thinking of the society that brings such rebuff, we cannot wash our hands of responsibility for the unjust treatment homosexuals receive. We profess to be a loving, caring, non-judgmental community, and our practice should parallel our preachments.

This does not mean we have no convictions, and we put the stamp of approval on everything that comes along. In Shakespeare's play *Hamlet*, Ophelia began distributing flowers indiscriminately only after she had lost her mind.[5] It seems to me that there are several ways in which a conscientious Christian can respond and still be both loving and intelligent. We begin by recognizing the enormity of the issue. The larger the island of knowledge, the longer is the shoreline of wonder and amazement at how intricate the whole subject actually is. Human sexuality is infinitely complicated, and we simplify it at our own peril. I have read many books, countless magazine articles and news releases relating to homosexuality, and I have only begun to scratch the surface in regard to being adequately informed. I sometimes wish I could be as sure of anything as some people are of everything.

Truly, a little learning is a dangerous thing. Henry Wheeler Shaw, an American humorist who lived in the last century, wrote under the pseudonym of Josh Billings. He said some whimsical, but pertinent things that deserve reflection. For example, "It ain't so much that folks don't know," he said, "but it's that they know so much that ain't so."[6] There are people who, if not liars, do seem to live a great deal of the time on the wrong side of the facts. Mark Twain spoke of an acquaintance by saying of him, "His ignorance covered the whole earth like a blanket and there was hardly a hole in it anywhere."[7]

There are so many myths circulating in regard to homosexuality that it is difficult to disengage fiction from fact. For instance, the implication that all homosexuals are "child molesters," "sickies" and "immoral characters" reflects unfounded prejudices that have no basis in fact. The belief that a homosexual can be known by body build, dress, voice or mannerisms is sheer, unmitigated nonsense. The assumption that homosexuals cannot live useful, happy, productive lives is disproven in the lives of thousands of lesbians and homosexuals.

There are many theories as to how sexual preferences originate, but they are not documented enough to be conclusive. Nor are homosexuals mentally ill as some would contend. The Trustees of the American Psychiatric Association voted unanimously to remove homosexuality from the list of mental illnesses. Many states have already lifted homosexuality out of the category of crime, and whether or not you call it a sin depends upon your definition of the word "sin." God made us as sexual beings. When we express those sexual inclinations, is it sinful per se? What is it that makes sexual expression legitimate or illegitimate?

A conscientious Christian resolves to be as intelligent as she knows how to be. She takes seriously the words of the Apostle Paul: "Don't let the world squeeze you into its mold, but let God remold your mind from within."[8] God gave us our minds, and he intended that we use them. We are to love God with heart, soul and mind. Unfortunately there are those who enjoy the comfort of opinion without the discomfort of thought. Everyone has a right to his own opinion, but no one has a right to be wrong in the facts. So often it seems the world is divided between the good people and the bad people. The good people determine which is which. It is not *who* is right, but *what* is right.

We praise the person who has the courage of his convictions, but any bigot or fanatic can do that. Greater praise should be reserved for those who have the courage to continually reassess their conclusions and alter them if new evidence would warrant it. How firmly we are willing to hold to outmoded concepts. Mark Twain offered wise counsel for us all. "You ought to get [your brain] out and dance on it. That would take some of the rigidity out of it."[9] An intelligent and honest response is to get all of the facts from all of the sides, analyze, compare, decide and then act. We must try to see the issues as clearly as possible.

The key question is what society stands to gain or lose if it gives sanction to homosexual lifestyles. The conservative argument seems to point to two major threats that the acceptance of a homosexual lifestyle presents to society: an erosion of the family as we know it–already embattled in a fight against disintegration–and the distortion of sexual values and behavior of the impressionable young.

The liberal says that the acceptance of the validity of a homosexual lifestyle gives to society a kind of institutional tolerance of those who are sexually different, and a more just treatment of those who are homosexual or lesbian.

As Christian people, we turn to the Bible for guidance and counsel. The Bible, generally simple and relatively easy to understand in many places, is nonetheless a complex and complicated book. No book is used, abused and misused more than the Bible. Its pages, like marriage, are not to be entered into unadvisedly or lightly, but reverently, discreetly, soberly and in the love of God.

We are all familiar with Anita Bryant and her campaign against homosexuality. The Bible is the arsenal from which she draws her ammunition for battle. Anita Bryant is an attractive, sincere and earnest person. She says, "I do not hate homosexuals. I love them. But I do hate homosexuality."[10]

I do not fault her zeal; I would that all were so zealous in propagating what they believe. I do not impugn her motives, but I quarrel with her interpretation of the scriptures. She lifts Bible verses out of context and leaps to unwarranted conclusions. For instance, she makes much of Leviticus 20:13 which reads, "If a man lies with a male as with a woman, both of them have committed an abomination; they shall be put to death, their blood is upon them." But what would she do about the law as stated in Leviticus 22:4-5? It states that we cannot touch the dead, and if we do, we are made unclean until the evening, and only after a bath and sunrise can we eat again. Those who resort to the proof text method of Bible usage become like a cat in a skein of yarn, so entangled that they cannot work their way out.

I think, without question, Anita Bryant has done us a grave disservice. She has inflamed national prejudices, fostered fear and hatred, and distorted the scriptures to her own ends. Her assertions of the dangers homosexuality present to society are patent nonsense. Her comment that the California drought was proof of God's displeasure with San Francisco's gay community is preposterous to the nth degree. Colin Morris has rightly pointed out that the Bible has declined in authority because of our insistence upon treating it like a one volume encyclopedia of universal salvation. Name your problem, and the Bible pundits will fire off a string of texts that they claim offer an infallible solution to it.

The Bible is not a time capsule buried two thousand years ago and preprogrammed by God to bellow forth at the touch of a button, instant answers to any question that history may throw up. I suspect the world is getting fed up with well meaning Christians scurrying around applying proof texts like sticking plaster to society's running sores.

A further question occurs: Should a sexual ethic be based solely on Biblical teachings for a Christian? I believe not. God's revelation to humankind did not cease when the Bible went to press. Should we close our eyes and minds to the insights of sociology, philosophy, psychology, psychiatry or psychoanalysis? We do so to the detriment of our own growth and understanding. The Bible writers were limited by the knowledge of their day. Many assumptions about human sexuality written in the Bible are obsolete or disproven by subsequent research.

I think it is important to remember that we do not worship the Bible. We worship the God the Bible reveals. We worship the God who makes a self-disclosure in the events enshrined in the Bible. The gift is not to be confused with wrappings that enclose it. The high office of Biblical scholarship is to disentangle those elements that are universal, abiding and essential. To read the Bible intelligently is to come to an awareness of those enduring realities that hang resplendent and clear in the skies after the fogs of an earlier morning have burned away. In the fullness of time, God sent his son, the Christ, and it is specifically in Him that we judge the validity of our faith. Nothing is binding on us that does not square with the life and spirit of Jesus. His insights into the nature of God, humankind, life and death are as valid today as they were then.

Jesus said nothing at all about homosexuality. It remains for us to make a subjective judgment as to what his conclusions in the matter would be. I cannot be sure, but it is crystal clear to all that the fundamental attitude that characterized the life of Jesus was charity, love and acceptance. The Christian faith is ultimately not a word of judgment, but of grace. His teachings confirm that no human thought, act or condition–homosexual or heterosexual–can take us beyond God's love and care.

As for me, I affirm a heterosexual lifestyle. I recommend it enthusiastically. I rejoice in my wonderful wife and fine sons. It is for me the most satisfying and fulfilling of all human relationships imaginable. But would it not be arrogant for me to insist that it be the lifestyle for all? For someone else, life's commitments and relationships may take another form. Do I, in my own frailty and sin, have justification in pointing the accusing finger at another?

No, it is not our calling as followers of the Christ to cast the stone of judgment, but to offer the helping, healing hand of love and reconciliation. It is not ours to assign blame, but to accept responsibility for ourselves and to act with charity toward others. It is not ours to proceed self-righteously and vindictively, but to walk humbly, penitently and searchingly toward the truth that will surely set us free. To this end we dedicate ourselves this day.

May God deliver us from the cowardice that shrinks from new truth, from the laziness that is content with half-truths, and from the arrogance that thinks it knows all truth.

Making Goodness Attractive

⚬❦⚬

The greatest foe of Christianity is not atheism, agnosticism or even Communism, as is commonly supposed. It is men and women who, having entered the Christian Life, have never had Christianity enter them enough to help them to be the joyful, radiant and attractive persons they were intended to be.

Nothing impedes the expansion of Christianity like a dull, negative, lifeless representative of the cause. At the same time, nothing is more attractive and inviting than a radiant, zestful Christian–someone who makes religion fun. Too long we have been schooled to think of religion as a duty to be performed rather than an adventure to be enjoyed. We have been carrying our religion, though it ought to be carrying us.

There are thousands who have the picture of goodness as something that exists best in cloisters and has to do with black clothing, long-faced sobriety and insipid quietness. No wonder there are so many fun-loving, red-blooded persons for whom Christianity has no appeal. They have been given a misconception, a counterfeit.

Those of us in the ministry have often been guilty of promoting this misconception. The stained glass window voice, the pontifical air, the avoidance of humor and the somber aspect all help create the image of Christianity as a joyless religion. How unfortunate when someone returns to his home and writes in a letter to a friend, as did one great American, "Have been to church and am not depressed."[1] What a sad commentary that this was unusual enough to deserve recording.

Poets and painters are also partly to blame for this false emphasis. We read Goethe, the German writer, who says, "Christianity is the religion of sorrow."[2] The poet Swinburne, missing the mark as usual, wrote:

> *Thou hast conquered pale Galilean.*
> *The world has grown gray with thy breath.*[3]

Look at Christian art. How many, if any, pictures have you seen of Jesus smiling? Too often he is depicted on canvas as a somber, grave and joyless person. The artists are not so much revealing Christ as themselves.

But, some might object that Jesus was a man of sorrows and acquainted with grief. He said, "Now is my soul troubled and what shall I say?"[4] and "My soul is exceeding sorrowful even unto death."[5] He spoke further of the necessity of self-denial. True, but to conclude from this that Christianity is a religion of sorrow is to make a judgment before all of the evidence is in. Such conclusions are not likely when the New Testament is seen in its entirety.

The word gospel means "good news." Angels who proclaimed good tidings of great joy heralded the birth of Jesus. His first public appearance was at a wedding where he made the guests happy. His last public appearance, according to the gospel of John, was around a campfire. No words were more frequently on his lips than:

> *Be of good cheer.*[6]
> *Let not your heart be troubled.*[7]
> *Be not anxious.*[8]
> *Be not afraid.*[9]
> *Rejoice and again I say rejoice.*[10]

It is not likely that he would have attracted and appealed to children as he did if he had been a dour, gloomy, morose person. They flocked around him to share his smile and hear his stories. He criticized the Pharisees because their interpretation of religion had become savorless, dull, mechanical and routine. They were intended to be the salt of the earth. Salt was put into lamps to give them sparkle; it was used to flavor food. The Jews were to give flavor, and bring luster and light to life. The insipid, stale life would have no appeal.

Jesus did not sadden; he gladdened life about him. The common people heard him gladly. He spoke of imprisoned possibilities encouraged the good, awakened the sleeping beauty; and gave hope and cheer. His was a liberating life. There was plenty of thunder and lightning in his preaching or speaking, but there was lots more sunshine in it. It was not a pinched, cramped, inhibiting message that he preached. "I came to bring life and life abundant."[11] There is no conflict between Jesus, Man of Sorrows, and Jesus, the Man of Joy. Joy and sorrow are not alien and antagonistic. They both spring from the same capacity for deep response, feeling and sensitivity.

No one with all of his faculties would be continuously cheerful. It has been well said that a pessimist is someone who has to live with an optimist. And yet, we believe that the general tenor of our lives ought to be happiness and not sorrow.

> *This is my Father's world;*
> *why should my heart be sad?*
> *The Lord is king; let the heavens ring.*
> *God reigns, let the earth be glad.*[12]

"But," someone may say, "it's all very well to be cheerful and pleasant, but when you are surrounded by insurmountable problems, that isn't so easy to do." That is true. Sometimes, I wonder how some people stand up at all under so much adversity. Yet, it was after the Apostle Paul was flogged, stoned, shipwrecked, beaten and jailed that he wrote, "Rejoice in the Lord always, and again I say rejoice."[13] It was near the end of a life of continuous physical suffering and pain that Robert Louis Stevenson wrote:

> *If I have faltered more or less*
> *In my great task of happiness;*
> *If I have moved among my race*
> *And showed no glorious morning face;*
> *If beams from happy human eyes*
> *Have moved me not; if morning skies,*
> *Books, and my food, and summer rain*
> *Knocked on my sullen heart in vain;*
> *Lord, thy most pointed pleasure take*
> *And stab my spirit broad awake.*[14]

Pale, haggard and bedridden though he was, his religion demanded of him an inextinguishable kindliness.

We cannot drive people into goodness. They must be lured by its attractiveness. Too often, in the name of Christ, we admonish, advise, exhort, lecture and preach. But, it is not mainly by these methods that the job gets done. It is not by compulsion and coercion that we accomplish our aim. The little girl had the right idea when she prayed, "Oh God, make all the bad people good and all the good people interesting."

If we were as wise as Satan, we would see this. "Satan," said the Apostle Paul, "fashions himself as an angel of light."[15] He makes evil appealing. Dr. Fosdick wrote:

> *Satan dresses war in pomp and uniform and sets it moving to martial music, calls it by high names of patriotism and loyal sacrifice. He dresses drunkenness in gaiety and makes it seductive with good fellowship, the clink of glasses, the lilt of song. He dresses licentiousness in the appearance of liberty, adventure, and gay self-expression. He doesn't mainly force men into evil, coerce or legislate into it. He attracts them into evil.[16]*

How beautifully he packages his wares! What beautiful ribbons! How many have succumbed to his wiles only to find they have only an empty box. What seemed to promise joy brings only sorrow. He makes evil attractive and lures men by his wiles. Dr. Keate, headmaster and terror of the boys at Eton, missed the point by far in his famous lecture given to those boys. "It is your duty to be pure in heart. If you are not pure in heart, I will flog you."[17]

Juliette Low, leader of the Girl Scout movement, was on the right track when she said to those who were to lead the Girl Scout troops:

Give the girls fun and give them instruction. If you can't give them both, give them fun, and they'll come back for instruction![18]

There is no fun in medicine, but there is medicine in fun. "A merry heart doeth good like medicine."[19]

Radiance of spirit is not a cosmetic applied to the surface of life, nor is it a whistling in the dark or an unrealistic view of life or failure to recognize things as they actually are. Happiness and joy have deep roots. They come when we meet the necessary conditions.

Jesus revealed what some of those conditions are in the Sermon on the Mount. "Blessed, or happy," said Jesus, "are the poor in spirit."[20] He refers to the humble, the teachable. Life for those who are humble is a continuously exciting adventure. The humble are learners. They don't take self too seriously. They know we are all ignorant, only in different ways. They are not easily offended because they do not believe themselves to be models of perfection.

"Blessed are they that mourn,"[21] those who are sensitive to the sins of self and society. Their lament is the first step toward improvement. The man who thinks he has already arrived tries to go nowhere. He is perfectly satisfied with things as they are.

"Blessed or happy are the meek."[22] Meekness is not weakness or cowardice, nor spineless passivity. It is power under control–a life submitted, committed, surrendered to

God's way. It is a life that is willing to believe and bet its life that in all things God does work for good with those who love Him. Stevenson said, "I believe in the ultimate decency of things. Yea, though I should wake in hell I should still believe it."[23] His happiness and joy was based on his belief in the love and goodness of God.

"Happy are those who hunger and thirst after righteousness."[24] These are the people for whom goodness is more than a mild craving, a passing fancy. Serenity and peace belong ultimately to those who persevere to the end in an effort to achieve the good life. "Let's not be weary in well doing for in due season we shall reap if we faint not."[25]

"Blessed are the merciful."[26] "To err is human, to forgive divine."[27] The one who does forgive, removes enmity and ill will from his own life, and knows a peace and calm otherwise impossible. He cleans the channel for reconciliation with the one who has offended.

"Blessed are the pure in heart."[28] He refers to those who live with singleness of purpose–to do God's will. They are people committed totally, wholeheartedly and completely to God, serving Him without reservation.

These are but a few of the conditions underlying the radiant life. The peace that passes understanding, of which the Bible speaks, is achieved by recognition of and conformity to these conditions. There is a correlation between holiness and happiness. We cannot do wrong and feel right.

The joy and serenity that we can come to know does not reveal itself as a raucous, backslapping, glad-handing, artificial goodwill, but as a pleasantness that makes us fit to live with. It is expressed in a sympathetic and understanding attitude toward others. The prayer of our lives could well be:

> *God, give me sympathy and sense,*
> *And help me keep my courage high;*
> *God, give me calm and confidence.*
> *And—please—a twinkle in my eye.*
> *Amen.*[29]

Notes

Rev. Dr. Dale Turner created these sermons for delivery at the University Congregational Church in Seattle, WA. Original printed sources for borrowed material have been cited wherever possible.

Life's Imperfect Alternatives

1. James, *The Will to Believe and Other Essays in Popular Philosophy,* 31.

2. Scudder, ed., "The Present Crisis," *The Complete Poetical Works of James Russell Lowell,* 68.

3. Original printed source unknown. For information on Lady Nancy Astor (1879-1964), see *Nancy Astor: A Biography* by Anthony Masters (New York: McGraw-Hill, 1981).

4. Original printed source unknown. For further development of Henry Drummond's decision-making philosophy, see his book of sermons, *The Ideal Life* (Cincinnati: Jennings and Graham, 1897).

5. Harrison and Gilbert, eds., *The Speeches of Abraham Lincoln,* 86.

6. Original printed source unknown. For further development of Henry Drummond's decision-making philosophy, see his book of sermons, *The Ideal Life* (Cincinnati: Jennings and Graham, 1897).

7. Ibid.

8. Ibid.

9. Ibid.

10. Wiggin and Smith, eds., "Opportunity," *Golden Numbers: A Book of Verse for Youth*, 608.

11. Original printed source unknown. For further development of Henry Drummond's decision-making philosophy, see his book of sermons, *The Ideal Life* (Cincinnati: Jennings and Graham, 1897).

Where Life's Victories Are Won

1. Matt. 6:20.

2. Mark 1:35.

3. Matt. 6:6.

The Purpose of Life

1. Hein, "I'd Like," *Grooks*, 49.

2. Original printed source unknown. For more information on Isaac Watts (1674-1748), see *Isaac Watts: His Life and Writings, His Homes and Friends* by Edwin Paxton Hood (London: The Religious Tract Society, 1875).

3. Morrison, "Rugby Chapel," *Masterpieces of Religious Verse*, 299.

4. Anonymous.

5. Original printed source unknown. For more information on John Wanamaker (1838-1922), see *The Business Biography of John Wanamaker* by Joseph H. Appel (New York: AMS Press, 1970).

6. Phil. 3:13.

7. Morrison, "My Name Is Legion," *Masterpieces of Religious Verse,* 274.

8. Masefield, "The Everlasting Mercy," *Poems,* 114.

9. Original printed source unknown. See this and other quotations by Oscar Wilde (1854-1900), English playwright and poet, at www.llywelyn.net.

10 Original printed source unknown. For more information on William James (1842-1910), see *Genuine Reality* by Linda Simon (New York: Harcourt Brace, 1998).

11. Guest, "Myself," *Collected Verse of Edgar Guest,* 724.

12. 1 Thess. 5:17.

13. Anonymous.

14. Original printed source unknown. For more information on Adlai Stevenson (1900-1965), see *Adlai Stevenson of Illinois* by John Bartlow Martin (Garden City, NY: Doubleday, 1976).

15. Original printed source unknown. For more information on Charles Mayo (1898-1968), see *Mayo: The Story of My Family and My Career* by Charles Mayo (Garden City, NY: Doubleday, 1968).

16. Original printed source unknown. See *The Words of Gandhi* edited by Richard Attenborough (New York: Newmarket Press, 1982).

17. Original printed source unknown. For more information about G. K. Chesterton (1874-1936), see *Chesterton: Man and Mask* by Garry Wills (New York: Sheed and Ward, 1961).

18. Morrison, " A Bag of Tools," *Masterpieces of Religious Verse,* 306.

The Difference One Life Can Make

1. Kessinger, Saxon White, "Indispensable Man," published by The Nutmegger Club in 1959. Reprinted with the author's permission.

2. Morrison, "Break, Break, Break," *Masterpieces of Religious Verse,* 285.

3. Miller, *Why We Act That Way,* 58.

4. A modified form of a Latin proverb.

5. Paxton, *Short Quotations of D. L. Moody,* 62.

6. Matt. 25:21.

7. Original printed source unknown.

8. Van Doren, *Nathaniel Hawthorne,* 140.

9. Pollock, *Wilberforce,* 27.

10. Emerson, *Essays,* 62.

11. Attributed to Alfred E. Smith (1873-1944). Original printed source unknown. For more information about Alfred E. Smith, see *Alfred E. Smith: The Happy Warrior* by Christopher M. Finan (New York: Hill and Wang, 2002).

12. Howell, *The Steel Industry in War Production,* 112.

13. Morrison, "Lend a Hand," *Masterpieces of Religious Verse,* 416.

Developing an Intelligent Faith

1. Original printed source unknown. For more information about H. L. Mencken (1880-1956), see *Disturber of the Peace: The Life of H. L. Mencken* by William Raymond Manchester (Amherst: University of Massachusetts Press, 1986).

2. Original printed source unknown. For more information about Harold Macmillan (1894-1986), see *Macmillan: A Study in Ambiguity* by Anthony Sampson (New York: Simon and Schuster, 1967).

3. Goethe, *Maxims and Reflections,* iii.

4. Job 38:2.

5. Matt. 5: 21a, 22a.

6. 2 Tim. 2:15.

7. Original printed source unknown. For more information about Bob Harrington, also known as the Chaplain of Bourbon Street, see www.thechaplain.com.

8. Thurber, *James Thurber: Writings and Drawings,* 190.

9. Original printed source unknown. For more information about Sir William Osler (1849-1919), see *The Life of Sir William Osler* by H. Cushing (Oxford: Clarendon Press, 1926).

10. Attributed to Frank Leahy (1908-1973), a Notre Dame University football coach. Original printed source unknown.

11. Original printed source unknown. For more information about Harry Truman (1892-1972), see *The Autobiography of Harry S. Truman* by Harry S. Truman (Boulder: Colorado Associated University Press, 1980).

12. Original printed source unknown. For more information about Bailey Smith and references to this quote, see www.answers.com.

13. Original printed source unknown. For more information about Will Durant (1885-1981), see *A Dual Autobiography* by Will and Ariel Durant (New York: Simon and Schuster, 1977).

Handling Our Handicaps

1. Phil. 4:11.

2. Original printed source unknown. For more information about Le Baron Russell Briggs (1855-1934), see *Dean Briggs* by Rollo Walter Brown (New York: Harper and Bros., 1926).

3. Fosdick, *On Being a Real Person,* 140.

4. Original printed source unknown. For more information about Charles W. Eliot (1834-1926), see *Between Harvard and America: The Educational Leadership of Charles W. Eliot* by Hugh Hawkins (New York: Oxford University Press, 1972).

5. Luke 15:8-10.

6. Original printed source unknown. For a listing of Harry Emerson Fosdick's works, see *Harry Emerson Fosdick: Persuasive Preacher* by Halford R. Ryan (New York: Greenwood Press, 1989), 155-73.

7. Matt. 26:39.

Dare to Stand Alone

1. Hamilton, *Mythology,* 150.

2. Original printed source unknown. For a complete compilation of Ralph Waldo Emerson's works, see *The Complete Writings of Ralph Waldo Emerson* (New York: Wm. H. Wise, 1929).

3. Eph. 4:14.

4. Rom. 12:2.

5. Original printed source unknown.

6. Riesman, Glazer and Denney, *The Lonely Crowd,* 21.

7. Chesterfield, *The Letters of Philip Dormer Stanhope, Earl of Chesterfield.*

8. Robinson, *Kansas: Its Interior and Exterior Life,* 60.

9. Emerson, *Essays,* 48.

10. Ibid., 51.

11. Ibid., 55.

12. Dan. 3.

13. Dan. 6.

14. Matt. 21:12-13; Mark 11:15-19; Luke 19:45-58.

15. Morrison, "Be Strong!" *Masterpieces of Religious Verse,* 308.

16. Sankey, "Dare to Be a Daniel," *My Life and the Story of the Gospel Hymns,* 134.

17. Prayer attributed to St. Ignatius (1491-1556). Original printed source unknown. For more information about St. Ignatius, see *Soldier of the Church: The Life of Ignatius Loyola* by Ludwig Marcuse and Christopher Lazare (New York: Simon and Schuster, 1939).

The Power of Doubt

1. Guest, "Had Youth Been Willing to Listen," *Collected Verse of Edgar A. Guest,* 677.

2. Original printed source unknown. For more information about George McDuffie (1790-1851), see *George McDuffie* by Edwin L. Green (Columbia, SC: The State Co., 1936).

3. Original printed source unknown.

4. Original printed source unknown.

5. Morrison, "In Memorium," *Masterpieces of Religious Verse,* 387.

6. Tillich, *Dynamics of Faith,* 22.

7. Bainton, *Here I Stand: A Life of Martin Luther,* 361.

8. Matt. 23:23.

9. Original printed source unknown. For a listing of Harry Emerson Fosdick's works, see *Harry Emerson Fosdick: Persuasive Preacher* by Halford R. Ryan (New York: Greenwood Press, 1989), 155-73.

10. May, *Paulus: Reminiscences of a Friendship,* 71.

11. Matt. 23:23.

12. Paine, *Mark Twain: A Biography,* Vols. III and IV, 1092.

13. Huxley, *Life and Letters of Thomas Henry Huxley*, Vol. 1, 235.

The Grace of Receiving

1. Original printed source unknown. For more information about George Bernard Shaw (1856-1950), see *Bernard Shaw: His Life, Work, and Friends* by St. John G. Ervine (New York: Morrow, 1956).

2. Mark 10:45.

3. Matt. 26:6-13; Mark 14:3-9; John 12:1-8.

3. John 14:6.

4. John 1:11.

5. Gal. 2:20.

6. Rev. 3:20.

7. Morrison, "O Little Town of Bethlehem!" *Masterpieces of Religious Verse,* 155.

You Are as Good as Your Words

1. Rasmussen, ed., *The Quotable Mark Twain: His Essential Aphorisms, Witticisms and Concise Opinions,* 61.

2. Mahoney, "Don Juan," *The English Romantics: Major Poetry and Critical Theory,* 396.

3. Gilbert, *Finest Hour 1939-1941,* Vol. VI of *Winston S. Churchill,* 468.

4. Morrison, "Just for Today," *Masterpieces of Religious Verse,* 70.

5. Luke 7:31.

6. Mark 12:37.

7. John 7:46.

8. St. Augustine, *On the Trinity,* Book VI, Chapter X, Section 12, www.newadvent.org/fathers (accessed May 10, 2005).

9. 1 Cor. 13:1.

10. Matt. 7:29.

11. Emerson, *The Complete Writings of Ralph Waldo Emerson,* 1039.

12. Hawthorne, *The Great Stone Face and Other Tales of the White Mountains,* 30.

13. Ibid.

14. Prov. 4:23.

15. Phil. 4:8.

When We Don't Get What We Want

1. Phil. 3:13.

2. Acts 16:7.

3. Phil. 4:11.

4. Wayne, *Wild Is Love.*

5. Baum, *Grand Hotel,* 45.

6. Original printed source unknown. For more information about Charles W. Eliot (1834-1926), see *Between Harvard and America: The Educational Leadership of Charles W. Eliot* by Hugh Hawkins (New York: Oxford University Press, 1972).

7. Original printed source unknown. For more information about Samuel Johnson (1709-1784), see *Life of Johnson* by James Boswell. Edited by R. W. Chapman. Corrected by J. D. Fleeman (Oxford: Oxford University Press, 1998).

8. Fosdick, *On Being a Real Person,* 55.

9. Original printed source unknown. For more information about Merton S. Rice (1872-1943), see *Preacher Mike: The Life of Merton S. Rice* by Elaine Rice Chabut (New York: The Citadel Press, 1958).

10. Hutchinson, ed., "Character of the Happy Warrior," *Wordsworth: Poetical Works,* 386.

11. Matt. 26:39.

12. Ibid.

13. Dukore, ed., *Not Bloody Likely! And Other Quotations from Bernard Shaw,* 28.

14. Original printed source unknown. For more information about Peter Milne (1834-1924), see *Peter Milne of Nguna, New Hebrides* by Alexander Don (Dunedin: Foreign Missions Committee, 1927).

15. Morrison, "Your Place," *Masterpieces of Religious Verse,* 360.

Giving Away the Sleeves of Your Vest

1. 2 Sam. 24:24.

2. Maxey, *Sermon Illustration,* 8.

3. Original printed source and author unknown.

Gift Suggestions

1. A modification of a Mother Goose rhyme.

2. Original printed source unknown. For more about Liston Pope (1909-1974), see www.library.yale.edu.

3. Gibran, "Giving," *The Prophet,* 19.

4. Emerson, *The Works of Ralph Waldo Emerson in One Volume,* 264.

5. Wylie, "The Art of Generosity," *Reader's Digest,* 101.

6. Original printed source unknown.

7. Ibid.

8. Fosdick, *The Living of These Days,* 36.

9. Original printed source unknown. For more information about St. Augustine (354-430), see *Augustine* by Christopher Kirwan (London: Routledge, 1991) or *A Select Library of the Nicene and Post-Nicene Fathers of the Christian Church Series,* Vol. 4, edited by Philip Schaff and Henry Wace (Grand Rapids: Eerdmans, 1971).

10. Original printed source unknown. For more information about Flip Wilson (1933-1998), see *Revolution Televised: Prime Time and the Struggle for Black Power* by Christine Acham (Minneapolis: University of Minnesota Press, 2004).

11. Original printed source unknown. For more information about Johann Wolfgang von Goethe (1749-1832), see *Goethe* by Irmgard Wagner (New York: Twayne Publishers, 1999).

12. Attributed to Matthew Prior (1664-1721). Original printed source unknown. For more information on Matthew Prior, see *The Life of Matthew Prior* by Francis Bickley (Norwood, PA: Norwood Editions, 1977).

13. Original printed source and author unknown.

14. Original printed source unknown. For more information about Billy Sunday (1862-1935), see *Billy Sunday Was His Real Name* by William Gerald McLoughlin (Chicago: University of Chicago Press, 1955).

15. Original printed source unknown. For more information about George Eliot (1834-1926), see *All-in-All: A Biography of George Eliot* by LouAnn Gaeddert (New York: Dutton, 1976).

16. Attributed to Otto von Isch. Original printed source unknown.

17. Original printed source and author unknown.

18. Morrison, "The Human Touch," *Masterpieces of Religious Verse,* 390.

Networking for Peace

1. Original printed source unknown. For more information about Omar Bradley (1893-1981), see "General Omar Bradley," produced by Lou Reda Productions, A&E Home Video, 1994.

2. Tse-Tung, *Selected Works of Mao Tse-Tung,* 225.

3. Original printed source unknown. For more information about Thomas Edison (1847-1931), see *Edison: A Biography* by Matthew Josephson (New York: J. Wiley, 1992).

4. Original printed source unknown. For more information about Thomas Paine (1737-1809), see *The Life of Thomas Paine* by Moncure Daniel Conway (New York: B. Blom, 1970).

5. Stevenson, *An Inland Voyage,* 36.

6. Attributed to Henri Bergson (1859-1941). Original printed source unknown. For more information, see *Henri Bergson* by Jacques Chevalier (New York: AMS Press, 1969).

7. Original printed source unknown. For more information about Thomas Paine (1737-1809), see *The Life of Thomas Paine* by Moncure Daniel Conway (New York: B. Blom, 1970).

8. Original printed source unknown. For more information about Ralph Bunche (1904-1971), winner of the 1950 Nobel Peace Prize, see http://nobelprize.org.

9. Eisenhower, ("TV Talk with Prime Minister Macmillan," August 31, 1959).

10. Camus, *Resistance, Rebellion and Death,* 272.

11. Pais, *Einstein Lived Here,* 175.

12. Overstreet, "Stubborn Ounces," *Hands Laid Upon the Wind,* 15.

13. Morrison, "Lend a Hand," *Masterpieces of Religious Verse,* 416.

What the World Needs Now

1. David, *What the World Needs Now Is Love and Other Love Lyrics,* 15.

2. Albert Schweitzer (1875-1965) quoted by photographer Yousuf Karsh, see "The Good, the Great and the Gifted" exhibition at www.nga.gov.an (accessed March 9, 2005).

3. Original printed source unknown. For more information on Pierre Teilhard de Chardin (1881-1955), see *Spirit of Fire: The Life and Vision of Teilhard de Chardin* by Ursula King (Maryknoll, NY: Orbis Books, 1996).

4. Original printed source unknown. For more information about Emmet Fox (1886-1951), see *Emmet Fox: The Man and His Work* by Harry Gaze (New York: Harper, 1952).

5. Huxley, *Collected Essays,* 399.

6. Attributed to E. Joseph Crossmann. Original printed source unknown.

7. Original printed source and author unknown.

8. Original printed source and author unknown.

9. Gibran, *Wisdom of Gibran: Aphorisms and Maxims,* L.

10. Original printed source and author unknown.

11. Original printed source and author unknown.

12. Fromm, *The Art of Loving,* 19-44.

13. Rom. 13:9.

14. Rooney, "Tribute to Harry Reasoner," *60 Minutes*, August 11, 1991, CBS R-#2336.

15. Attributed to Charles Douglas Jackson. Original printed source unknown.

16. Simpson, ed., *Simpson's Contemporary Quotations,* 4034.

17. Original printed source and author unknown.

18. Original printed source unknown. For more information about Dorothy Parker (1893-1967), see *Dorothy Parker: What Fresh Hell Is This?* by Marion Meade (New York: Penguin Books, 1989).

19. Original printed source unknown. For more information about Calvin Coolidge (1872-1933), see *The Autobiography of Calvin Coolidge* by Calvin Coolidge (Plymouth: Calvin Coolidge Foundation, 1989).

20. Original printed source unknown. For more information about Luther Burbank (1899-1926), see *A Gardener Touched with Genius* by Peter Dreyer (New York: Coward, McCann & Geoghegan, 1975).

21. George, ed., "Love," *The Family Book of Best Loved Poems,* 3.

22. Gibran, "Marriage," *The Prophet,* 15-16.

23. Original printed source unknown. For more information about Johann Wolfgang von Goethe (1749-1832), see *Goethe* by Irmgard Wagner (New York: Twayne Publishers, 1999).

24. Original printed source and author unknown.

25. Original source unknown. For more information on G. K. Chesterton (1874-1936), see *Chesterton: Man and Mask* by Garry Wills (New York: Sheed & Ward, 1961).

26. Cook, *The Book of Positive Quotations,* 81.

27. Attributed to Anselm of Canterbury (1033-1109). Original printed source unknown. For more information about St. Anselm, Archbishop of Canterbury, see *Anselm: The Joy of Faith* by William Henry Shannon (New York: Crossroad, 1999).

28. Gardner, "To Virgins, to Make Much of Time," *The New Oxford Book of English Verse,* 243.

29. David, *What the World Needs Now Is Love and Other Love Lyrics,* 15.

30. Kinney, "A Cold Within." The poem was written in the 1960's by James Patrick Kinney and first published in *The Liguorian,* a Catholic magazine. The poet's widow wishes to see the poem widely circulated.

31. Morrison, "A Bag of Tools," *Masterpieces of Religious Verse,* 306.

Creative Controversy

1. Original printed source unknown. For more information about G. K. Chesterton (1874-1936), see *Chesterton: Man and Mask* by Garry Wills (New York: Sheed and Ward, 1961).

2. Ibid.

3. Davis, ed., "Essay on Criticism," *Pope: Poetical Works,* 64.

4. John 8:32.

5. Neider, ed., *The Autobiography of Mark Twain,* 247.

6. Abbott, *Henry Ward Beecher,* 412.

7. Original printed source unknown. For more about Henry Ward Beecher (1813-1887), see *Henry Ward Beecher* by Lyman Abbott (New York: Chelsea House, 1980).

8. Morrison, "Mourn Not the Dead," *Masterpieces of Religious Verse,* 474.

Probing Our Prejudices

1. Original printed source unknown. For more about Ralph W. Sockman's (1889-1970) opinions on social issues, see *Date with Destiny* by Ralph W. Sockman (New York: Abingdon-Cokesbury Press, 1944).

2. John 1:43-47.

3. Spinoza, *A Spinoza Reader: The Ethics and Other Works,* 204.

4. Original printed source unknown. For more information about Winston Churchill (1871-1947), see *Churchill: A Life* by Martin Gilbert (New York: Holt, 1991).

5. Huxley, *Life and Letters of Thomas Henry Huxley,* Vol. 1, 235.

6. Original printed source unknown. For more about the life of Benjamin E. Mays (1894-1984), see *Born to Rebel* by Benjamin E. Mays (New York: Charles Scribner's Sons, 1971).

7. Ibid.

8. Original printed source unknown. For more information about James E. K. Aggrey (1875-1927), see *The Life of Dr. J. E. K. Aggrey* by L. H. Ofosu-Applah (Accra, Ghana: Waterville Publishing House, 1975).

9. Matt. 22:39.

10. Morrison, "Lend a Hand," *Masterpieces of Religious Verse,* 416.

Amnesty

1. Original printed source unknown. For more information about Robert H. Schuller (1926-), see *Goliath: The Life of Robert Schuller* by James Penner (New York: Harper Paperbacks, 1993).

2. Daniel J. Evans was governor of Washington from 1965 to 1977.

3. Attributed to Albert Einstein (1879-1955). Original printed source unknown. For more information about Albert Einstein, see *Einstein: A to Z* by Karen C. Fox (Hoboken, NJ: J. Wiley, 2004), or *Einstein: The Passions of a Scientist* by Barry R. Parker (Amherst, MA: Prometheus Books, 2003).

4. Original printed source unknown. For more information about John Milton (1608-1674), see *John Milton: A Sketch of His Life and Writings* by Douglas Bush (New York: Macmillan, 1964).

5. Pamphlet published by the World Without War Issues Center, Berkeley, CA. Reprinted by permission of the author, Robert Pickus.

6. Harris, (statement at the hearing before the Subcommittee on Administrative Practice and Procedure of the Committee on the Judiciary, United States Senate, 92nd Congress, 2nd session, February 20, 1972).

7. Original printed source unknown.

Loneliness

1. Billy Graham, "Morality in the United States" (address to the Commonwealth Club of California, San Francisco, CA, Sept. 8, 1972), www.commonwealthclub.org/archive/20thcentury/72-09graham-speech.html (accessed Jan. 21, 2005).

2. Original printed source unknown. For other quotes by Faith Baldwin (1893-1978), see *Women in American History* by Encyclopaedia Britannica at http://search.db.com/women (accessed May 17, 2005).

3. Ps. 23:2.

4. Original printed source unknown. For more information about Johann Wolfgang von Goethe (1749-1832), see *Goethe* by Irmgard Wagner (New York: Twayne Publishers, 1999).

5. Hammarskjold, *Markings,* 85.

6. Original printed source unknown. For more information about Reinhold Niebuhr's (1892-1971) philosophy of love, see *Love and Justice: Selections from the Shorter Writings of Reinhold Niebuhr* (Louisville: Westminster John Knox Press, 1992).

7. Matthiessen, "Each and All," *The Oxford Book of American Verse,* 70.

8. "Loneliness Can Kill You," *Time,* 5 Sept. 1977, 45.

9. Hassall, *Rupert Brooke,* 395.

10. Morrison, "The Human Touch," *Masterpieces of Religious Verse,* 390.

11. Eliot, ed., *The Confessions of St. Augustine,* 1.

12. Josh. 1:9.

13. Isa. 43:2.

14. Ps. 46:1-2.

15. Original printed source unknown.

16. Deut. 33:27.

17. Ps. 23:4.

18. John 15:15.

19. Heb. 13:5.

20. Matt. 28:20.

Conquering Fear

1. King, *Strength to Love,* 202.

2. Parrott, Hubler and Telfer, eds., *Shakespeare: Twenty-Three Plays and the Sonnets,* 1.3.43. References are to act, scene and line.

3. Original printed source unknown.

4. Fosdick, *On Being a Real Person,* 110.

5. Original printed source unknown. For a listing of Harry Emerson Fosdick's works, see *Harry Emerson Fosdick: Persuasive Preacher* by Halford R. Ryan (Greenwood Press, 1989), 155-73.

6. John 12:24.

7. Schneider, ed., "The Rime of the Ancient Mariner," *Samuel Taylor Coleridge: Selected Poetry and Prose,* 63.

8. Heslop, *Five Hundred and One Sermon Illustrations,* 8.

9. Bunyan, *The Pilgrim's Progress,* 48.

10. Original printed source unknown. For more information about Mark Twain (1835-1910), see *Mark Twain: A Biography* by Albert Bigelow Paine (New York: Harper & Bros., 1912).

11. Attributed to Peter Marshall (1902-1949). Original printed source unknown. For more information about Peter Marshall, see *A Man Called Peter: The Story of Peter Marshall* by Catherine Marshall (New York: Avon Books, 1994).

12. Original printed source unknown.

13. "Her Name Is Julia," web.ukonline.co.uk/m.gratten/Names/Julia.htm (accessed April 2005).

14. Stange, "Rabbi Ben Ezra," *The Poetical Works of Robert Browning,* 383.

15. Parrott, Hubler and Telfer, eds., *Shakespeare: Twenty-Three Plays and the Sonnets,* 3.1.78-82. References are to act, scene and line.

16. Kern and Hammerstein, *Show Boat: Vocal Selections,* 31.

17. Anonymous.

18. Stevenson, *Vailima Letters,* 183.

19. 2 Tim. 1:7.

20. Morrison, "Overheard in an Orchard," *Masterpieces of Religious Verse,* 86.

21. Ibid., "The Gate of the Year," 92.

Dealing with Irritability and Depression

1. Original printed source and author unknown.

2. Original printed source unknown. For more information on Peanuts cartoons, see United Feature Syndicate, Inc. at www.unitedmedia.com/comics/peanuts.

3. Peterson, *Lincoln in American Memory,* 185.

4. Fisher and Hawley, *A Few Buttons Missing: The Case Book of a Psychiatrist.*

5. Schneider, ed., "The Rime of the Ancient Mariner," *Samuel Taylor Coleridge: Selected Poetry and Prose,* 69.

6. Parrott, Hubler and Telfer, eds., "Sonnet XXIX," *Shakespeare: Twenty-Three Plays and the Sonnets,* 1094.

7. Bunyan, *The Pilgrim's Progress,* 48.

8. Attributed to Eleanor Roosevelt. (Modified by Dr. Turner.) Original printed source unknown. For more information about Eleanor Roosevelt (1884-1962), see *The Autobiography of Eleanor Roosevelt* (New York: Da Capo Press, 1992).

9. Nesbit, *The Value of a Smile,* (no page numbers used).

Grief

1. Neider, ed., *The Autobiography of Mark Twain,* 192.

2. Thompson, *Essays* in Vol. III of *Francis Thompson: Poems and Essays,* 10.

3. Attributed to Mencius (371 B.C.-289 B.C.), a Confucian sage. Original printed source unknown. For more information, see *Mencius,* translated by D. C. Lau (Hong Kong: The Chinese University Press, 2003).

4. Bayly, *The View from a Hearse,* 42.

5. Minquass proverb.

6. Eccles. 3:4.

7. Original printed source unknown. For more information and quotes by Charles Reynolds Brown (1862-1950), see www.answers.com.

8. Westberg, *Good Grief: A Constructive Approach to the Problem of Loss,* 48-49.

9. Wilder, *The Angel That Troubled the Water,* 149.

10. Morrison, "Pleasure and Sorrow," *Masterpieces of Religious Verse,* 436.

11. Ibid., "The Inevitable," 292.

12. Rom. 8:31, 35, 37.

Suicide

1. Day, *The Long Loneliness: The Autobiography of Dorothy Day,* 253.

2. Original printed source unknown. For more quotations, see *Josh Billings, His Sayings* by Josh Billings (New York: AMS Press, 1972).

3. Eliot, *Collected Poems,* 53.

4. Fosdick, *The Living of These Days: An Autobiography,* 73.

5. Exod. 20:13.

6. Aquinas, *Summa Theologica,* Vol. 1, "The Sin of Suicide," Reply Objection 3, at www.csulb.edu, (accessed May 4, 2005).

7. Original printed source unknown. For more information about John Wesley (1703-1991), see *John Wesley* by Stanley Ayling (Cleveland: William Collins Publishers, 1979).

8. Original printed source unknown.

9. Friedman, *Encounter on the Narrow Ridge: A Life of Martin Buber,* 80. (A corrected version of the incident mentioned here. Incorrect versions are widely circulated.)

10. Morrison, "God's Pity," *Masterpieces of Religious Verse,* 86.

11. Thoreau, *Walden,* 8.

12. Johnson, ed., "VI," *The Complete Poems of Emily Dickinson,* 433.

Finding Our Way Through a Sexual Wilderness

1. Original printed source unknown. For more information about Albert Einstein (1879-1955), see *Einstein: A to Z* by Karen C. Fox, (Hoboken, NJ: J. Wiley, 2004) or *Einstein: The Passions of a Scientist* by Barry R. Parker (Amherst: Prometheus Books, 2003).

2. Scudder, ed., "The Present Crisis," *The Complete Poetical Works of James Russell Lowell,* 68.

3. Chinese proverb.

4. Matt. 5:28.

5. Lewis, *Mere Christianity,* 96.

6. Spinoza, *A Spinoza Reader: The Ethics and Other Works,* 265.

7. Luke 18:13.

8. Original printed source unknown. For more about the life of Henry Ward Beecher (1813-1887), see *Henry Ward Beecher* by Lyman Abbott (New York: Chelsea House, 1980).

9. Eliot, ed., *The Confessions of St. Augustine,* 129.

10. Ibid., 136.

11. 2 Cor. 6:2.

Genetic Experimentation

1. Original printed source unknown. For more information about Arthur Compton (1892-1962), winner of the 1927 Nobel Prize in Physics, visit http://nobelprize.org.

2. Einstein, *The World As I See It,* 24-28.

3. Excerpt from Martin Van Buren's letter to Andrew Jackson on January 31, 1829. See *The Jackson and Van Buren Papers* by William MacDonald (Worcester: American Antiquarian Society, 1907).

4. Rom. 8:28.

5. Excerpt from Thomas Jefferson's letter to Thomas Seymour in 1807. See *The Jeffersonian Cyclopedia,* Vol. 43, edited by John P. Foley (New York: Funk and Wagnalls, 1990).

6. Guest, "Had Youth Been Willing to Listen," *Collected Verse of Edgar A. Guest,* 677.

7. Original printed source unknown. For more information about Thomas Edison (1847-1931), see *Edison: A Biography* by Matthew Josephson (New York: J. Wiley, 1992).

Obscenity

1. Bainton, ed., *The Art of Authorship,* 87-88.

2. Morris, *Include Me Out! Confessions of an Ecclesiastical Coward,* 43.

3. Ibid.

4. Ibid., 43-44.

5. "Sex as a Spectator Sport," *Time,* 11 July 1969, 61.

6. Morton, ed., *Hilaire Belloc's Stories, Essays and Poems,* 413.

7. Original printed source unknown. For more information about James Cagney (1899-1986), see *Cagney* by John McCabe (New York: Carroll & Graf, 1999).

8. Original printed source unknown. For more information about Malcolm Boyd (1923-), see *As I Live and Breathe: Stages of an Autobiography* (New York: Random House, 1970).

9. Matt. 23:27.

10. Luke 10:30-32.

11. Luke 18:11.

12. John 2:13-16.

13. John 8:3-11.

14. Matt. 23:14.

15. Matt. 23:23.

16. Morris, *North Toward Home,* 423.

17. Matt. 25:42-45.

18. Luke 18:13.

19. Rev. 22:17.

Drinking

1. Prov. 20:1.

2. 1 Tim. 5:23.

3. Original printed source unknown. For more information about Thomas Edison (1847-1931), see *Edison: A Biography* by Matthew Josephson (New York: J. Wiley, 1992).

4. Parrott, Hubler and Telfer, eds., *Shakespeare: Twenty-Three Plays and the Sonnets,* 2.3.291-293. References are to act, scene and line.

5. Original printed source unknown. For more information about Ogden Nash (1902-1972), see *The Life and Rhymes of Ogden Nash* by David Stuart (Lanham, MD: Madison Books, 2000) and *The Pocket Book of Ogden Nash* (New York: Pocket Books, 1962).

6. Original printed source unknown. For more information about Will Rogers (1879-1935), see *Never Met a Man I Didn't Like: The Life and Writings of Will Rogers* by Joseph H. Carter (New York: Avon, 1991).

The Christian Faith and Homosexuality

1. Original printed source unknown. For more information about Robert H. Schuller (1926-), see *Goliath: The Life of Robert Schuller* by James Penner (New York: Harper Paperbacks, 1993).

2. Original printed source unknown. For more information about G. K. Chesterton (1874-1936), see *Chesterton: Man and Mask* by Garry Wills (New York: Sheed and Ward, 1961).

3. See "Kinsey and the Homosexual Revolution" at www.leaderu.com and "Prevalence of Homosexuality: Brief Summary of U.S. Studies" at www.indiana.edu.

4. The twenty million-person estimate apparently originated from a brochure that was produced and widely distributed by One, Inc./HIC in 1966, Don Slater, editor. HIC has since retracted that statement. More information is available from the Tangent Group, www.tangentgroup.org/history/newsletters/newsletter33.html.

5. Parrott, Hubler and Telfer, eds., *Shakespeare: Twenty-Three Plays and the Sonnets,* 4.5.175-186. References are to act, scene and line.

6. Original printed source unknown. For quotations by Josh Billings, see *Josh Billings: Hiz Sayings* by Josh Billings (New York: Carleton, 1866).

7. Neider, ed., *The Autobiography of Mark Twain*, 247.

8. Rom. 12:2.

9. Paine, *Mark Twain: A Biography*, Vols. III and IV, 1092.

10. Original printed source unknown. For more information about Anita Bryant, see *A New Day* by Anita Bryant (Nashville: Broadman Press, 1992).

Making Goodness Attractive

1. Stevenson, "Letter to Mrs. Sitwell, June 1875," Vol. 1 of *The Letters of Robert Louis Stevenson*.

2. Original printed source unknown. For more information about Johann Wolfgang von Goethe (1749-1832), see *Goethe* by Irmgard Wagner (New York: Twayne Publishers, 1999).

3. Dobree, ed., "Hymn to Proserpine," *Swinburne: Poems,* 43.

4. John 12:27.

5. Matt. 26:38.

6. John 16:33.

7. John 14:1.

8. Matt. 6:25.

9. Josh. 1:9.

10. Phil. 4:4.

11. John 10:10.

12. *Hymns for the Family of God,* Selection 6.

13. Phil. 4:4.

14. Morrison, "The Celestial Surgeon," *Masterpieces of Religious Verse,* 359-60.

15. 2 Cor. 11:14.

16. Original printed source unknown. For a listing of Harry Emerson Fosdick's works, see *Harry Emerson Fosdick: Persuasive Preacher* by Halford R. Ryan (New York: Greenwood Press, 1989), 155-73.

17. Fosdick, *Living Under Tension: Sermons on Christianity Today,* 131.

18. Original printed source unknown. For more information on Juliette Low, see *Lady from Savannah: The Life of Juliette Low* by Gladys Denny Schultz and Daisy Gordon Lawrence (Philadelphia: Lippincott, 1958).

19. Prov. 17:22.

20. Matt. 5:3.

21. Matt. 5:4.

22. Matt. 5:5.

23. Stevenson, *Vailima Letters,* 183.

24. Matt. 5:6.

25. Gal. 6:9.

26. Matt. 5:7.

27. Davis, ed., "Essay on Criticism," *Pope: Poetical Works,* 79.

28. Matt. 5:8.

29. Bryant, comp., "A Prayer," *Sourcebook of Poetry,* 544.

References

Abbott, Lyman. 1980. *Henry Ward Beecher*. New York: Chelsea House.

Bainton, George, ed. 1890. *The Art of Authorship*. New York: Appleton.

Bainton, Roland H. 1950. *Here I Stand: A Life of Martin Luther*. Nashville: Abingdon Press.

Baum, Vicki. 1967. *Grand Hotel*. Translated by Basil Creighton. New York: Dell.

Bayly, John. 1972. *A View from the Hearse*. New York: New Family Library.

Bryant, Al, comp. 1968. *Sourcebook of Poetry*. Grand Rapids, MI: Zondervan.

Bunyan, John. 1933. *The Pilgrim's Progress*. Philadelphia: John C. Winston.

Camus, Albert. 1961. *Resistance, Rebellion, and Death*. Translated by Justin O'Brien. New York: Alfred A. Knopf.

Chesterfield, Philip Dormer Stanhope. 1892. *The Letters of Philip Dormer Stanhope, Earl of Chesterfield*. London: George Allen & Unwin.

David, Hal. 1970. *What the World Needs Now and Other Love Lyrics*. New York: Trident.

Davis, Herbert, ed. 1966. *Pope: Poetical Works*. London: Oxford University Press.

Day, Dorothy. 1980. *The Long Loneliness: The Autobiography of Dorothy Day*. New York: HarperSanFrancisco.

Dobree, Bonamy, ed. 1961. *Swinburne: Poems*. Baltimore: Penguin Books.

Drummond, Henry. 1897. *The Ideal Life*. Cincinnati: Jennings and Graham.

Dukore, Bernard F., ed. 1986. *Not Bloody Likely! And Other Quotations from Bernard Shaw*. New York: Columbia University Press.

Einstein, Albert. 1949. *The World As I See It*. New York: Philosophical Library.

Eisenhower, Dwight D. 1959. "TV Talk with Prime Minister Macmillan," August 31. Dwight D. Eisenhower Library, Abilene, KS.

Eliot, Charles W., ed. 1965. *The Confessions of St. Augustine*. Translated by Edward B. Pusey. New York: P. F. Collier and Son.

Emerson, Ralph Waldo. 1929. *The Complete Writings of Ralph Waldo Emerson*. New York: Wm. H. Wise.

Emerson, Ralph Waldo. 1883. *Essays*. Boston: Houghton Mifflin.

Fisher, James T., and Lowell S. Hawley. 1951. *A Few Buttons Missing: The Case Book of a Psychiatrist*. Philadelphia: J. B. Lippincott.

Fosdick, Harry Emerson. 1958. *The Living of These Days: An Autobiography*. New York: Harper and Row.

Fosdick, Harry Emerson. 1941. *Living Under Tension: Sermons on Christianity Today*. New York: Harper and Bros.

Fosdick, Harry Emerson. 1943. *On Being a Real Person*. New York: Harper and Row.

Friedman, Maurice. 1991. *Encounter on the Narrow Ridge: A Life of Martin Buber*. New York: Paragon House.

George, David L., ed. 1952. *The Family Book of Best Loved Poems*. Garden City, NY: Doubleday.

Gilbert, Martin. 1983. *Finest Hour 1939-1941*. Vol. VI of *Winston S. Churchill*. Boston: Houghton Mifflin.

Graham, Billy. 1972. "Morality in the United States." Address to the Commonwealth Club of California, San Francisco, CA, Sept. 8, www.commonwealthclub.org/archive/20thcentury/72-09graham-speech.html (accessed January 2005).

Guest, Edgar A. 1934. *Collected Verse of Edgar A. Guest*. Chicago: Contemporary Books.

Hamilton, Edith. 1942. *Mythology*. New York: The New American Library.

Hammarskjold, Dag. 1964. *Markings*. Translated by Leif Sjeborg and W. H. Auden. New York: Alfred A. Knopf.

Harris, David. 1972. Statement at the hearing before the Subcommittee on Administrative Practice and Procedure of the Committee on the Judiciary, United States Senate, 92nd Congress, 2nd session, February 20.

Harrison, Maureen, and Steve Gilbert, eds. 2005. *The Speeches of Abraham Lincoln*. Carlsbad, CA: Excellent Books.

Hassall, Christopher. 1964. *Rupert Brooke*. New York: Harcourt, Brace and World.

Hawthorne, Nathaniel. 1935. *The Great Stone Face and Other Tales of the White Mountains*. Boston: Houghton Mifflin.

Hein, Piet. 1966. *Grooks*. Garden City, NY: Doubleday.

"Her Name Is Julia," web.ukonline.co.uk/m.gratten/Names/Julia.htm (accessed April 12, 2005).

Heslop, W. G. 1955. *Five Hundred and One Sermon Illustrations.* 3rd ed. Butler, IN: Higley Press.

Howell, Max Don. 1955. *The Steel Industry in War Production.* Washington, DC: Industrial College of the Armed Forces.

Hutchinson, Thomas, ed. 1971. *Wordsworth: Poetical Works.* London: Oxford University Press.

Huxley, Leonard. 1900. *Life and Letters of Thomas Henry Huxley,* Vol. 1. London: Macmillan.

Hymns for the Family of God. 1976. Nashville: Paragon Association.

James, William. 1956. *The Will to Believe and Other Essays in Popular Philosophy.* New York: Dover.

Johnson, Thomas H., ed. 1960. *The Complete Poems of Emily Dickinson.* Boston: Little, Brown.

Kern, Jerome, and Oscar Hammerstein II. 1927. *Show Boat: Vocal Selections.* Milwaukee: Hal-Leonard Corp.

King, Martin Luther, Jr. 1963. *Strength to Love.* New York: Walker.

Lewis, C. S. 1960. *Mere Christianity.* New York: Macmillan.

"Loneliness Can Kill You." 1977. *Time* (September 5): 45.

Mahoney, John L. 1978. *The English Romantics: Major Poetry and Critical Theory.* Lexington: D. C. Heath.

Masefield, John. 1967. *Poems.* New York: Macmillan.

Matthiessen, F. O. 1950. *The Oxford Book of American Verse.* New York: Oxford University Press.

May, Rollo. 1973. *Paulus: Reminiscences of a Friendship.* New York: Harper and Row.

Miller, John Homer. 1946. *Why We Act That Way*. New York: Abingdon-Cokesbury Press.

Morris, Colin. 1968. *Include Me Out! Confessions of an Ecclesiastical Coward*. Nashville: Abingdon Press.

Morris, Willie. 1967. *North Toward Home*. Boston: Houghton Mifflin.

Morrison, James Dalton. 1948. *Masterpieces of Religious Verse*. New York: Harper and Row.

Morton, J. B., ed. 1963. *Hilaire Belloc's Stories, Essays and Poems*. London: Everyman's Library.

Neider, Charles, ed. 1959. *The Autobiography of Mark Twain*. New York: Harper and Row.

Overstreet, Bonaro W. 1955. *Hands Laid Upon the Wind*. New York: Norton.

Paine, Albert Bigelow. 1912. *Mark Twain: A Biography*, Vols. III and IV. New York: Harper and Bros.

Pais, Abraham. 1994. *Einstein Lived Here*. Oxford: Clarendon Press.

Parrott, Thomas Marc, Edward Hubler and Robert Stockdale Telfer, eds. 1966. *Shakespeare: Twenty-Three Plays and the Sonnets*. New York: Charles Scribner's Sons.

Paxton, Sam, comp. 1961. *Short Quotations of D. L. Moody*. Chicago: Moody Press.

Peterson, Merrill D. 1994. *Lincoln in American Memory*. New York: Oxford University Press.

Pollock, John. 1977. *Wilberforce*. New York: St. Martin's Press.

Rasmussen, R. Kent, ed. 1998. *The Quotable Mark Twain: His Essential Aphorisms, Witticisms and Concise Opinions*. Chicago: Contemporary Books.

Riesman, David, Nathan Glazer and Reuel Denney. 1961. *The Lonely Crowd*. New Haven, CT: Yale University Press.

Robinson, Sara T. L. 1856. *Kansas: Its Interior and Exterior Life*. Boston: Crosby Nichols.

Rooney, Andrew A. 1991. "Tribute to Harry Reasoner." *60 Minutes*, August 11. CBS R-#2336.

Sankey, Ira David. 1906. *My Life and the Story of the Gospel Hymns*. New York: Harper and Bros.

Schneider, Elisabeth, ed. 1964. *Samuel Taylor Coleridge: Selected Poetry and Prose*. New York: Holt, Rinehart and Winston.

Scudder, Horace E., ed. 1925. *The Complete Poetical Works of James Russell Lowell*. Boston: Houghton Mifflin.

"Sex as a Spectator Sport." 1969. *Time,* (July 11): 61.

Simpson, James Beasley, comp. 1988. *Simpson's Contemporary Quotations*. Boston: Houghton Mifflin.

Spinoza, Benedict de. 1994. *A Spinoza Reader: The Ethics and Other Works*. Edited and translated by Edwin Curley. Princeton: Princeton University Press.

Stange, G. Robert. 1974. *The Poetical Works of Robert Browning*. Boston: Houghton Mifflin.

Stevenson, Robert Louis. 1994. *The Letters of Robert Louis Stevenson*. Vol. 1. New Haven, CT: Yale University Press.

Stevenson, Robert Louis. 2000. *Vailima Letters*. Electronic Classic Series Publication. Hazelton, PA: Penn State.

Stevenson, Robert Louis. 1991. *An Inland Voyage*. Heathfield, England: Cockbird Press.

Thompson, Francis. 1969. *Essays*. Vol. III of *Francis Thompson: Poems and Essays*. Edited by Wilfred Meynell. Freeport, NY: Books for Libraries Press.

Thoreau, Henry D. 1950. *Walden*. New York: Harper and Row.

Thurber, James. 1996. *James Thurber: Writings and Drawings*. New York: The Library of America.

Tillich, Paul. 1957. *Dynamics of Faith*. New York: Harper Torchbooks.

Tse-Tung, Mao. 1961. *Selected Works of Mao Tse-Tung,* Vol. II. Oxford: Pergamon Press.

Van Doren, Mark. 1966. *Nathaniel Hawthorne*. New York: Viking Press.

Wayne, Dorothy "Dotty." 1960. *Wild Is Love*. Nashville: Capitol Records.

Westberg, Granger E. 1962. *Good Grief: A Constructive Approach to the Problem of Loss*. Philadelphia: Fortress Press.

Wiggin, Kate Douglas, and Nora Archibald Smith, eds. 1908. *Golden Numbers: A Book of Verse for Youth*. New York: McClure.

Wilder, Thornton. 1928. *The Angel That Troubled the Waters and Other Plays*. New York: Coward-McCann.

Wylie, Ida Alexa Ross, 1954. "The Art of Generosity." *Reader's Digest* (June): 101.